GAME DEVELOPMENT

BUSINESS AND

LEGAL GUIDE

ASHLEY SALISBURY

PREMIER PRESS

GAME DEVELOPMENT

Premier

Press

Publisher: Stacy L. Hiquet

Senior Marketing Manager: Martine Edwards

Marketing Manager: Heather Hurley

Manager of Editorial Services: Heather Talbot

Acquisitions Editor: Mitzi Koontz

Developmental Editor/Project Editor: Sandy Doell

Technical Reviewers: Jim Eberz, Li Reilly, Myra Packman, Jeff Carton, Kirk Owen, Fred Fierst, Jeff Hilbert, Dave Meiselman, and Dave Steiner

Interior Layout: William Hartman

Cover Designer: Mike Tanamachi

Indexer: Sharon Shock

Proofreader: Sara Gullion

ISBN: 1-59200-042-8

Library of Congress Catalog Card Number: 2003101211

Printed in the United States of America

03 04 05 06 07 BH 10 9 8 7 6 5 4 3 2 1

Premier Press, a division of Course Technology
25 Thomson Place
Boston, MA 02210

I have an incredible family,
and this book is for them.

Acknowledgments

I'd like to thank my chapter reviewers: Jim Eberz, Li Reilly, Myra Packman, Jeff Carton, Kirk Owen, Fred Fierst, Jeff Hilbert, Dave Meiselman, and Dave Steiner.

A big thanks to all of the industry vets who agreed to let me interview them for this book: Glyn Anderson, Matt Bellows, Keith Boesky, Dave Christensen, Gordon Dawson, Mark DeLoura, Graeme Devine, Mr. Hart and the Yahoo Games team, Todd Hollenshead, Bob Hopkins, Rob Huebner, Jamie Leece, Ken Levine, Fred Malmberg Gene Mauro, Benoit De Maulmin and Alex Carré de Malberg, American McGee, Joe Minton, Tim Morten, Frank Pape, David Perry, Scott Pink, Ted Price, Mark Rein, Brian Reynolds, Dan Rogers, John Romero, Jason Rubin, Suzan Rude, Dan Scherlis, Kathy Schoback, Bernie Stolar, Jonathan Strause, Steve Wall, and Greg Zeschuk.

To everyone who taught me how to be a lawyer: Lisa Rothblum, Fred Fierst, Jenny Bourbeau, Karen Collins, Anne Haynes, Jonathan Kane, Jeff Kinder, Diane Kleber, Janet Lussier, John Pucci, and the inimitable Margalee Riggan.

To the RX family for all their encouragement.

And to the two ladies without whom none of this would have been possible: Sandy Doell and Mitzi Koontz.

About the Author

Ashley Salisbury is an attorney (www.gamelawyer.com) who has worked in the interactive entertainment industry since 1998. After graduating Harvard Law School, she worked in McKinsey & Co.'s organization design practice group before starting a consulting firm providing product development, business strategy, and legal services to broadband entertainment companies and clients including Intel, TBWA/Chiat Day, Univision.com, and venture capital funds. She has produced multi-million-dollar software entertainment projects and lectured to film producers and television network programming executives on leveraging brands in digital media.

Since 2000, her legal practice has focused almost exclusively on interactive entertainment and domestic and international intellectual property licensing for clients at home and abroad, working with companies such as Eurocom Developments, Irrational Games, Paradox Entertainment, Mirage Studios (administrators of the Teenage Mutant Ninja Turtles property) and Shiny Entertainment while at Fierst & Pucci LLP. She holds an AB from Princeton University where she studied English literature and architectural theory. She can be reached at Salisbury@GameLawyer.com.

CONTENTS AT A GLANCE

CONTENTS

CHAPTER 3

FINANCING A GAME DEVELOPMENT

CHAPTER 5

A PRIMER ON INTELLECTUAL PROPERTY 181

CHAPTER 6

THE PUBLISHING CONTRACT ▪▪▪▪▪▪▪▪▪▪▪▪▪▪▪ 243

Work for Hire Publishing Agreement 252

For Content 270

CHAPTER 7

LICENSING ∎∎∎∎∎∎∎∎∎∎∎∎∎∎∎∎∎∎∎∎∎∎∎∎∎∎∎∎∎ 299

Letter from the Series Editor

My original goal for this Game Development series was that it be the one-stop authority for all things game related. This *Game Development Business and Legal Guide* fills out the series with what will undoubtedly become the definitive work in the areas of business law and finance for game development, new media, and technological intellectual property in general. My initial desire for this book came from my experiences running software companies myself and knowing that when it comes to legal and business issues you want to learn as *little as possible* from experience! I would rather read about how to properly protect myself contractually than find out in court! This is a book that both a game developer (or related new media developer) and lawyer (or related fields) can read, feeling comfortable with both the legal and business aspects that inevitably crop up with intellectual property such as games and other digital art forms.

As a businessperson there are only three things you ever need to worry about:

1. Liability

2. Taxation

3. Liability!

Liability is directly related to legal issues, and knowing how to protect yourself is the best defense against litigation and other unpleasant events that you will find yourself partaking in if you ever do get involved in the management or founding of a game development or related company.

What we set out to do with *Game Development Business and Legal Guide* was walk you through all the different aspects of game development (from both development and business points of view). Then we examine each aspect from a legal standpoint and keep you involved with the kinds of issues you should be aware of. For example, you want to start a game company? Great! What kind of entity should you select? C-corporation, sub-chapter S, LLC (limited liability), or maybe a partnership? What about a sole proprietorship? Wait a minute—what about taxes? Bank accounts? Liability? Investors? Stock options? The confusing list goes on and on.

All right, great, you have a company. Now you want to license an engine; what does that mean? Can you modify it? What's it going to cost? Is it worth it? What if you make your own engine? Can you protect it?

If you are a lawyer, knowing the pitfalls in digital new media and IP that your clients will stumble on will help you better direct them and make the best use of their legal budgets.

I just finished reading through the final version of this book and Ashley Salisbury has done a wonderful job of making such dry and tedious material interesting, fun, and engaging. Not to mention the poor editor, Sandy Doell, who had to translate a lot of the legal jargon. I demand that, if you have anything to do with business, licensing, or intellectual property, you read this book. If you don't learn something new, I will be very surprised. Ashley represents a very small group of lawyers in the country that knows anything about this kind of law and, moreover, can give practical advice on how to apply it in the form of a book that you don't need a law degree to understand.

In closing, I highly recommend this book to everyone, even if you don't deal with business operations, legal, or licensing—it's good stuff to know. In fact, there are a lot of companies I wish knew the difference between a copyright and a patent. Do you? If not, for that alone, please read this book!

Sincerely,

André LaMothe
Series Editor
Premier Game Development Series

INTRODUCTION

HOW TO USE THIS BOOK

The goal of this book is to give game developers a reasonably in-depth introduction in lay language to the legal issues they will face in their business, from choosing a business entity to finance, human resources, intellectual property protection, publishing contract negotiation, and licensing. I have gone into a lot of detail in this book because

   (i) having worked with developers, I know that most of you are smart enough to understand the concepts; and

   (ii) having worked with developers, I know that most of you are smart enough to know that this book does not make you capable of handling your own legal affairs. Just as a good cookbook does not make you Julia Child, this book does not make you a lawyer or even close to it.

This book can help you in two important ways: it can make you more efficient when dealing with your lawyers; and it can sensitize your legal radar so that you recognize danger before it blows you up.

I am trusting you to be big boys and girls and *hire lawyers*. And not just one lawyer; you'll probably need different lawyers for different situations like general business affairs, human resources, securities, taxes, contract negotiation, bankruptcy, and litigation. You are not a lawyer, and unless you want to learn a new definition of pain as you are slowly digested over a period of a thousand years, you won't try to act like one. I understand that no one likes to hire or pay lawyers, but no one likes going to the gym, either—you do it because it's how you stay healthy.

CHAPTER I

118 Things to Know about Running a Game Development Company

In Action

Defunct Software is a reputable game developer that has shipped six SKUs over the past three years, mostly on time and mostly well reviewed. Morale is generally high, and the fact that Defunct is located in the geographically remote town of Podunk, Pacifica contributes to a collegial atmosphere. Their most recent game, *LicensedGame,* was intended to be a magnum opus. Spec extensions and work on what were, at the time, new platforms (PS2 and Xbox) led to uncharacteristic production delays. Caught up in production fever, management of Defunct poured company money in to cover the delays, reasoning that the game would be so great, it would pay for itself in new contracts.

After a death march to the finish line of its PS2/Xbox/PC release "*LicensedGame,*" Defunct Software ran clean out of money. The CEO had been hunting for new projects since alpha, but wasn't able to close a deal in time to make payroll. The owners of Defunct decided to close the company before it amassed debts that it couldn't pay off.

After the company folded, the lead game designer (Pat), tech lead (Dusty), art lead (Alex), and executive producer (Dana) met over beers, pinochle, and Orbital to talk about their future. Three Anchor Steams later, Pat started free-associating a storyline about the freehand characters that Dana's roommate Jean (a graphic novelist and close associate of the Defunct group) had plastered all over the living room. Jean, who had been baking a Frito pie in the kitchen, walked out and started correcting Pat's story:

"No, he killed her twin sister, not her mother. They had been born three months early and incubated in an experimental light womb that caused their pre-conscious brain waves to fuse so that they couldn't distinguish between who was me and who was my sister. They didn't understand that they were two people."

"Hmmm. Yes, yes…of course. Then we could insert a parallel level that she gets sucked into whenever…" and so on through much of the night. Before long, the group had fleshed out a solid backstory and final mission for a game. The group, including Jean, decided to meet again the next night to see if the idea only sounded good after too much alcohol, or if they had the basis of something interesting.

As she walked home, Dana became convinced that this group would be credible to publishers. They had complementary strengths—technology, art, design, and project management. They had shipped a lot of product on almost every platform, most of it on time. More important, they had shipped it together; they were an old team.

At their next meeting, Dana started the discussion. "Look," she said, "we're young, none of us have babies or big mortgages to cover, and it's not like we've been living large in Podunk. My guess is you've all got a pretty fat nest egg, too. We should look for other jobs, obviously, but that could take months. Why not use the lag time to see what we can come up with?" They agreed to start sending out resumes but to work on a game design for one week without making any decisions.

After interviewing dozens of folks, the overall picture painted was so bleak that I thought about calling this book "Bring the Pain" or, as one executive suggested, "Don't Quit Your Day Job." The fact is, like any fun and creative job, there's a lot of competition, and you've got to have a surfeit of talent and a willingness to make a lot of sacrifices. As usual, the question boils down to: "Is the view worth the climb?" If you are interested in making the climb, here are one hundred and eighteen pearls to help you do it.

3 Things to Know about Your Publisher

LIVE INFOGRAMES
STOCK INFORMATION

INFOGRAMES

CLICK HERE

Figure 1.1

Infogrames stock information appears on its Web site's home page.

#1 What Being a Public Company Means

If your publisher is a publicly traded company, it makes predictions to Wall Street about how much revenue the publisher expects to earn each quarter. The stock price of the publisher can rise and fall depending on how close it comes to meeting (or exceeding) that number.

The author would like to thank Jeff Hilbert of Digital Development Management (www.digdevmgmt.com) for his assistance in preparing the company illustration appearing at the head of every chapter.

Those quarterly revenue predictions are based on the assumption that X, Y, and Z games will be getting released in that quarterly "window." If you are the developer of game X, and your production schedule slips and game X doesn't go out, your publisher is left with what is known as a "revenue hole." In other words, if your game doesn't ship on time, the publisher won't earn the revenue on that game, and it may not meet its quarterly projections.

Time is money, literally. So when a company misses its quarterly projection, its share price can suffer. Even if the publisher will release game X in the next quarter and may make up the difference in its next quarter, there is a premium on predictability and on getting money today versus tomorrow. Furthermore, the market can only handle so many games at a time, so slotting more releases into a window may cannibalize sales away from the publisher's other games.

#2 What Dealing with the Console Manufacturer Means

As you may know, console manufacturers look to license fees (paid by publishers) for a large chunk of their profits. They also exercise significant influence over the games released on their platforms, which takes some control over the development and manufacturing process out of the publisher's hands. Pieces of the process owned by the console manufacturer:

- Console manufacturers usually must give their approval of the concept for a game.
- A manufacturer may choose to cancel a game at the QA stage, after significant development.
- They can also cancel the game in its final form (though this is rare), or tell the publisher to go back and change it.
- They actually manufacture the game.

All of these approvals and processes take time, and a publisher has to factor those delays into its scheduling.

#3 What They Have to do to Get Onto a Shelf

In addition to other roles, the publisher provides the service of marketing and distributing the actual packaged product. Packaged product is usually sold to retailers directly or through a distributor (sort of like a catalog where the retailers shop).

A retailer's help can make a big difference in a game's sales. For example, games placed at eye level on the shelf (children's or adults, as relevant) are more likely to grab a customer's attention than games placed at foot level. Retailers can include your game in their advertising circular, or place promotional posters in the store, or feature your game in a big display like an *end-cap*.

Furthermore, retail real estate—often collectively known as *shelf space*—is a limited and very valuable asset. A retailer can only carry so many games on the shelves it has allotted for games. A publisher's job is to get as much of that shelf space as it can, at the most desirable level, along with any other retailer support it can negotiate.

How does a publisher get support from a retailer? Frequently, with cold hard cash—whether as *MDF* ("marketing development funds"), paying for advertising in the circulars, paying extra for premium space and end-caps, and so on.

This influence can only go so far. A retailer needs to get a certain return per square inch of shelf space per month. If a game isn't selling, the retailer can't afford to have it hogging up shelf space, so it sends back any product that doesn't "sell through" after a certain period of time, which seems to get shorter and shorter, or simply refuses to even stock titles it doesn't think will sell.

Figure 1.2

Wal-Mart sells 25% of all video games in the U.S. market.

115 Things To Know about Running Your Company

The next 115 tips were culled from my own experience as well as that of many of the most successful people in the game industry. Everyone has a different opinion, and every company has different needs, but these were some common themes and advice voiced.

Getting Started

#4   The pitch build is everything, so keep the company stuff like a Web site or a business card and stationery to a minimum until you're one month away from showing your work.

#5   The scale of pitch materials from cheapest to most expensive is: A. Design plus storyboards; B. Animated game mockup; C. A rendered .AVI; D. Playable demo with art and music; E. Full level/mission demo.

#6   If you're really strapped and looking to prove yourself, try using a free engine off the Web or modding another game to incorporate yours. Check the licenses to make sure you're allowed to make this use of the software.

#7   Get your attorney and accountant sooner rather than later.

#8   If your landlord wants you to personally guarantee the lease, ask if he'll take a letter of credit from your publisher instead.

#9   There are tools out there to help you build your prototype. Some, like virtools, cost $5K to $10k; others can be found free or under GPL on the Web.

#10   Two excellent resources: www.gamasutra.com and www.igda.org. Game-specific legal tips can be found in the famous last words column at idga.org and at www.gamelawyer.com. Take a look at www.gdconf.com, which always has interesting speeches from the previous Game Developer's Conference. Biz Dev, Inc. has a great series called Publishers Speak that asks major figures in publishing everything you want to know but couldn't get within 10 feet to ask. Check it out at www.bizdev-inc.com under "Publications."

Figure 1.3

*The IGDA is dedicated to help-
ing independent game developers. They've got a great Web
site at www.igda.org.*

#11   Starting on smaller platforms like GBA and wireless is good if you're learning. You can buy GBA emulators and developer tools to experiment. If you're looking to get into level design or programming, handheld and wireless is great; if you're an artist or a team look-ing to get a PC or console development engagement, your publisher needs to see the abili-ty to handle massive amounts of art assets. If you're more advanced, try doing a PC game demo or buying one of the Linux-based PlayStation 2 developer kits and making a pitch build with that.

#12   If possible, choose co-founders who can roll up their sleeves and program.

#13   Join a successful developer before you do it on your own.

Finance

#14   One pet peeve of publishers is "chasing milestones": A developer overspends on the cur-rent project, hunts down another, and takes his best (if not most) people off the first proj-ect to get the second one going, leaving the publisher to "chase" the last milestones.

#15   Publishers' missing milestones and late payment is the rule of the biz. If you want to sur-vive, maintain a cash cushion.

#16   If you are building an innovative product or technology into your game, budget at least 1.5 times the expected cost for that component.

#17   You have to impress a game agent as much as you have to impress a publisher.

#18   If you want to be bought out, you'll need a history of good titles that have come out on time, great technology that can be leveraged into other games, and a professional attitude (no shouting at publishers).

#19   You have to be incredibly well-organized to use completion bonding. You can't change your mind about what the game's going to be.

#20   If you do self-fund, expect around 50 percent of net wholesale as a royalty.

Human Resources

#21   Avoid long hours, unclear reporting structure, and unclear decision-making.

#22   If you're hiring a manager, the candidates should be interviewed by everyone they'll be managing. Be sure you've got your employees' buy-in before hiring anyone.

#23   Hiring for the long run means starting people at reasonable salaries. Many game developers have very low turnover, but you're still expected to give raises, so keep this in mind when setting salaries.

#24   Run it like a company, not a clubhouse. People have to be accountable. Fire those who don't fulfill their responsibilities. Publicize policies and enforce them equally.

#25   Don't poach. At least, don't poach from those with whom your company has good relations.

#26   Have regularly scheduled meetings by team, executive level, and any other logical grouping. Face to face communication is the grease that makes a company's wheels run smoothly.

#27   Always offer people the opportunity to contribute new game ideas at any point.

#28   Pay yourself and your people reasonably but not exorbitantly.

#29   Talent is important, but a compatible personality is just as important. When colleagues like each other, life is a lot easier for everyone.

#30   There are lots of ways to pay people. Try giving an expense account for games. It's a cheap thrill that makes your employees more effective.

#31   Do you tell your employees about trouble? Most developers tell their employees what is going on when their actions can help solve the problem but try to avoid distracting employees with other issues.

#32   Don't forget—people are not machines. Employees have spiritual and emotional needs as well as financial ones, and part of your job as manager is to meet those needs (or hire someone who can).

#33 There are two camps when it comes to office design: those who like open bullpen styles and those who believe in having a door that can be closed. The bullpen almost guarantees sufficient team communication, and the individual office almost guarantees greater productivity. One effective compromise: bullpens with quiet rules.

Figure 1.4

If you've got a bullpen-style office, noise-canceling headphones can help developers stay in the alpha state (tie optional).

#34 Delegate. Just because you *can* do it yourself doesn't mean that you *should*.

#35 Don't get emotional. When someone says something that makes you want to rip her head off, stop and ask yourself, "WHY did she say that" and "What is my GOAL." That will keep you calm and help you find the solution.

#36 Just because you're the CEO, don't think you get a big salary before you've earned anything.

#37 Stress is very hard on your health. You can only go one month at crazy hours before you start to lose your health and your judgment.

#38 Starting a company in an area far from talent will make it difficult to attract and retain employees.

#39 If you have to have layoffs, make sure you go far enough to save the company.

#40 Hire a full time office manager and IS person at your earliest convenience, which probably shouldn't be any later than hiring your sixteenth employee.

#41 Everyone should be an at-will employee.

#42 If you think there's a problem, there's a problem.

#43 The boss should get an annual review by the employees.

Publisher Relations

#44   If you want to work in a platform that you haven't shipped, your best bet is to make a prototype that is functional on that platform.

#45   Self-funding can backfire: If a manager at the publisher took a $4M bet on a project, he'll be very concerned with recouping because that product reflects on him personally. The publisher might not put as much money behind your product if it doesn't have to worry about recouping on it.

#46   Pitch materials for next game four to eight months before production starts.

#47   Don't fight for every inch with your publisher—it can poison the relationship.

#48   If you are signing a long-term contract, put some thought into your share of revenue from subscription services, wireless games, and digital distribution.

#49   The more risk the publisher takes, the less lucrative your deal is.

#50   If you stop development, it's considered a hostile act. A hostile act amounts to shooting yourself in the foot.

#51   Self-funding your games is only so appealing to a publisher because its financial risk comes from two ends: developing the game and spending the money to market and distribute it. As one publisher said: "Even if we get a free product, getting it out the door is expensive."

#52   While you can contract for some kind of marketing minimum, marketing dollars are generally decided *after* a product is developed. What makes a publisher want to throw down for your product? 1. A good game; 2. For which they own the sequel and franchise rights; 3. That had a sexy E3 demo; and 4. Has gotten consumers and retail buyers interested.

#53   Publishers want to see experience developing for a given platform; if you are trying to break into a new platform, make it easier for the publisher to say yes by getting yourself licensed by the manufacturer.

#54   When a publisher is evaluating your company, it wants to see a tool that enables non-technical staff to put an asset into the game, hit a button, and be able to see that asset running in-game on a console, without having to run to a programmer.

#55   Publishers look at the compatibility of your technology to the product: does your renderer match the art style the project needs, is your animation motion-capture if it's a realistic fighting game, and so on.

#56   Console manufacturers want publishers to release games that show off their console's unique properties. Publishers want to see that you understand the peccadilloes of each platform and have ideas for how you're going to highlight those unique properties with your game.

#57   If you want to work on consoles, publishers like to see low-level microcode skills, which often help optimize the code for the console.

#58   Remember the international and the port market when making your game. Build your game to be modular and port-friendly, and you increase the odds of getting into other platforms. For international: Schedule your localizations so that U.S. and international releases can happen concurrently. During development isolate all localizable elements, including audio and video. QA needs to test on different hardware running different local preferences. Don't forget that it's not just your game that gets localized; you'll need to translate the box, sales material, and anything else used to sell the game. Check out Octagon's white paper on maximizing international revenue from games: http://www.octagon1.com/resources/wtpapersframe.htm.

#59   Don't make a game that copies another game; you should be able, in one sentence, to persuade the publisher and the consumer of your game's unique selling properties. Maybe two sentences.

#60   Extra features don't always make a game better.

#61   Always have the ability to audit.

#62   Own your technology. Full stop.

#63   Publishers want teams with experience, but what they really want is teams with experience *together* (experience meaning shipped product). As one executive put it: "I don't even care if they put it out with a small publisher; I want to see a team get through one battle before we sign them."

#64   Publishers will generally only develop a game that has sequel and franchise potential (and where they own the rights to those sequels/franchises).

#65   The decision to produce your game happens by committee, and usually that committee is international. In other words, the European product development/sales and marketing group has to look at the sell sheet and say, "I think we can sell 60K of this game." From there, it is often a cost-benefit analysis: how many copies in total does the company think it can sell, at what marketing, distribution, and development cost, and how much profit does that leave?

#66   Publishers, developers, and retailers are all feeling similar pain right now: the cost of development is going up, team size is going up, the price for games probably won't go up, and shelf space is bursting with too much product.

#67   Contract terms may not translate to behavior.

#68   If the deal sounds too good to be true, it might be. Find out if the publisher has been paying milestones.

#69   Even when your publisher is stepping on your toes, try to avoid the adversarial legal approach if possible. That said, sometimes the adversarial legal approach is the only one that works.

#70   A publisher doesn't want to feel like its milestone payment is all that stands between your company and bankruptcy. If you do find yourself in this position, some developers advocate letting the publisher know so that they understand a late milestone payment equals no payroll equals no game. Other developers think it is best to camouflage this as best you can because it may negatively impact your ability to get other development assignments from the publisher.

#71   Many developers create a pitch build based on an original idea, but with an eye toward working on a license. One developer noted that, frequently, the purported reason for the meeting is to show the latest prototype, but it's really to talk about what license the publisher needs developed.

#72   Why go with a publisher at all? Publishers are a huge help managing the worldwide retail channel. They add value to that process—they have the relationship with manufacturing, logistical support in simultaneous launch, managing receivables from buyers. This isolates the developer from the publishing risk.

#73   Piracy is a big problem, and it's getting bigger.

Production

#74   Consider outsourcing.

#75   Many developers cautioned against spending beyond your budget because you think you will make it back in royalties. "Never happens," was one successful developer's terse dismissal.

#76   Constantly set your external producer's expectations. Most problems with external producers are the result of mismatched expectations. Easy example: If you're going to be late, or later, the consequences will be immeasurably better if you are honest with yourself and your producer (instead of deluding yourself that you'll catch up).

#77   Corollary: Bad news probably shouldn't go from producer to external producer. It may make more sense and reduce miscommunication by having the CEO or executive producer communicate the news directly to the external producer's boss.

#78   When your external producer changes more than once during a project, that may mean you should be communicating with his boss and having the boss review the milestones to ensure continuity for your company.

#79   It's important to expect things to go wrong during production because it's human nature to be optimistic and underbudget/underschedule.

#80   Have one person, a good communicator, designated as the initial point of contact for all publishing side personnel (production, sales and marketing, and others).

#81   Have clear deliverables with objective standards (where possible). Be sure you and the publisher know exactly what the deliverables are.

#82   At this point, developers need to have at least a passing knowledge of all platforms.

Figure 1.5

Developers may want to think about how to share revenue from subscription services such as Xbox Live.

Figure 1.6

A developer should aspire to proficiency with all available platforms.

#83   If you're developing a new toolset, it may not be best to make the tools sequentially. Try building a prototype, which requires taking a first pass at most of those tools and will help you figure out how much time and money it will take to build those tools.

#84   Eat your vegetables before dessert. Pre-production can make or break a development. Plan it out, make benchmarks, devise visual tools to track progress, give *everything* a contingency plan.

#85   When pacing the milestones, put the hardest work up front. The back end is always difficult, so do what you can to make it easier.

#86   Ask for a seasoned external producer, even if it means sharing him or her with another project. As one developer put it: "If the person you're negotiating with doesn't respect that desire, you're talking to the wrong publisher."

#87   Prototypes beat 100-page design documents any day; it's hard to predict fun on paper.

#88   Keep the timeline visual, with graphs. Video game developers hate to read and hate to read repetitive documents. Speak their language; make it visual.

#89   Pre-production should articulate all of the assets and have contingency plans. If you've designed for 60 widgets, but it's taken you nine months to build 7 widgets, the pre-production plan should dictate that the widget count is cut or widget production is outsourced.

#90   Keep an eye on other games coming out, and delegate this responsibility to your team. Don't get caught where your game is redundant.

#91   Always make your technology modular and scalable.

#92   Consider having an in-house sound studio when you can afford it.

#93   Put in a high fringe benefit amount.

#94   Put in more software and hardware maintenance and expense fees than you can imagine. Everyone always ends up buying more hardware.

#95   1.25 to 1.5 times what you think you need is what you'll use.

#96   Keep your external producer updated because the decision to cancel or fund further if you're in trouble is heavily influenced by the producer. Get to know them well as people.

#97   Ninety percent of the budget is personnel.

#98   Before expanding into more teams, remember that managing two projects can be 6 times as hard, and three projects can be 20 times as hard.

#99   If you make a prototype for your pitch build, you can save yourself time and money by making it scalable into the full game.

#100   It is hard to hear criticism about your product when you are working so hard to get it made, but there are three groups to take seriously, even if you don't implement their advice: developer relations at the console manufacturer, developer relations at the publisher, and consumer testing (which can start at around 30 percent). Every suggestion deserves a rational response, at the very least: "I hear you and this is why we aren't doing/can't do that."

#101   Nobody knows what didn't make it into the game at the end of the day. If you're falling behind, be ruthless: cut length and scope, like missions, levels, and characters.

Licensing

#102   If you're working on a licensed film or television property, see what kind of assets you can get from the producer to incorporate in your game.

#103   Strategy guides are a huge part of the licensing revenue.

Figure 1.7

*Strategy guides are a
big part of licensing
revenue.*

#104   If you're hiring an entertainment agent, have someone make a realistic assessment of opportunities for your property, devise a strategy for pursuing them, and assess the time and resources it will take to pursue them. You only have so much time to spend chasing opportunities, so beware the agent who blows sunshine up your skirt.

#105   Many developers create their own technology and decide not to go to the effort of marketing it for licensing (which has an uncertain return) and instead create it with an eye toward recycling it through three or four games (which is a more predictable return).

#106   Be careful if you're making original properties that you realize the potential for licensing into OEM and entertainment.

#107 Be proactive if there's a license you really want. Movie companies are interested in your ideas. Your most persuasive pitch will have funding (or bonding) and a publisher behind it.

#108 If you want to work with Hollywood, get hip-waders and a damn good lawyer..

#109 If you are releasing a product abroad and don't know the market, get a distributor you can trust. Look at who else they distribute, contact trade associations like the IDGA to see if they've been the subject of an enforcement action. You can also try asking local counsel specializing in the field.

#110 Include mod license language and restrictions in the game's end user license agreement as well as with any tool kits.

Wireless

#111 The lack of standardization in mobile devices is a problem, but not necessarily an expensive one. The main difference is usually re-sizing your graphics, changing the I/O, and porting to the applicable language (like Brew, J2ME, or Simbian).

Figure 1.8

The lack of standardization in mobile headsets makes wireless game development somewhat more complex.

#112   External producers for wireless games may not be as seasoned as those you are used to.

#113   Hardware testing used to be expensive, but the trend now is for carriers to subsidize the testing houses, bringing the cost down dramatically.

#114   Expect the carriers to be very involved in the process.

#115   Carriers worldwide are providing content providers with up to 80 percent of purchase revenue. It is unclear if this will be the profit split in the future.

#116   The publisher's role in wireless gaming: 1. Provide development fees ($10K to 60K) against royalties and 2. provide an "in" with the carrier. Many carriers won't listen to pitches from independent developers because of high volume of submissions.

#117   Standardization of technology is unlikely anytime soon.

#118   The market for licensed product is still germinal, and prices have yet to settle.

CHAPTER 2

FIRST STEPS

First Steps in Action

Everyone had certain ideas about how not to run the company. Because Pat, Dusty, Jean, and Alex needed to be working full time on the prototype, and because Dana had the most experience dealing with publishers ("and human beings," added Pat), it was decided that she would be the CEO and would be responsible for putting the company together around the team.

The thorny topic of allocating company ownership and control came up. Everyone took turns saying what he thought his main contribution to the new company would be, and what he thought was fair compensation for that contribution. Dana and Dusty had spoken privately earlier that day about company allocations. The two of them agreed that they could probably insist on a bigger share of the pie given the value of their contributions—Dana's publishing contacts and Dusty's technical facility would generally fetch more on the job market than the art and game design skills of Jean, Pat, and Alex. However, they both felt that they would prefer working in a cooperative environment where everyone felt equally valued, and would be willing to risk the consequences of having five equal owners. "I know it's probably moronic from a business point of view, and I blame the year I spent on a kibbutz after college," Dusty said, "but I'd rather try it this way." Dana also raised concern about giving Jean an equal share of the company, since none of them had ever worked with her before. "Maybe we can work it out so that no one actually owns the founders' stock for three or four years?"

Dana proposed a five-way equal split with four-year monthly vesting. This sounded good to everyone and they gave Dana the go-ahead to figure out a structure for the company. All five of them also agreed to put $5,000 apiece into the company for its initial capitalization.

"What do we call it?" asked Dusty. "She needs something to tell the lawyer." Much murmuring ensued.

"Nothing hypergothic or manic-depressive," Alex pleaded, "I don't want our logo to look like it came off of a dungeon entrance."

"How about an anagram of our initials?" suggested Jean.

"D-D-J-A-P. That's not very promising," said Pat, "A double d and a racial epithet."

"Then leave off the epithet," said Dana. "Let's call it Double D Development." Everyone thought this was utterly hilarious, and so it stuck.

No fool, that Dana, her first move was to get the names of a couple of local corporate lawyers with experience taking care of small, cash-starved businesses. She set up initial consultations (free) with two attorneys, Michael Rahn and Eva Tinder. After Dana explained Double D's situation to each of them, the two attorneys had roughly the same basic advice and estimated costs of getting the business up and running, but Dana had a better rapport with Michael. She reported back to the team, who agreed that—all other things being equal—Dana would be having the most contact with the lawyer and should work with whomever she was most comfortable. The team retained Michael on behalf of Double D.

Dana and Michael decided that the best structure for Double D would be an S-corporation because it would be quicker to get up and running than an LLC, but would also offer limited liability protection and pass-through taxation. Furthermore, since all of the owners will be employees, they may be eligible for some tax benefits. Michael also mentioned that the company may eventually be interested in reorganizing as a C-corporation and there are tax advantages to doing that as an S-corporation rather than as an LLC.

Michael explained that the other documents Dana would need right away were all of the corporate filings, a set of bylaws, a stock purchase agreement, and employment agreements for the founders. When Michael asked how the ownership would be allocated, Dana told him that the group was pretty dead set on splitting the stock five ways equally. She also said that the founders wanted their stock to vest over four years. Michael agreed that this was a good idea and told Dana that the group should file 83(b) elections within 30 days of the award date. He told Dana that his office could help prepare the documents for the founders.

Michael asked Dana if she was sure everyone understood the impact of the equal ownership decision—that a gang of three could control the company with its majority. Dana asked if there were ways that everyone could share equally but without the risk of three owners hijacking the company. Michael suggested that the bylaws could be written to require a supermajority vote (for example, requiring 80 percent of the votes) for certain actions, like firing a founder.

Michael took this information and drafted articles of incorporation, bylaws, and a restricted stock purchase agreement that he thought would fit with this consensus-driven company. He e-mailed the documents to every founder and scheduled a meeting with the group to go over the agreements and answer any questions.

The decision to start a company brings so much complexity and change that it can be easy to feel overwhelmed. Between the personal changes involved in self-employment and concern over lining up and executing the actual work product, structuring the business can be overlooked.

This chapter outlines the first three steps any nascent company should take.

Decide Ownership Stakes

This is one of the first tests of a management/founding group's ability to run a venture. Addressing questions of value, worth, and control—Who deserves what? When should they get it? Who has ultimate decision-making authority?—can hit primal nerves, and must be done tactfully and rationally. This section will give you a list of questions to get the discussion started and help you evaluate your respective contributions as unemotionally as possible.

Choose an Entity for Your Business

How your business organizes itself legally—as a corporation, LLC, or partnership—affects the taxation, administration, and asset protection of your business, among other effects. This section will describe the behavior, benefits, and detriments of each entity type and help you determine which is most appropriate for your business.

Issue the Ownership Stakes

Once you have decided how the company will be owned and controlled, and know which entity makes the most sense for the business, the ownership stakes must be distributed to the founders, and the rules of owning those stakes must be established in an agreement. These rules are primarily occupied with the purchase and sale of ownership, addressing issues such as what happens when a founder becomes disabled, or wants to sell his stake to an outsider.

You will get an overview of the legal issues and concerns surrounding each, and can see a sample restricted stock purchase agreement at the end of the chapter.

The author would like to thank Jim Eberz of Meiselman, Denlea, Packman, and Eberz P.C. (www.mdpelaw.com) for his assistance with preparing this chapter.

DECIDING OWNERSHIP STAKES

The three core questions in allocating ownership among a group of founders are

- Who deserves what?
- When should they get it?
- Who has ultimate decision-making authority?

Who Deserves What?

Now is a good time to understand how each of your co-founders understands his individual role and contribution, as well as how he sees the contributions of others. To focus the discussion during negotiations, ask each party to answer the following questions:

- What will each founder contribute up front? A respected name in the industry? Cash? Fundraising experience and contacts? Property, real or intellectual? Other rights (such as an exclusive license to a property or a development contract)?
- What will each founder contribute in the near future? More cash? Real or intellectual property (say, the development of an engine)? Sweat equity? Experience? A network? (These contributions are always "discounted" slightly to reflect the bird in hand/two in the bush principle of future returns).
- How should you value each of those contributions in light of the company's individual needs? In valuing the contributions, a useful index is to consider the opportunity cost of each donor. If a founder is donating cash, what return could he expect from other forms of investment? For someone donating experience, what is that experience worth on the job market? For one donating intellectual property, what would a license for that IP bring?
- If you plan to share ownership with employees, or have yet to hire key personnel who will require some stake in the company, what share of the company needs to be set aside for future employees? (Generally 10 to 20 percent—an experienced CEO alone will require 5 to 10 percent.)
- Do you plan to raise capital in the future? How much, when, and in roughly how many rounds? Many, if not most, game developers fund their operations with retained earnings. However, some elect to fund expansion plans (development of new IP, breaking into new businesses) with outside investment.

NOTE

Some developers elect to isolate new ventures, and even every game, with a separate business entity. Example: A development company, Devco, wants to develop an original IP called *NewGame*, but needs to raise $300,000 to fund a prototype. Rather than selling a piece of Devco and all of its assets to investors in the *NewGame* property, Devco creates a new wholly-owned subsidiary corporation called NewGame, Inc. and sells shares of that company to investors. This strategy has pros and cons for both sides, but it has the effect of making sure that investors are impacted only by the success or failure of *NewGame* and not the success or failure of other Devco operations.

- Professional investors will frequently demand as much as 40 to 60 percent in an early fund raising round, though this number should be significantly lower for a developer with a track record and, best of all, a development contract.

- Finally, carefully consider if there are any parties who may emerge "out of the woodwork" to lay a claim to the company or its IP. Think back on everyone with whom you talked over a story idea or game design, everyone who worked on code that became part of your engine, or anyone to whom any founder said anything that could have been construed as a promise of involvement in the venture. 'Tis a far far better thing to pay 1 or 2 percent up front than to have a release held up by litigation.

TIP

A new business is everyone's baby, and it is not uncommon for everyone to think he gave birth to it. Like Solomon, the founders' job is not to split the baby, but to devise a plan whereby the baby remains intact and all the parents are adequately motivated to act in its best interest. It seems obvious, but can get lost in the deal-making shuffle: Never negotiate a deal that is too lean to keep your counterparty happy for at least the next three years.

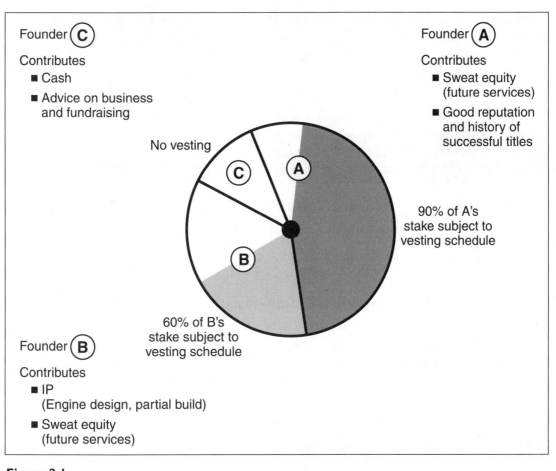

Figure 2.1

Founders must decide both how much each equity each will own and whether that equity is subject to vesting.

When Should They Get It?

After deciding each founder's share of the company, you should consider the timing of actual transfer of ownership. Frequently, the ownership agreement (see the "Ownership Agreements" section later in this chapter) will state that founder-employee stakes will *vest* over time, meaning that, while the entire amount is allocated to the stakeholder, he will only gain full legal ownership to the stake after a certain period of employment.

Example: Devco, Inc. is a corporation with four founders who plan to share the *equity* (stock) equally. Founders A & B will be contributing services, Founder C will contribute cash up front.

Founder C, since he has performed his contribution, receives ownership of all of his stock. Founder A, because he has a very prestigious name in the industry, will be receiving part of his stake free and clear and part subject to *straight line vesting*. Founder B will receive his stock subject to a *modified cliff vesting* schedule. According to the schedule, each will get

Founder	Signature of Shareholder's Agreement	End of Year One	End of Year Two	End of Year Three	End of Year Four
C (fully vested)	100%	—	—	—	—
A (vests at the end of every month)	10%	22.5%	22.5%	22.5%	22.5%
B (vests at the end of every year until Year Three; monthly vesting for Years Three and Four)	5%	5%	10%	40%	40%

Why Use Vesting Schedules?

The idea behind vesting is to defer delivery of ownership until the grantee has delivered all of the services contemplated by the parties when they signed the agreement. When ownership is granted in consideration for future services, there is risk that the services will not be rendered. Vesting matches that risk by allocating the full amount of ownership to be granted, but only delivering the amount proportionate to the delivery of services.

Vesting gives those working for the company an incentive to continue working for the company, and it keeps ownership of the company in the hands of those most interested in the success of the company—the employees. Two scenarios in which vesting can be a helpful tool:

Scenario One: A founder-employee leaves the company earlier than anticipated.

What if you start a company, give each of the founders one quarter of the equity, and then after three months, one of them quits, gets fired, or goes otherwise AWOL? Is he then entitled to 25 percent of everything the company makes going forward? Probably not. Where a founder will be contributing sweat equity, the other founders will probably want to protect the company by enforcing vesting and giving the company rights to re-purchase any stock that has vested.

Scenario Two: A founder wants to prove himself and gradually earn more control of the company.

What if one of the founders is relatively unproven, but the other founders believe he has much potential and want to keep him happy if he works out well? Here is another scenario where a wisely drafted ownership agreement will help all of the parties achieve their goals. A *steep* vesting cliff (most vesting is deferred for a few years and then granted in larger chunks) can give the other founders time to evaluate the young turk's progress while giving said turk the comfort that his efforts have a clearly defined reward.

Who Has the Final Word?

Ownership bears two primary benefits: profits and control. While the two are often intermingled, they can be separated if it suits the owners. This may be desirable where a party wishes to make a *passive* investment (an investment not accompanied by significant effort in the venture, such as employment) and does not want to exercise control in the venture. Different owners have different preferences: a cash investor will probably be more interested in return on investment, while a sweat equity investor may be more concerned with control.

How is control exercised? The answer to this question varies with entity type. Each business entity has its own prescribed method of control and management of the business, described below. For example, a corporation divides control among three groups: the shareholders, the directors, and the executives. Shareholders elect directors for a term. Directors hire and fire executives. A founder seeking control would be well advised to have not only ownership of shares, but a voting agreement guaranteeing him one (or more, which he can fill with an ally) seat(s) on the board, particularly if he is an executive. It is important to match the dynamics of your founding group (if indeed there is more than one founder) to the management mechanics of the entity.

Be aware that you may not be granted the final say in a company simply by virtue of owning the largest stake in the venture. Every business entity (covered in detail below) has some mechanisms by which minority owners can restrict the majority's ability to take certain actions (such as terminating the minority owner, or the majority owner's selling his or her stake to an outsider).

CAUTION

In some respects, the most important negotiations are not over money but over the provisions of the agreement governing relations among the business owners. These are covered in the "Issuing Ownership: Owners' Agreements" section, later in this chapter.

CHOOSE A BUSINESS ENTITY

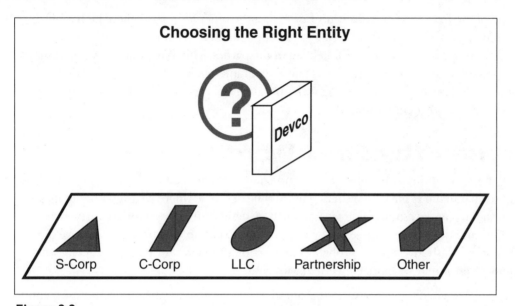

Figure 2.2

Finding the right fit will save you taxes and time.

Now that you have some idea how you will be splitting the pie, it's time to decide the flavor. The government authorizes different forms under which businesses can be organized and operated, with each form (or *entity*) having its own rules regarding ownership, taxation, management, required documentation, and liability. The primary forms in the United States are

- The corporation
- Limited liability company ("LLC")
- Partnership
- Sole proprietorship

This section introduces the major distinctions and varieties of the corporation, LLC, and partnership, as well as finding the entity most suitable to your enterprise's needs. Fortunately, you can always reorganize—often tax-free—as a different entity if those needs change.

> **NOTE**
> Because sole proprietorships are generally inappropriate for a development company, they will not be covered here.

Figuring out the best kind of entity for your business will help your company:

1. Protect owner and employee personal assets from company liabilities.
2. Minimize taxes by using losses to offset gains, avoid corporate-level tax (i.e. "double taxation"), and pass the money into your pocket at long term capital gains ("LTCG") rates, which top out at 20 percent, instead of ordinary income ("OI") tax rates, which can climb to 38.6 percent.
3. Gain access to the financing sources you need by organizing in a financier-friendly form.
4. Create a clearly defined ownership pool that can be divided among founders, financiers, and employees.
5. Operate efficiently with third parties, such as suppliers, customers, and employees.

The biggest differences among the entities are the following:

Corporations are treated as separate legal entities, almost like a person, that are owned by other separate legal entities (shareholders). The major benefit of this is that anyone suing or collecting from a corporation can only collect from the corporation's assets (except in very limited circumstances, see "The Corporation: C-Corporations: Liability" section)—so your company's creditors couldn't take your house if the company ends up unable to pay its bills. The major detriment of the separate entity theory is that every dollar you earn as a corporation will be taxed twice: the corporation pays tax on its income, and shareholders pay tax on money distributed to them as dividends or stock value appreciation. S-corporations, which avoid the double tax, are discussed in "The Corporation: S-Corporations" section.

Partnerships, LLCs, and S-corporations have the bonus of "pass-through" taxation, meaning that all income is passed tax-free through the entity to the owners, who then pay tax on the distributions. These entities have other drawbacks—greater exposure to company liabilities and onerous ownership restrictions, respectively—that are discussed in depth later in this chapter.

CAUTION

DOUBLE CAUTION: State law generally governs business organization and operation. These can vary significantly, so I can't urge you strongly enough to consult a local attorney. Understanding the vagaries of state law (and you may have to comply with the laws of more than one state) isn't easy, so don't go it alone.

The Corporation

There are two types of corporations, the *C-corporation* and the *S-corporation*, so named for the Internal Revenue Code subchapters governing each. The two share many of the same structures: the company is owned in units of equity called shares; shareholders control the company indirectly via an elected board of directors, who hire and fire the executives that run the company. The main difference is one of taxation; an S-corporation passes its profits (and losses) through to its shareholders, escaping the double taxation. Of course, as the IRS giveth, it also taketh away; S-corporation status is accompanied by some onerous restrictions that must be carefully weighed against the tax boon.

C-Corporations

C-corporations are most appropriate if your company:

- *Is widely held (more than 75 shareholders).* Other business entities limit ownership to 75 or fewer entities.
- *Wants to offer inexpensive options to attract employees.* C-corporations can issue different classes of stock with different privileges and prices, making it possible for employees to pay less for shares than outside investors.
- *Plans to raise money from corporations or investment funds.* Some business entities restrict ownership to natural persons, and others carry tax burdens for certain kinds of investors.
- *Expects owner/investor turnover.* Transferring ownership is simplest in a corporation, more complex in a partnership.
- *Employs shareholders as salaried employees or service providers.* Investor-employees can avoid the double-tax by taking profits as (reasonable) salary, which is deductible from corporate income.

Ownership and Restrictions

The C-corporation has almost no restrictions on who or what entities may own the business. The corporation is considered a separate legal being and may be owned by any number of shareholders, including only one. Foreign parties and other business entities may own the C-corporation. Because the corporation is wholly distinct from its owners and exists as a separate legal entity, it survives all changes in ownership, including the death or ouster of a founder.

Management

One of the virtues of both types of corporations is that management procedures are largely standardized by law. Certain variations are possible, but this standardization gives a level of comfort and transparency to investors.

Control is divided among three groups: *shareholders, directors,* and *officers.* Shareholders are the actual owners of the corporation. The board of directors is something like a council of elders, composed of people with admired business experience who may or may not be shareholders. The officers and executives of the corporation are employees of the corporation who run it on a day-to-day basis. The shareholders elect a board of directors. The board of directors is responsible for the high-level strategic management of the company and makes most of the major decisions, including hiring (and firing) of officers. The officers (for example, the CEO, president, and CTO) then manage day-to-day operations. Crucial decisions affecting the corporation, such as a sale of substantially all of the corporation's assets, are decided by shareholder vote.

State statutes mandate certain officer positions, generally a president, treasurer, and secretary. In most states, one person can hold all positions and is not subject to any ownership qualifications.

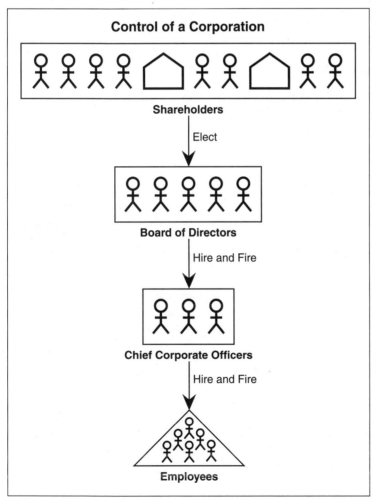

Control of a Corporation

Shareholders

Elect

Board of Directors

Hire and Fire

Chief Corporate Officers

Hire and Fire

Employees

Figure 2.3

Corporate control is divided among shareholders, the board of directors, and the officers.

Taxation

Ay, here's the rub. In exchange for all the flexibility and attractions of the C-corporation, the IRS exacts what is known as "double taxation." The corporation's profits are taxed once at the entity level, and then shareholders pay tax on whatever gain they receive.

The corporation must pay a federal tax on its profits of 15 to 34 percent. One common way to mitigate this bite is for shareholders who are also employees/service providers to distribute earnings to themselves in the form of legitimate salaries, which are deductible from corporate income. A closely held, owner-operated C-corporation can thereby gain many of the benefits of C-corporation status while minimizing the tax consequences.

Corporations distribute earnings in one of two ways: as dividends or as an appreciation in the value of the business, which usually translates into an increased share value. A corporation may decide to issue dividends if it has ready capital and profits in excess of its requirements for growth. While this confers the benefit of current income to shareholders, dividends are taxed at the shareholder's OI tax rate. If the corporation reinvests the money and the share price appreciates, the shareholder gains two tax benefits:

1. She pays no tax until the sale of the share.
2. Any appreciation in the share price will be taxed at the LTCG rate if the stock is held onto for more than one year, or at an even lower rate if the stock qualifies for the small business corporation exemption (see sidebar: "Small Business Corporation stock").

Getting Money Out of a C-Corporation

> **Assume**
> Corporate tax rate = 34%
> Ordinary income tax rate = 38.6%
> LTCG = 20%
> STCG = 38.6%

For $1 of profit paid out as:

	Dividends	Share Value Appreciation	Salary to Shareholder
Corporation Pays	$.34 ↓ $.66 to SH	$0 if profit reinvested ↓ $1 to SH	$0 ↓ $1 to SH
Shareholder Pays	$.25 ($.66 of OI)	Nothing until sale of shares. At time of sale, if the stock is held ≥ 12 months, SH pays LTCG rate of 20%. ≤ 12 months and SH pays STCG of 38.6%	$.38 ($1 of OI)
Total Tax Paid	$.59	$.20 – $.38	$.38

Figure 2.4

Tax planning is required to minimize double taxation of C-corporation profits.

Liability

With some exceptions, shareholders, directors, and officers are protected from the corporation's liabilities by what is known as "the corporate veil." If the company goes bankrupt, creditors cannot look past the corporation's assets to the owners for satisfaction of debts. If money damages are awarded to a party suing the corporation, that party cannot look to the owners for the award. Generally, shareholders can only be held liable for the debts of the corporation if a court finds that they used the corporation to intentionally perpetrate a fraud or injustice.

Seven Simple Liability Precautions

Normally, creditors of a corporation may only look to the assets of the corporation, not the shareholders, to satisfy debts. This is what is known as the "corporate veil." The corporate veil can be *pierced* (disregarded), however, where a court finds that shareholders used the corporation to fraudulent or unjust ends (the *alter ego* doctrine, where the shareholders use the corporation as their alter ego to perpetrate fraud). The court's goal is to prevent crooks from exploiting the corporate laws to escape personal liability.

To make it more unlikely that a court will find a reason to pierce your company's corporate veil, and to maintain good personal/corporate financial hygiene:

1. Be sure that the company is adequately capitalized and insured, taking into account the risks of the business. For game developers, this might include having a cash cushion against a publisher's delay in paying a milestone and a general liability insurance policy, as well as all state and federally mandated insurance.

2. Don't use corporate assets for personal reasons. In other words, don't take the corporate car on a kayaking trip to Baja (unless there is some legitimate business purpose for the trip, such as a company outing).

3. Don't commingle corporate and personal assets. This means keeping separate business and personal checking accounts; don't pay your personal bills from the company till, even if you reimburse the company.

4. Keep a separate set of books and records for the corporation and your own personal assets.

5. Avoid self-dealing and sweetheart deals. Keep your nose extra-clean when it comes to dealings between the corporation and any major shareholder or

director by fully disclosing any potential conflicts of interest in written corporate records and getting approval from disinterested board members or an appropriate third party.

6. Be sure that all corporate actions requiring proper, papered authorization receive it from the board of directors or shareholder. This means obtaining, recording, and holding onto shareholder and board authorization. Conduct shareholders' meetings and board meetings regularly (at least once per year) and keep accurate minutes in corporate records.

7. All contracts for the corporation should be signed with the corporation's name above the signature line, and the name and title of the person signing below the signature line. This makes it apparent to the other parties to the contract that they are dealing with a corporation and not the person, and they should expect to have recourse only to the corporation's assets should something go amiss with the contract.

Documents Required

A corporation requires certain documents to be prepared and filed with the company state's secretary of state as well as the IRS. After the initial filings, there are sundry ongoing requirements to operating a corporation, such as conducting board meetings, taking minutes of those board meetings and approving them, and so forth. Your attorney can review these with you and set up a system to make it easier for you to remain compliant. Furthermore, there are certain agreements like the shareholders' agreement (see heading "Shareholders' Agreement," this section) that are not mandated by law but are highly recommended for proper functioning of the corporation.

> ### CAUTION
> **Consulting an attorney early in this process will save you money and heartache in the long run. She will help you figure out the capital structure, ownership distribution, and equity incentive plan best fitting your needs, as well as help you develop tax-efficient strategies.**

CERTIFICATE OF INCORPORATION/ARTICLES OF INCORPORATION

The Certificate of Incorporation (COI) must be filed with the secretary of state of the state in which you will be incorporating (not necessarily the same as your principal place of business) to inform the government of your company's vital stats. Requirements for this document vary from state to state, but most require:

- Name.
- Business Purpose. For most states, this can be as general as "engaging in any lawful activity for which corporations can be organized in the state."
- Authorized Capital. This is the number of shares that the corporation can issue, their par value (usually $.01), and classes of stock, if more than one. Since it is common to issue preferred stock to later investors (see discussion below) you may want to authorize "blank-check" preferred stock (if your state allows it) to avoid the expense of amending the articles. Blank-check preferred stock states that preferred stock is authorized and shall have the rights, preferences, and privileges that the board sets in board resolutions.
- Agent's name and address. Service of process sent to this address will be deemed received, so rather than using the address of an individual associated with the corporation, hire one of the companies that provides this service inexpensively. The worst-case scenario would be that process is served on an agent no longer associated with the company and a default judgment is entered against your company.
- Indemnification. Indemnification is protection (usually reimbursement and legal defense) the corporation gives certain individuals against liabilities arising from their activities on behalf of the corporation. Here is where you specify the indemnifications that the corporation will furnish its officers, directors, employees, and agents.

The following provisions may or may not be permitted in your state of organization; if permitted and you desire their use, include them in your certificate:

- Supermajority requirements. More than a simple majority is required for shareholder or director actions. State the threshold percentage.
- Cumulative voting (see the "Where to Incorporate" section that follows).
- Preemptive rights. Right of an investor to buy enough of any future rounds of financing to maintain his or her current percentage (also known as the "kiss of death").

BYLAWS

Bylaws set out the nuts and bolts of a corporation's administrative functions. The bylaws establish, among other things:

- Where the corporation will be located.
- When, where, and how stockholders' meetings will occur.
- How stock certificates will be issued, paid for, and transferred.

- How many directors the corporation will have, what powers they will have, how they will be elected, and how and when they will meet.
- Officer positions of the corporation, how they will be elected, what their powers will be.

ACTION BY INCORPORATOR

This is a simple, vital step that must be completed to effect incorporation. It can be done as soon as the COI is filed with the secretary of state. It is a short document in which whomever is named as the incorporator on the original COI (frequently your attorney's assistant) adopts the bylaws, appoints the first directors, and then resigns.

At its first meeting, the board of directors should appoint officers, authorize the issuance of stock to the founders, establish a bank account, and authorize payment of expenses. At the same meeting, or soon thereafter, the board should do the following:

- Adopt a standard non-disclosure agreement and other proprietary information forms for all employees and consultants.
- Draft an employee stock/option purchase plan (if applicable).
- Adopt a restricted stock purchase agreement imposing vesting and a right of first refusal on employee stock/option grants.
- Set a fiscal year.
- Agree on tax status (C or S).

If your board is far-flung, your state may allow what is known as an "action by unanimous written consent," which allows actions to be taken if all directors sign a document approving same.

SHAREHOLDERS' AGREEMENT

The shareholders' agreement establishes rules of ownership, most of which have to do with transferring ownership. Some individual clauses are covered in this chapter in the section "Owners' Agreements." A sample shareholders' agreement can be found at the end of this chapter.

EMPLOYMENT AGREEMENTS

If any of the founders or shareholders will be employed by the company, an employment agreement setting out the terms of their relationship with the company should be negotiated, signed, and referenced in the shareholders' agreement.

Small Business Corporation Stock

The IRS has created tax incentives for investment in new small businesses under sections 1202, 1244, and 1045 of the Internal Revenue Code. These sections allow for up to three major tax savings to investors in a qualifying small business ("QSB"):

■ A 50 percent exclusion of any gain realized by the investor upon the sale of the stock (Section 1202 of the Code);

■ Deferral of the gain realized by the investor if the investor "rolls over" such gains by purchasing additional QSB stock (Section 1045 of the Code); and

■ If the investor loses money on the investment, re-characterization of any capital losses as ordinary losses (Section 1244 of the Code).

To qualify for a 50 percent reduction in the capital gains tax due upon sale of your QSB stock, the stock must meet all of the following criteria:

1. The corporation must be a domestic "C" corporation.

2. The stock must have been issued after August 11, 1993.

3. The stockholder must have received the stock as an original issue.

4. The aggregate gross assets of the corporation must not have exceeded $50,000,000 at the time of and immediately after the issuance of the stock.

5. At least 80 percent of the assets, by value, of the corporation must have been used in active trade or business.

S-Corporations

S-corporations are most appropriate for businesses that:

■ *Are closely held.* An S-corporation can have no more than 75 shareholders.
■ *Will not have any corporate or international investors.*
■ *Will generate initial losses that shareholders can use against their taxable income.*
■ *Plan to distribute most profits immediately to shareholders.* A company that reinvests most of its profits can minimize its corporate-level income tax. If the shareholders intention is to take profits out of the company as cash instead of reinvesting them to grow the company, then they will prefer a pass-through entity that does not have a corporate level income tax.

- *Will not offer preferentially priced options to attract employees.* An S-corporation can have only one class of stock, meaning that employees will have to pay the same price for shares as outside investors.
- *Will not be able to distribute a significant amount of corporate income to shareholders by means of salary.* Salaries are deductible from corporate income, creating a way for shareholders to avoid the corporate-level tax. If this option is not available, the presence or absence of corporate-level income tax becomes a major issue.

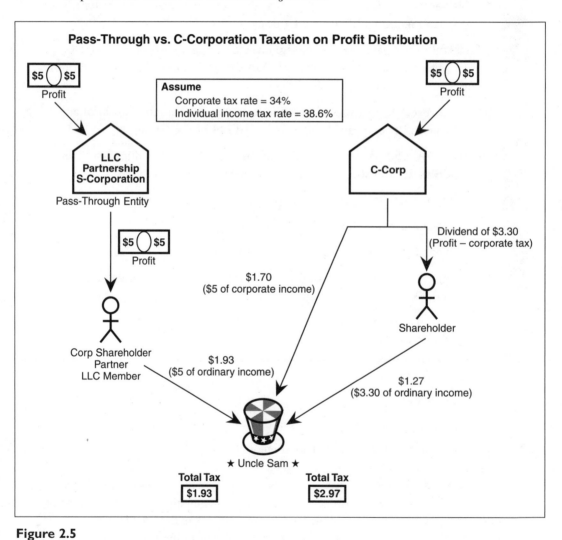

Figure 2.5

Pass-through entities may offer tax advantages to company owners.

Ownership Restrictions

S-corporations can have no more than 75 shareholders, all of whom must be individuals (though there are some allowances for tax-exempt trusts and estates) living in the United States.

Developers who plan to raise money must consider this limitation carefully, since corporations (e.g. publishers) and foreigners form a large part of their investor audience.

Another limitation is the S-corporation's ability to issue only one class of stock, which complicates the matter of incentive equity. (See the "Ownership of a Corporation" section in this chapter). Many developers do not find this a serious burden and opt to

> **TIP**
>
> S-corporations are easily converted into C-corporations as needed, for instance in a situation where a foreign entity or corporation wishes to buy the S-corporation.

use other means to create employee incentives, such as profit-sharing plans, royalty participation pools, and bonus plans, see the Sharing the Wealth sidebar in Chapter 4, "Staffing Up." To avoid employees' owing tax on their receipt of shares, they must pay the same price as the investors.

Management

The S-corporation has management procedures that are largely standardized by law.

Control is divided among three groups: *shareholders*, *directors*, and *officers*. Shareholders are the actual owners of the corporation. The board of directors is something like a council of elders, composed of people with admired business experience who may or may not be shareholders. The officers and executives of the corporation are employees of the corporation who run it on a day-to-day basis. The shareholders elect a board of directors. The board of directors is responsible for the high-level strategic management of the company and makes most of the major decisions, including hiring (and firing) of officers. The officers (for example, the CEO, president, CTO) then manage day-to-day operations. Crucial decisions affecting the corporation, such as a sale of substantially all of the corporation's assets, are decided by shareholder vote.

State statutes mandate certain officer positions, generally a president, treasurer, and secretary. In most states, one person can hold all positions and is not subject to any ownership qualifications.

Taxation

The S-corporation entity does not owe federal tax on its profits. All profits and losses flow through to its shareholders, who then owe income tax (or receive deductions) on those distributions at the shareholder's ordinary income tax rate.

> **NOTE**
>
> Owner-employees of an S-corporation may be eligible for reductions in their self-employment tax.

Many investor/founders like the S-corporation as an initial choice because they can deduct some or all of the losses generated by the company from income they generate through other avenues. There are many restrictions on this practice, and it requires the counsel of a solid tax planner to accomplish effectively.

Unlike the other pass-through entities (LLC and partnership), owners of an S-corporation may not decide amongst themselves how to allocate profits and losses; all profits and losses must be allocated by share ownership. Differential allocation is desirable in circumstances where, for instance, an S-corp will be generating tax losses for the first few years, and a large stakeholder (say, a founder) will not have enough income to use all of the loss, whereas a minority shareholder (say, an angel investor) will. Under the IRS rules regulating S-corporations, the minority shareholder will only be able to declare that portion of the corporation's loss corresponding to his or her ownership percentage in the company.

Quick example: Founder A owns 65 percent of the stock and earns $30,000 in income. Founder B owns 20 percent of the stock, but also works at another company and earns $400,000. The company generates losses of $100,000 in its first year. Founder A has a $65,000 loss that he can deduct from his income, but because he only has $30,000 in income, $35,000 goes unused. Founder B has a $20,000 loss that she applies against her $400,000 income, but she sure could use that extra $35,000 loss to deduct against her salary. Alas, she can't; S-corporations do not allow for differential loss allocation.

CAUTION

There are many assumptions and qualifications in this example—it should not be used as a blanket application of the tax law.

Two more limitations on using the S-corporation's losses:

- A passive shareholder (one who does not work for the company) cannot deduct the losses from most income. The losses are considered capital losses and are only useful against the investor's capital gains.
- Deductions are limited to the shareholder's *basis* in his stock. An easy way to think of basis is as your total cost paid for the stock. So if you have only paid $10 for your stock, you can only use $10 worth of deductions.

A potentially graver consequence of S-corporation taxation is that shareholders must declare their share of corporate profits *whether or not said profits have been distributed.* Thus, a cash squeeze could arise for an investor if the corporation retains profits but the shareholder must pay taxes on the profit.

Quick Example: Use the numbers from the example above, but change the $100,000 loss into a $100,000 gain. If the corporation stockpiles all of the profit, Shareholder A will feel the pinch of owing income tax on both his $30,000 salary and his $65,000 share of the profits, even though he has not received any of that money.

Liability

With some exceptions, shareholders, directors, and officers are protected from lawsuits and personal liability arising from their actions in connection with the company by what is known as "the corporate veil." If the company goes bankrupt, creditors cannot look past the corporation's assets to the owners for satisfaction of debts. If money damages are awarded to a party suing the corporation, that party cannot look to the owners for the award. Generally, shareholders, directors, and officers can only be held liable for the debts of the corporation if a court finds that they used the corporation to intentionally perpetrate a fraud or injustice. See Sidebar: Seven Simple Liability Precautions in this chapter for tips on how to keep your veil intact.

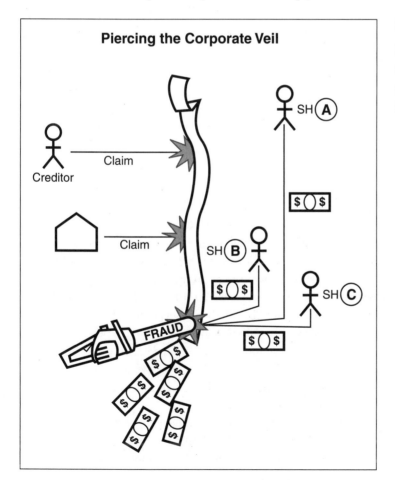

Piercing the Corporate Veil

Figure 2.6

Fraudulent conduct may result in officer and/or shareholder liability.

Documents Required

A corporation requires certain documents to be prepared and filed with the company state's secretary of state, as well as the IRS. After the initial filings, there are sundry ongoing requirements to operating a corporation, such as conducting board meetings, taking minutes of those board meetings and approving them, and so forth. Your attorney can review these with you and set up a system to make it easier for you to remain compliant. Furthermore, there are certain agreements like the shareholders' agreement (see heading "Shareholders' Agreement," this section) that are not mandated by law but are highly recommended for proper functioning of the corporation.

> **CAUTION**
>
> Consulting an attorney early in this process will save you money and heartache in the long run. She will help you figure out the capital structure, ownership distribution, and equity incentive plan best fitting your needs, as well as help you develop tax-efficient strategies.

You will need to obtain the following documents to set up an S-corporation.

CERTIFICATE OF INCORPORATION/ARTICLES OF INCORPORATION

The Certificate of Incorporation must be filed with the secretary of state of the state in which you will be incorporating (not necessarily the same as your principal place of business) to inform the government of your company's vital statistics. Requirements for this document vary from state to state, but most require:

- Name.
- Business Purpose. For most states, this can be as general as "engaging in any lawful activity for which corporations can be organized in the state."
- Authorized Capital. This is the number of shares that the corporation can issue, their par value (usually $.01), and classes of stock, if more than one. Because it is common to issue preferred stock to later investors (see discussion below) you may want to authorize "blank-check" preferred stock (if your state allows it) to avoid the expense of amending the articles. Blank-check preferred stock states that preferred stock is authorized and shall have the rights, preferences, and privileges that the board sets in board resolutions.
- Agent's name and address. Service of process sent to this address will be deemed received, so rather than using the address of an individual associated with the corporation, hire one of the companies that provides this service inexpensively. The worst-case scenario would be that process is served on an agent no longer associated with the company and a default judgment is entered against your company.
- Indemnification. Indemnification is protection (usually reimbursement and legal defense) the corporation gives certain individuals against liabilities arising from their activities on behalf of the corporation. Here is where you specify the indemnifications that the corporation will furnish its officers, directors, employees, and agents.

The following provisions may or may not be permitted in your state of organization; if permitted and you desire their use, include them in your certificate:

- Supermajority requirements. More than a simple majority is required for shareholder or director actions. State the threshold percentage.
- Cumulative voting (See "Where to Incorporate" section).
- Preemptive rights. Right of an investor to buy enough of any future rounds of financing to maintain his or her current percentage (also known as the "kiss of death").

Bylaws

Bylaws set out the nuts and bolts of a corporation's administrative functions. The bylaws establish, among other things:

- Where the corporation will be located.
- When, where, and how stockholders' meetings will occur.
- How stock certificates will be issued, paid for, and transferred.
- How many directors the corporation will have, what powers they will have, how they will be elected, and how and when they will meet.
- Officer positions of the corporation, how they will be elected, and what their powers will be.

A sample of corporate bylaws is included at the end of this chapter.

Action by Incorporator

This is a simple, vital step that must be completed to effect incorporation. It can be done as soon as the COI is filed with the secretary of state. It is a short document in which whomever is named as the incorporator on the original certificate of incorporation (frequently your attorney's assistant) adopts the bylaws, appoints the first directors, and then resigns.

At its first meeting, the board of directors should do the following:

Appoint officers

Authorize the issuance of stock to the founders

Establish a bank account

Authorize payment of expenses.

At the same meeting, or soon thereafter, the board should:

Adopt a standard non-disclosure agreement and other proprietary information forms for all employees and consultants

Draft an employee stock/option purchase plan (if applicable)

Adopt a restricted stock purchase agreement imposing vesting and a right of first refusal on employee stock/option grants

Set a fiscal year

Agree on tax status (C or S)

If your board is far-flung, your state may allow what is known as an "action by unanimous written consent," which allows actions to be taken if all directors sign a document approving same.

SHAREHOLDERS' AGREEMENT

The shareholders' agreement establishes rules of ownership, most of which have to do with conditions of transferring ownership. Some individual clauses are covered in this chapter in the section "Owners' Agreements." A sample shareholders' agreement can be found at the end of this chapter.

IRS election

S-corporation status is elected by filing form 2553 with the IRS, along with written consent of all shareholders, before the fifteenth day of the third month of the taxable year of the corporation for which S status is desired. A corporation must meet all of the requirements over the course of the entire year; otherwise, the election is deemed ineffective until the next year.

Where to Incorporate

You may have noticed that far more companies are incorporated in Delaware than appear to "reside" there. This is largely due to Delaware's well-established body of corporate law that strongly favors the corporation and gives management more power and discretion than the laws of some other states. If you elect to organize in Delaware, you will probably also have to file as a foreign company in the state of your company's principal place of business. The downside to incorporating in Delaware is that your company will have to comply with tax and regulatory requirements of both states and will incur additional expenses in filing and maintenance expenses such as employing a local Delaware *agent*.

An agent is a person legally authorized to act on behalf of your company. This kind of agent acts as your company's local presence for official communications. The state in which you incorporate needs to have a person within its borders through whom it can give your company official, binding communication, such as service of process.

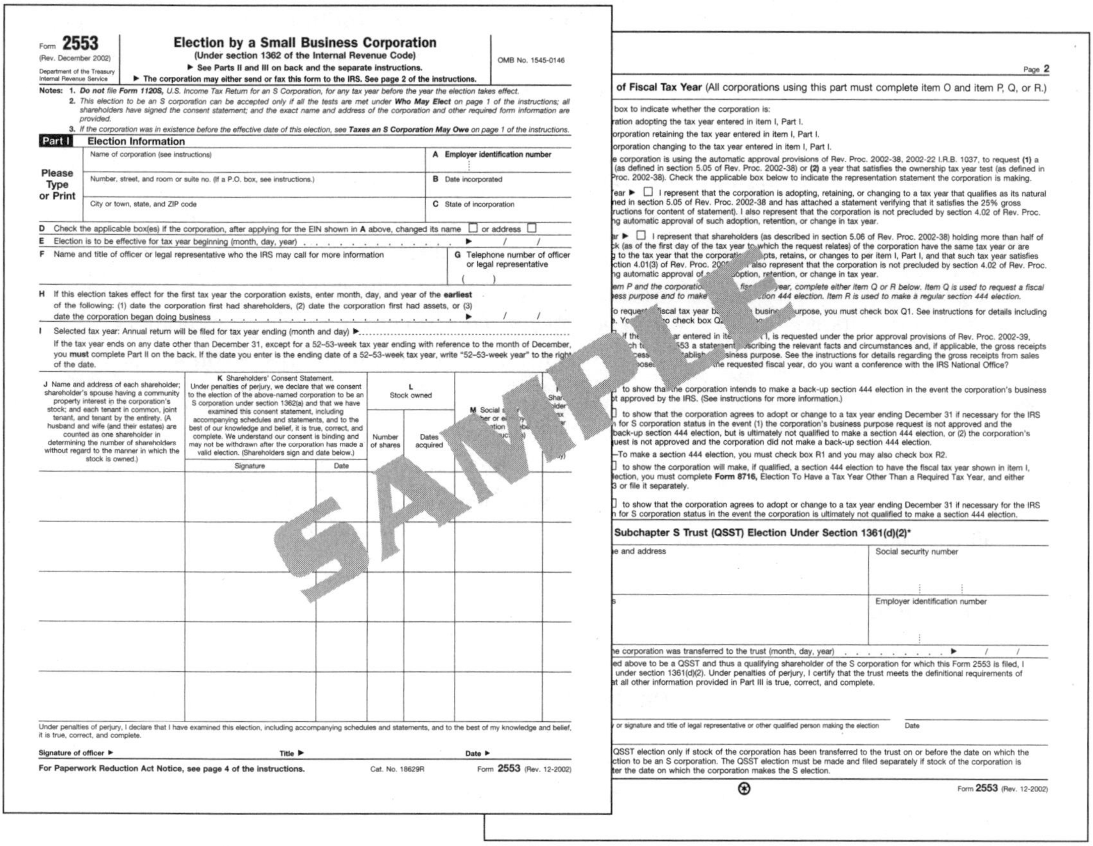

Form **2553** (Rev. December 2002) Department of the Treasury Internal Revenue Service

Election by a Small Business Corporation
(Under section 1362 of the Internal Revenue Code)
▶ See Parts II and III on back and the separate instructions.
▶ The corporation may either send or fax this form to the IRS. See page 2 of the instructions.

OMB No. 1545-0146

Notes: 1. *Do not file Form 1120S, U.S. Income Tax Return for an S Corporation, for any tax year before the year the election takes effect.*
2. *This election to be an S corporation can be accepted only if all the tests are met under Who May Elect on page 1 of the instructions; all shareholders have signed the consent statement; and the exact name and address of the corporation and other required form information are provided.*
3. *If the corporation was in existence before the effective date of this election, see Taxes an S Corporation May Owe on page 1 of the instructions.*

Part I Election Information

Please Type or Print — Name of corporation (see instructions); Number, street, and room or suite no. (If a P.O. box, see instructions.); City or town, state, and ZIP code
A Employer identification number
B Date incorporated
C State of incorporation

D Check the applicable box(es) if the corporation, after applying for the EIN shown in A above, changed its name ☐ or address ☐
E Election is to be effective for tax year beginning (month, day, year) ▶ / /
F Name and title of officer or legal representative who the IRS may call for more information
G Telephone number of officer or legal representative ( )
H If this election takes effect for the first tax year the corporation exists, enter month, day, and year of the **earliest** of the following: (1) date the corporation first had shareholders, (2) date the corporation first had assets, or (3) date the corporation began doing business ▶ / /
I Selected tax year: Annual return will be filed for tax year ending (month and day) ▶
If the tax year ends on any date other than December 31, except for a 52–53-week tax year ending with reference to the month of December, you **must** complete Part II on the back. If the date you enter is the ending date of a 52–53-week tax year, write "52–53-week year" to the right of the date.

J Name and address of each shareholder; shareholder's spouse having a community property interest in the corporation's stock; and each tenant in common, joint tenant, and tenant by the entirety. (A husband and wife (and their estates) are counted as one shareholder in determining the number of shareholders without regard to the manner in which the stock is owned.)
K Shareholders' Consent Statement. Under penalties of perjury, we declare that we consent to the election of the above-named corporation to be an S corporation under section 1362(a) and that we have examined this consent statement, including accompanying schedules and statements, and to the best of our knowledge and belief, it is true, correct, and complete. We understand our consent is binding and may not be withdrawn after the corporation has made a valid election. (Shareholders sign and date below.) Signature / Date
L Stock owned: Number of shares / Dates acquired
M Social security number or employer identification number

SAMPLE

Under penalties of perjury, I declare that I have examined this election, including accompanying schedules and statements, and to the best of my knowledge and belief, it is true, correct, and complete.
Signature of officer ▶ Title ▶ Date ▶
For Paperwork Reduction Act Notice, see page 4 of the instructions. Cat. No. 18629R Form **2553** (Rev. 12-2002)

Page **2**
... of Fiscal Tax Year (All corporations using this part must complete item O and item P, Q, or R.)
... Subchapter S Trust (QSST) Election Under Section 1361(d)(2)*
Form **2553** (Rev. 12-2002)

Figure 2.7

IRS form 2553.

Points on which state laws vary:

- Types of consideration (payment) that can be used to buy stock
- Enforceability of voting agreements (agreements that essentially allow certain shareholders to elect a certain number of board seats)
- Ability of fewer than all shareholders to act by written consent
- Ability to stagger director elections (rather than having all directors up for election at once)
- Indemnification of officers and directors
- Validity of "poison pill" (anti-takeover) measures
- Shareholder appraisal rights (discussed in Chapter Three)

If your corporation is privately held (that is, not publicly traded) and it meets the 50/50 test (more than 50 percent of the shares are owned by California residents and more than 50 percent of the business is conducted in California), you will be subject to California corporate governance laws, which have a few quirks worth noting:

- California corporations may pay dividends or buy back shares only to the extent of the corporation's accumulated earnings.
- Privately held corporations must allow cumulative voting. Under cumulative voting, every shareholder receives that number of votes equal to the number of shares owned multiplied by the number of directors to be elected. This can give minority shareholders power to elect directors. Example: DevCo has 100 outstanding shares of voting stock—Shareholder A owns 20 percent, Shareholder B owns 80 percent, and five board members are up for election. Shareholder A will have 20 votes to distribute as she sees fit over the nominees for the five board slots, Shareholder B has 80 to do likewise. Shareholder A can therefore be guaranteed one director of her choosing on the board if she places all 200 votes with one nominee.
- Staggering of board elections is prohibited; all directors must be elected annually, creating more potential for radical change.

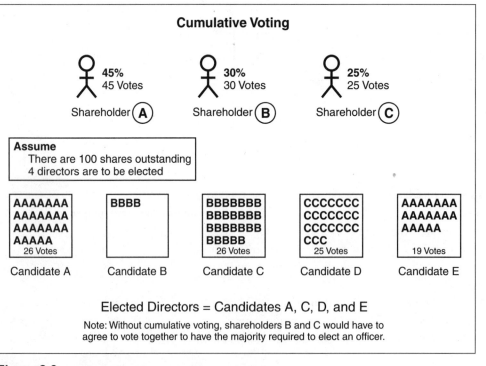

Cumulative Voting

Shareholder (A) 45% / 45 Votes
Shareholder (B) 30% / 30 Votes
Shareholder (C) 25% / 25 Votes

Assume
There are 100 shares outstanding
4 directors are to be elected

Candidate A	Candidate B	Candidate C	Candidate D	Candidate E
AAAAAAA AAAAAAA AAAAAAA AAAAA 26 Votes	BBBB	BBBBBBB BBBBBBB BBBBBBB BBBBB 26 Votes	CCCCCCC CCCCCCC CCCCCCC CCC 25 Votes	AAAAAAA AAAAAAA AAAAA 19 Votes

Elected Directors = Candidates A, C, D, and E

Note: Without cumulative voting, shareholders B and C would have to agree to vote together to have the majority required to elect an officer.

Figure 2.8

Cumulative voting can prevent tyranny by the majority.

Limited Liability Company

A limited liability company (LLC) is most appropriate for those companies that:

- Will not need to issue incentive equity to attract employees.
- Do not plan to raise money from an investment fund.
- Are considering organizing as a partnership or S-corporation.
- Will not qualify for the QSBC capital gains reduction.

The limited liability company is a relatively recent, very popular addition to the roster of corporate entities. It combines the most desirable qualities of the limited partnership and S-corporation while eliminating some of those entities' more obvious drawbacks. Unlike the limited partnership, the LLC does not require any one person to bear ultimate liability for the company's debts. Unlike the S-corporation, it may issue more than one class of ownership interest, may have more than 75 shareholders, any of whom may be non-U.S. residents or entities, and may freely allocate profits and losses among members for tax benefits.

Ownership Restrictions

The owners of an LLC are called "members," each owning a "membership interest." Unlike partnerships and S-corporations, corporate investors are allowed to own membership interests in an LLC. While investment funds are free to invest in LLCs, most will not because of unfavorable tax consequences to their tax-exempt investors (for example, pension funds).

Management

Most LLCs will appoint one or more "managing members," who will actively manage the company's business. Because there are not many statutorily required management structures or documents, there is much latitude in how an LLC is managed. This confers the benefit of hand-tooling the operating rules to suit the members, but also creates the need for a well-drafted custom operating agreement. Some of the key clauses to include in the operating agreement are discussed in the "Ownership Agreements" section in this chapter.

Taxation

The LLC is a pass-through entity. Corporate investors may be attracted to the form because LLCs allow for custom allocation of profits and losses to members. An LLC can also be incorporated, sometimes tax-free, at any time, making it a sound initial-stage entity form. A frequent strategy is for a company to organize as an LLC initially

NOTE

Venture and investment funds will generally not invest in an LLC due to tax implications for their investors.

if it expects to generate losses. After those losses have been allocated to early investors, the company can incorporate if necessary.

Liability

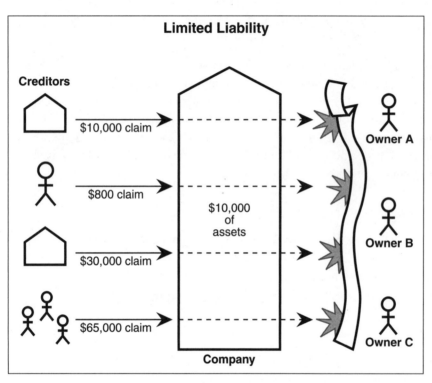

Limited Liability

Creditors

$10,000 claim

$800 claim

$10,000 of assets

$30,000 claim

$65,000 claim

Owner A

Owner B

Owner C

Company

Figure 2.9

Limited liability protects a company's owners from the debts of the company.

Members have no personal liability for the LLC's obligations, but—as with corporate directors—they remain liable for errors and omissions committed while acting in connection with the business.

Documents Required

- Certificate of formation. The certificate of formation (also referred to as "articles of organization" in California) is a short document, similar to the articles of incorporation filed for a corporation, filed with the secretary of state that sets forth the basic information of the business: name, address, agent for service of process, term, and governance (that is, will the LLC be governed by the members or by managers appointed by the members).

- Operating Agreement. As mentioned above, taking advantage of the LLC's flexibility requires careful documentation of relations between the members and the company. Boilerplate documents are strongly discouraged. See the "Ownership Agreements" section in this chapter for a discussion of these contracts.

Partnership

A partnership is most appropriate for businesses:

- *Whose founders desire to allocate profits and tax losses as they desire.*
- *With at least one founder willing to accept liability for the business' debts.* Partnerships require at least one partner to be a general partner personally liable for the debts of the partnership.
- *That do not expect to raise funds from foreigners or investment funds.* Partners must be persons, and partnership income carries tax burdens on foreigners that can be avoided by using a corporation.

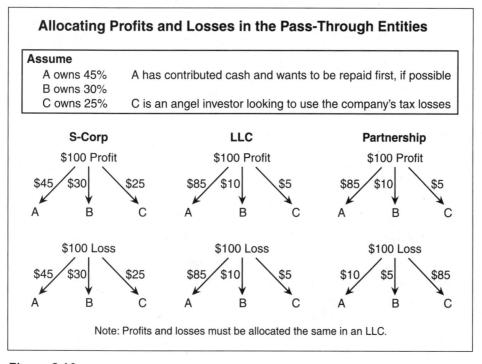

Allocating Profits and Losses in the Pass-Through Entities

Assume

A owns 45%   A has contributed cash and wants to be repaid first, if possible
B owns 30%
C owns 25%   C is an angel investor looking to use the company's tax losses

Note: Profits and losses must be allocated the same in an LLC.

Figure 2.10

Flexible profit and loss allocation is an attractive feature of the partnership.

Ownership Restrictions

A partnership must be owned by two or more persons, which includes individuals, partnerships, corporations, and other associations. While foreigners are not prohibited from becoming partners in a United States partnership, the partnership entity is unattractive to them because they will owe U.S. tax on any income generated from their partnership activity (no such tax is due on a foreign entity's profits from a U.S. corporation).

Partnerships do not tolerate owner turnover very well. Adding more partners is not difficult, but the partnership legally dissolves on the death or withdrawal of a general partner (see the "Partnership: Liability" section in this chapter, on the distinction between general and limited partners). Most partnerships contain a clause providing an alternative to liquidation, generally a buyout of the departing partner, followed by the election of a new general partner if necessary.

Management

A partnership creates an agent relationship between each partner and the partnership, meaning that every partner has the authority to act on behalf of the partnership. Any partner—limited or general—can obligate the partnership if that partner is acting with the scope of the partnership's business. A rogue partner could obligate you to a bad business deal, but probably not to a lease on a Ferrari. The potential for chaos and liability makes the selection of partners and the drafting of the partnership agreement particularly important. Some would draw a parallel to marriage, but we do not consider ourselves authorities on that topic.

Limited partners generally cannot participate in control of the partnership; otherwise, they risk being treated as general partners for liability purposes (see the "Partnership: Liability" section that follows).

Taxation

A partnership, like an S-corporation or an LLC, is a flow-through tax entity.

Probably the most attractive feature of the partnership is that losses and profits are freely allocable among partners. Unlike the S-corporation, in which profits and losses must be allocated by ownership, partners can gain tax advantages by agreeing to different arrangements. A situation where this may be desired is one in which a partner providing services wishes to give her share of a year's losses to a partner who donated cash. The best part is that profits can be allocated differently from losses. These arrangements can include preferred return systems, and may change over time.

There are limits to the utility of this flexibility. Passive losses (losses incurred by a partner who does not actively participate in the business) are not deductible from most forms of income. Since limited partners are generally assumed to be passive, limited partners will only be able to use the partnership losses against capital gains they may have incurred that year. Furthermore, a partner cannot claim a deduction greater than the amount of the partner's basis in his interest.

Liability

There are two forms of partnerships: general, and limited liability. In a general partnership, all partners have unlimited liability for the partnership's debts. In a limited liability partnership, there must be at least one general partner who accepts personal liability for the partnership's debts; all limited partners (none of whom may actively participate in the management of the partnership) are liable only to the extent of their contribution to the partnership. The general partner must take extra care when selecting partners, as every partner is a legal agent of the partnership and may transact business and create obligations on its behalf (see the preceding "Management" section).

The partnership is interesting because it is treated as a separate legal entity for some purposes, and not for others. A partnership can sue and be sued, and it may own property. However, the creditor of a partner would sue the partner's interest, not the partnership as a whole.

Documents Required

For a general partnership, no documents are required, merely a meeting of minds and intention to form a partnership. A limited partnership must file a certificate with the secretary of state and have a written partnership agreement.

All partnerships should have a written partnership agreement covering certain basic terms and eventualities, discussed in the following "Ownership Agreements" section.

Unlike corporate documents, which are reasonably standardized, the ownership, management, and profit-sharing relations among partners vary significantly, requiring carefully tailored agreements. Individualization equals attorney time, but it is usually necessary, as boilerplate forms are not likely to adequately reflect the partners' intent.

Added to the many dangers of engaging in business without a document clearly establishing ownership, intent, and eventualities is the application of state partnership laws in the absence of a written agreement. This can create undesirable outcomes due to provisions of law that may contradict the original intent of the parties (and, frequently, generally accepted notions of fairness). Partnership law is nowhere near as comprehensive as corporate law, meaning that partners will have a less established body of law to guide them in case of disputes.

Other Considerations

The following issues pertain to all businesses regardless of entity type:

Licenses

If you plan to do business or maintain an office outside your state of organization, it may be necessary to register as a foreign entity with the secretary of state for each state in which you will be conducting business. Furthermore, check with local counsel to understand any tax obligations you may incur, such as income or sales taxes. If you will have employees in states other than that which you are organized, your company may be subject to withholding worker's compensation, and other labor regulations.

Insurance

Unfortunately, insurance has become very expensive in the last couple of years, leading some companies to "self-insure." "Self-insuring" should always be used in quotation marks because it is a somewhat ironic term: it refers to the practice of putting money into a reserve/rainy day fund rather than paying premiums to a third-party insurer. Of course, the risk is that if disaster strikes when there is not enough money in the reserve, there is no coverage. Even with the limited liability afforded by many corporate entities, insurance is a good idea because

1. It protects the individuals working for the company against errors and omissions for which they would otherwise be personally liable.
2. Insurance can be the difference between a company's survival and its failure in case of fire, unexpected departures of owners who need to be bought out, or other devastating occurrences.

Don't expect investors to put money into a company with no limits to its exposure. Ask around for the name of a good insurance agent who works with other companies in the industry, and spend a bit of time with him explaining how your business operates.

You should consider the following coverage:

- General liability/product liability
- Fire and casualty
- Worker's compensation
- Errors and omissions coverage for officers/directors/management
- Business interruption
- Disability and life insurance for key personnel
- Insurance to fund a buyout in the event of death or disability of an owner

Name

Once you choose a name for your organization, you will first want to check its availability for business use with the secretary of state for each state in which you will be operating. Then, and only then, should you pursue trademarking the name. You can do a cursory check at the United States Patent and Trademark Office's website: www.uspto.gov, but you should ask your attorney to do a proper trademark search and registration as soon as possible. Few things are more irritating than having to change your company's name after the stationery, business cards, website, and a bit of brand equity have been established. A U.S. trademark only protects use of your mark in the U.S., so consult with your attorney to decide if you should pursue international registration (see Chapter 5, "A Primer on Intellectual Property and Licensing," for a discussion of global IP protection issues).

ISSUING OWNERSHIP STAKES

Once you have decided on an entity type and the allocations of ownership, profits, and control among founders, the next step is to issue the ownership stakes. In an LLC, the ownership unit is a *membership interest* owned by *members*, with one or more *managing members* who are most active in the management of the LLC. A partnership has *partners* who own *partnership interests*. A limited partnership will have *limited partners* who enjoy limited liability but little control and *general partners* who enjoy control but full liability for the partnership's debts. A corporation is owned by *shareholders* who own *stock*. Ownership of a corporation can bring other complexities, which will be covered in this section.

While the terms describing what it is one "owns" are different for each entity, they share many of the same legal issues and trouble spots that need to be addressed. Owners should have a written agreement in place laying down the owners' expectation in a number of areas: control; how ownership will be affected by certain events such as death, departure, and addition of new owners; and what to do when an owner wishes to sell. The "Ownership Agreements" section of this chapter covers the main scenarios and points to consider.

This section will explain:

- The form and special considerations of ownership in a corporation.
- Recommended provisions in ownership agreements.

Ownership of a Corporation: Equity

This section addresses issuing ownership in corporations, which will provide a good framework for understanding concerns of sharing ownership no matter what your entity type. Ownership comes in the form of shares of stock, which are also known as *equity*.

Tax Rules Regarding Stock and Stock Option Grants

The animating principle behind the IRS regulations regarding stock and option grants is that the government wants to encourage business development while preventing employees from getting a free ride by camouflaging all of their income as stock, which can be taxed at the lower long-term capital gains rates.

Taxpayers are taxed on the value of equity received. Value is determined in the IRS's eyes through "valuation events" like financing rounds. If they receive equity in exchange for services, they are taxed on the fair market value of the equity as though they had been given cash. If they are given options, they are taxed on the difference between the fair market value of the stock at time of election and the *exercise price* (what the person pays to exchange the option for an actual share of stock) of the option.

The goals, in descending order, of an equity incentive program, are

1. To get a bye on as much of the asset's value as possible.
2. To have as much equity appreciation qualify for LTCG treatment as possible, with a maximum rate of 20 percent, instead of OI, which has a maximum rate of 38.6 percent.
3. To defer the "taxable event," (the time when tax becomes due), as long as possible (thereby theoretically allowing the taxpayer to invest and receive interest/returns on that money during the interim).

To Founders

Generally speaking, founders and employees will receive common stock subject to vesting. Another incentive to incorporate early and issue stock is that if you wait until the eve of a financing—for instance, if you will be receiving an equity investment from a publisher—the IRS could deem it as discounted stock and tax you on the spread.

Stock Versus Options

Founders can take stock or options, but stock is generally the wiser choice for two reasons.

1. If a founder will not be an employee, she will not qualify for a tax-privileged option plan.
2. Capital assets such as stock must be "held" for a certain amount of time to gain special tax status, 12 months to be a LTCG and five years to be QSBC. Stock is a capital asset (assuming that it is vested or the owner has filed an 83(b) election, discussed in the 83(b) section, which follows), but stock options are not, meaning that holding periods only begin running when stock is purchased. If you qualify for the QSBC exemption (see Sidebar: Small Business Corporation Stock), you will want to start the five-year holding period as soon as possible.

Vesting

Vesting, where the company retains the right to repurchase some or all of a stock/option grant until certain dates, is a mechanism for the corporation to grant stock or options while retaining the right to repurchase them should the employee leave the company. *Cliff vesting* is the norm, whereby some amount of a grantee's stock will vest at the end of a long period, say, one year, and the remainder will vest monthly over, for example, the next three years.

> **NOTE**
>
> If the grantee leaves early, the company may repurchase the stock (or in the case of options, invalidate the options), at the lower of the employee's cost or the fair market value of the stock.

83(b) Election

The IRS only considers you to "own" stock that is not subject to a *substantial risk of forfeiture.* Stock or options subject to vesting is considered to be at a substantial risk of forfeiture, and therefore not actually owned until it vests.

At every vesting date, the IRS thinks of you as receiving income—subject to withholding and income tax—equal to the value of the stock *at the date of vesting* less whatever you pay for the vesting shares. This could result in unpleasant consequences if your stock's value experiences rapid gain over your vesting schedule.

83(b) Election

Assume
FMV at date of grant = $10
FMV at date of vesting = $20
Sale price = $35

Tax Due At:

	Date of Grant	Date of Vesting	Date of Sale
With 83(b) election	$10 ordinary income tax	$0	$25 long term capital gains tax
Without 83(b) election	$0	$20 ordinary income tax	$15 capital gains tax*

*Note that the shareholder may owe short term capital gains tax (up to 38.6%) because the holding period only began at time of *vesting*, not time of *grant*.

Figure 2.11

The 83(b) election can minimize the tax bite of vesting equity compensation.

Fortunately, the IRS allows you to escape this by filing an 83(b) election within 30 days of the initial purchase of your shares. An 83(b) election is an agreement to pay the amount of tax that would be due if the stock were not subject to vesting. Essentially, you pretend that you have received all of the stock at the date of the election, and pay whatever tax would be due if that were the case. Usually, it is zero, because you will be paying fair market value for the stock and, because there will not have been any appreciation in the stock's value, there will be no spread. LTCG tax will be due when the stock is ultimately sold.

Acceptable Consideration

It surprises many founders that they are required to furnish valid *consideration* (payment) for their stock, or face IRS income tax. State laws regarding acceptable consideration vary, so check your state statute for restrictions. Cash and most kinds of property with a documentable value are acceptable. Fortunately, founder stock is usually very inexpensive, $.01 per share, so cash-strapped entrepreneurs can afford to buy a stake in their own company. Some states allow past services, but others do not consider the promise of future services or other promissory notes to be valid.

If you are contributing property, you will want to avoid paying income tax on the value of the shares you receive by making a Section 351 election. This is available if and only if:

- The property is transferred solely in exchange for stock of the company; and,
- Immediately after transfer, all transferors (cash and property, not solely service providers) own stock with at least 80 percent of combined voting power of all classes of stock entitled to vote and at least 80 percent of total number of shares of each non-voting class.

If there will be more than one transferor, the transfers do not need to be simultaneous, but rights need to have been defined in an agreement and documents effecting the transfers need to be summarily executed.

You need to file a 351 election on your tax return to receive this treatment. If you do not qualify for a 351 election, you will likely pay income tax on the receipt of shares and qualify for capital gains treatment on any appreciation thereafter.

CAUTION

If a founder will be donating property, she should give assurances that she owns all rights in and to the property, *especially* if it's intellectual property. Otherwise, the company could be liable for damages to third parties caused by the use of the property, for example, if it were stolen. It is also a fine idea for the company to obtain guarantees and indemnifications from the transferor or third-party insurance in case problems arise.

To Investors

Later investors often receive convertible preferred stock or preferred stock with warrants. There are two main reasons for this:

1. Investors like preferred stock because it carries *payment priority* over common stock (preferred stockholders are paid back first) in case of bankruptcy. Some investors try to get upside participation as well in the form of conversions or warrants attached to the preferred stock.
2. The company wants to avoid having all of its equity priced at the valuation the investors paid, because it would be much more expensive for employees and founders to purchase. A company can point to the preferred stock's extra rights and show the IRS that the common stock should be valued at a significant discount, thus enabling the company to continue giving out common stock and options at advantageous exercise prices and minimizing the tax liabilities to their employees.

To Employees

An employee option plan is valuable to employees if

1. They receive stock options at a low valuation and can exercise and sell those shares at a later date; the grant is taxed at LTCG and not OI rates; and
2. The employee does not incur an undue or poorly timed tax obligation.

Qualifying vs. Non-Qualifying Stock Options

Assume
FMV at date of grant = $10
price = $10
FMV at exercise date = $20
sale price = $25

Tax Due At:

	Date of Grant	Date Exercised		Date Sold	
Qualifying	$0	$0		Sale price	$25
				Less price paid for option	$10
				LT Capital Gains	$15
Non-Qualifying	$0	FMV at exercise	$20	Sale price	$25
		Less price paid	$10	Less basis	$20
		Ordinary income	$10	Capital Gains	$5

Figure 2.12

Qualifying stock options can allow more of the option on value to classify or the lower LTCG rates.

The receipt of an option is not a taxable event. Only the exercise or sale of the underlying stock is. An option is not a capital asset, so in order to receive LTCG treatment on the underlying stock, the IRS requires you to hold it for at least 12 months from the time you exercise your right to purchase the stock.

There are two kinds of employee incentive option programs: those that qualify for favorable IRS treatment and those that do not. The benefit of qualifying is that the employee pays no ordinary income tax at exercise, and—even better—the employee defers the taxable event until *the underlying shares are sold.* The spread on the shares (fair market value less exercise price) will be taxed at LTCG rates if the stock—not the option—is held for more than one year from exercise, and two years from the date the option was granted. Otherwise, the employee faces OI tax on the spread. To qualify for this kind of tax treatment, the options must be granted to an employee, and the exercise price must be 100 percent of fair market value *at date of grant* (110 percent if grantee owns more than 10 percent of the corporation).

All other option grants are non-qualifying. When the grantee exercises, she recognizes OI on the spread, subject to income and employment withholding. Any additional gain in security is treated as capital gains.

Ownership Agreements

Ownership agreements are contracts that govern relations among owners of an enterprise including what owners can do with their shares/membership interests/partnership interests, how an owner leaves the company, and so forth. These are extremely important contracts as they set many of the ground rules for resolving conflict and allocating power, so be sure you have experienced counsel helping you.

Transferability of Ownership

All founders and founder-employees should sign a shareholders' agreement—sometimes referred to as a *stock purchase agreement* or *buy-sell agreement*—granting the company the ability to maintain ownership with the ship's current crew and to provide liquidity in particular situations as necessary. This agreement lays out the valuation methodology, order of purchaser priority (to whom the share is offered first, second, and so forth), and to whom a shareholder may sell in the event she leaves the company. The three primary means of regulating share ownership are the right of first refusal, the buy/sell, and the co-sale agreement.

- Under a right of first refusal, the company has first pick of any shares sold by the founder/employee at the price being offered to the founder/employee by a third party. This has the functional effect of parking the stock; no buyer wants to negotiate a price knowing that it will be offered to an outside party.

- The buy/sell agreement generally stipulates that:
  a. The shareholder may only transfer his or her shares in accord with the buy-sell agreement.
  b. Certain transfers to family (or other designated parties) are permitted, for instance, on death or disability of the shareholder.
  c. The company has the option or obligation to purchase the shares from the family/designated party for fair market value, and the transferee is obligated to sell. Pricing is difficult because there is no third party or liquidity event; appointing an account of mutual choosing is often helpful.

- A co-sale agreement is frequently used where parties are concerned about a majority owner selling his or her share to an outsider. This agreement allows other shareholders to replace a portion of the stake being sold with their own shares. Example: An outsider wants to buy all of the majority owner's 400,000 shares, and a 50/50 co-sale is in place. The other shareholder may sell 200,000 shares and the majority owner may sell 200,000 shares to the third party.

> **CAUTION**
>
> **Marriage, divorce, and death can give rise to spousal rights in the shares. Consult with the attorney preparing your shareholder's agreement about the marital property laws of the states in which shareholders reside to understand their effects on the company and other shareholders.**

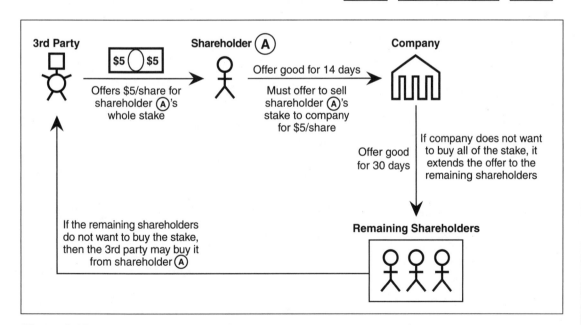

Figure 2.13

Illustration of the right of first refusal.

Partnership and LLC Considerations

Partnership and LLC agreements will have additional clauses peculiar to their form, including:

- Profit and Loss Allocation. Because profits and losses may be allocated according to owners' wishes, the partnership agreement and LLC operating agreement should set forth the proportions for allocations of profits and losses.

- Capital contributions. Partnerships and LLCs may have capital contribution requirements, which may require owners to commit to providing a set amount of supplemental funding should the company require it.

- Distributions. A partnership or LLC agreement will set up rules for how, when, and how much money is distributed to the owners. There are usually conditions, for example, only capital in excess of $X may be distributed. Such distributions are sometimes referred to as the "draw."

- Departure/Admission of new partners or members. Partnerships and LLCs tend to be closely held and intimately managed, making the departure or addition of new owners a big deal. To be sure that this process is managed carefully, the ownership agreements will usually set out the procedure for termination, voluntary withdrawal, and admission of new owners.

- Dissolution. Ownership of LLCs and partnerships is not as freely transferable as with a corporation. Generally, these entities legally dissolve on the departure of a member or partner, so the ownership agreements usually set out ways to continue the company's existence in case of legal dissolution.

SUMMARY

This chapter covered the first steps of organizing your company, which should happen in three steps:

- Decide ownership stakes. Sit down and figure out how the founders see their contributions and what level of ownership and control they expect. Think about whether a vesting schedule would make sense.
- Choose a business entity. Take a look at the business entity options available: the C-corporation, S-corporation, and LLC make the most sense for developers, because they give all of the owners limited liability protection.
- Issue the ownership. Once you know how you'll be allocating ownership and what business entity is best for your company, you'll need to execute an ownership agreement controlling relations among the owners.

The C-corporation is usually not appropriate for young companies because of its entity-level tax, but because most of the profits will be reinvested and/or paid to owners as salary, the entity tax becomes less of an issue. Furthermore, QSBC stock can cut the owners' capital gains tax in half if the stock is owned for five years or more.

The S-corporation offers a lot of the C-corporation's benefits but without the double tax. Ownership is limited to 75 or fewer individuals, however—which means no corporate investment. Lots of entrepreneurs start their companies as S-corporations so that they can deduct initial capital losses against their income and capital gains tax, reorganizing (tax-free) later as a C-corporation.

The LLC is another popular option for game developers. It has the benefits of an S-corporation without the limit on ownership. It also doesn't have all of the regulatory requirements of a corporation (annual meetings, filing minutes, and so on). However, there are some drawbacks to the LLC, such as the difficulty of transferring ownership or adding owners, and the lack of self-employment tax reductions that may be available to owner-employees of an S-corporation.

RESTRICTED STOCK PURCHASE AGREEMENT

This restricted stock purchase agreement ("Agreement") is made this _____ day of _____, 20_____ by and between Double D Development, Inc. ("Company") and Dana Darby ("Darby"), Alex Johns ("Johns"), Pat Ling ("Ling"), Dusty Trayle ("Trayle"), and Jean Zinter ("Zinter").

WHEREAS, Company is authorized to issue 20,000 shares of common stock of the company ("Common Stock") having no par value (all issued and outstanding shares of Common Stock being referred to as "Shares"), and

WHEREAS, Company hereby issues 15,000 shares of Common Stock to be purchased on this day by the Shareholders as follows:

Dana Darby _____ 3,000 Shares
Alex Johns _____ 3,000 Shares
Pat Ling _____ 3,000 Shares
Dusty Trayle _____ 3,000 Shares
Jean Zinter _____ 3,000 Shares

WHEREAS, the shares of Common Stock be purchased by the Shareholders (the "Shares") will be subject to certain terms, conditions, and restrictions on transfer as set forth in this Agreement; and

WHEREAS, the Shareholders agree to vote their shares for the officers of Company as follows:

_____ President

_____ Vice President

_____ Secretary

_____ Treasurer

WHEREAS, the Shareholders shall be appointed to the board of directors of Company (the "Board") so long as they continue to be Shareholders, and

WHEREAS, Darby, Johns, Ling, Trayle, and Zinter are concurrently entering into employment agreements with the Company (each an "Employment Agreement") and desire to provide for the continuity of the present successful and harmonious management of the Company, and

WHEREAS, each of the parties herein desires to make provision with respect to the ownership, transfer, or other disposition of his or her shares of the Company,

NOW, THEREFORE, in consideration of the mutual promises and agreements contained herein, the parties hereto agree as follows:

1. Definitions. For purposes of this Agreement:

   "Founding Shareholder" shall refer to any of Darby, Johns, Ling, Trayle, or Zinter.

   "Permitted Transferee" shall mean any guardian or conservator of a Shareholder, or any executor or administrator of the estate of a Shareholder.

   "Purchasing Shareholder," as defined in Section 3(B)(i)(c) hereof.

   "Remaining Shareholders" shall mean all other Shareholders of record at the time of a given event.

   "Shareholder" shall mean any person or entity now or hereafter owning any of the Shares and who is party to this Agreement, including without limitation, Darby, Johns, Ling, Trayle, and Zinter.

2. Vesting

   A. Schedule. So long as a Founding Shareholder remains an employee or director of the Company, one-forty-eighth (1/48th) of that Founding Shareholder's Shares will vest at the end of each partial or complete calendar month after the effective date of this Agreement. A Founding Shareholder will become fully vested in the Shares at the end of the 48th month from the effective date of this Agreement if she remains an employee of the Company throughout such period.

   B. Company Repurchase Right. Upon a Founding Shareholder's termination of employment, the Company shall have the right, in its sole discretion, to repurchase the unvested portion of the Founding Shareholder's Shares at the Founding Shareholder's original purchase price.

   C. Stock Power and Retention of Certificates. The Company may require the Founding Shareholder to execute and deliver to the Company a stock power in blank with respect to the unvested Shares and may, in its sole discretion, determine to retain possession of or escrow the certificates for unvested Shares. The Company shall have the right, in its sole discretion, to exercise such stock power in the event that the Company becomes entitled to any Shares. Notwithstanding retention of such certificates by the Company, the Founding Shareholder shall have all rights (including dividend and voting rights) with respect to the unvested Shares represented by such certificates.

   D. Taxes. To the extent the lapse of restrictions results in the receipt of compensation by the Founding Shareholder for tax purposes, the Company shall withhold from any cash compensation then or thereafter payable to the Founding Shareholder any tax required to be withheld by reason thereof. To the extent the Company determines that such cash compensation is or may be insufficient to fully satisfy such withholding requirement, the Founding Shareholder shall deliver to the Company cash in an amount determined by the Company to be sufficient to satisfy any such withholding requirement. If the Founding Shareholder makes the election authorized by § 83(b) of the Internal Revenue Code of 1986, as amended, the Founding Shareholder shall submit to the Company a copy of the statement filed by the Founding Shareholder to make such election.

E. Change in Control. The Company's option to repurchase set forth in Sections 2 and 3 hereof shall lapse immediately upon the occurrence of a "change in control" of the Company. For purposes hereof a "Change in Control" of the Company shall be deemed to occur if (i) any party other than a group including the Founding Shareholder whose shares are in question is or becomes the owner of securities with forty percent (40%) or more of the combined voting power of the Company's then outstanding securities, or (ii) the Shareholders approve a merger or consolidation of the Company with any other corporation in which, post-transaction, the Company holds less than fifty percent (50%) of the combined voting power of the voting securities of the merged entity, or (iii) the shareholders approve a plan of complete liquidation of the Company or an agreement for the sale or disposition by the Company of all or substantially all the Company's assets.

3. Voluntary Transfers.

A. No Shareholder shall pledge, grant a security interest in or otherwise encumber any Shares, whether with her consent or by operation of law, without the unanimous written consent of the remaining Shareholders and of Company ("Consent"), except as set forth below in this Agreement.

B. No Shareholder shall sell, assign, transfer or otherwise dispose of any of his Shares or enter into any contract to sell, assign, transfer or otherwise dispose of any Shares, whether voluntarily or by operation of law, except upon the following terms and conditions:

   i. Absent Consent, a Shareholder wishing to sell, transfer or assign or otherwise dispose of any Shares must first receive a bona fide offer for the purchase of such Shares from a third party, which offer may only be accepted by the Shareholder after satisfaction of the following terms and conditions:

      a. The Shareholder ("Offering Shareholder") shall provide notice to the Company of the third party offer ("Notice of Offer"), and Company shall forward copies of such Notice of Offer to Remaining Shareholders within seven (7) days of its receipt. The Notice of Offer shall serve as an offer, irrevocable for fourteen (14) days ("Company Offer Period"), to sell all of the Shares offered to the third party ("Offered Shares") to Company and an offer, irrevocable for an additional thirty (30) days ("Remaining Shareholder Offer Period") to sell shares not purchased by company to the Remaining Shareholders. The Notice of Offer shall state: (i) the terms of the proposed transfer, including the offered price per Share and the terms of payment, (ii) the name and address of the proposed transferee and (iii) the contemplated date of transfer, and shall contain a copy of the third party's offer.

b. If the Company elects to purchase the Offered Shares, it shall give written notice to Offering Shareholder ("Notice of Acceptance") and Remaining Shareholders within the fourteen-day offer period and shall, as promptly thereafter as practicable, pay the Offering Shareholder the Purchase Price as defined in Section 7 below and in accord with Section 9 below.

c. If the Company elects not to purchase the Offered Shares, the Remaining Shareholders shall have the right to purchase all, but not less than all of the Offered Shares by giving Notice of Acceptance and shall, as promptly thereafter as practicable, pay the Offering Shareholder the Purchase Price as defined in Section 7 below and in accord with Section 9 below (any such Shareholder giving Notice of Acceptance, a "Purchasing Shareholder"). In the event that more than one Purchasing Shareholder gives a Notice of Acceptance to purchase the number of Shares which is subject of the offer, each such Purchasing Shareholder shall purchase the number of Shares which is computed by dividing the number of Shares which is the subject of the offer by the number of Purchasing Shareholders.

d. If all the Offered Shares are not subscribed to be purchased pursuant to the terms hereof by the Company or a Purchasing Shareholder(s), then the Offering Shareholder shall have the right to sell or transfer the Offered Shares within sixty (60) days after the expiration of the Remaining Shareholder Offer Period upon the terms and to the party described in the Notice of Offer. If such Shares are not so transferred within such sixty (60) day permitted time period, such Shares shall again become subject to the restrictions contained in this Section 3 (and which Shares shall also remain subject to all of the other restrictions hereunder) in the hands of the Offering Shareholder.

e. Each and every transferee of such Shares shall take such Shares subject to the terms and conditions of this Agreement, and shall be deemed a Shareholder hereunder with respect to any subsequent disposition of such Shares by a transferee. No such transferee shall accept Shares and no Shares shall be transferred until such transferee becomes a party to this Agreement by executing one of the signature pages hereof in the space provided under the heading "Additional Shareholders." Upon execution of such signature page, such transferee's acceptance of such Shares and the transfer of such Shares on the records of the Company, such transferee shall be deemed to be a Shareholder within the meaning of this Agreement, and such transferee shall be bound by this Agreement to the same extent that the Founding Shareholders are so bound.

f. The provisions of Section 3 of this Agreement shall not be applicable to any transfer to a Permitted Transferee provided that prior to or simultaneously with a transfer each and every such Permitted Transferee becomes a party to this Agreement by signing and dating in the space provided under the heading "PERMITTED TRANSFEREE Shareholders." Upon any transfer in accordance with the preceding sentence, the transferee shall be deemed a Shareholder within the meaning of this Agreement and shall be bound by this Agreement to the same extent that the Founding Shareholders are bound.

g. Notwithstanding anything to the contrary contained in the Agreement, a Shareholder may pledge or otherwise grant a security interest in his portion of the Shares if required by a third party institutional lender, as security or guaranty of the Company's obligation in connection with a loan from such institutional lender to the Company.

4. Death of a Shareholder.
In the event of the death of a Shareholder, the legal representatives of said deceased Shareholder shall promptly give written notice of his death to the Company, and the Company must by written notice to the legal representatives of said deceased Shareholder within forty-five (45) days after receipt of such notice of death, elect to purchase all, but not less than all, of the Shares owned at the time of death by said deceased Shareholder for the Purchase Price set forth in Section 7 and upon the terms set forth in Section 9.

5. Transfers by Operation of Law.
Should a Shareholder: file a voluntary petition under any bankruptcy or insolvency law; petition for the appointment of a receiver; make an assignment for the benefit of creditors; be subject involuntarily to such petition or assignment; or, be subject to a third party's attachment or other legal or equitable interest in that Shareholder's Shares (other than by voluntary transfer or by pledge to an institutional lender in accordance with the provisions of Section 3.g), and such involuntary petition or assignment is not discharged within sixty (60) days after its date (all of the foregoing, hereinafter called a "Credit Event"), the Company shall have the right to elect to purchase all, but not less than all, of the Shares owned at the time of such credit Event by said Shareholder for the Purchase Price set forth in Section 7 and upon the terms set forth in Section 9.

This right to purchase shall continue for forty-five (45) days after the Company is given written notice of such Credit Event and may be exercised by notice to such Shareholder at any time within such period. With respect to any Shares not purchased by the Company pursuant to rights granted pursuant to this Section 5, any sale, transfer, pledge or any other disposition by any such receiver, petitioner, assignee or other person obtaining any such legal or equitable interest shall be deemed to be a disposition by the Shareholder pursuant to Section 3 hereof and shall be subject to the provisions thereof and the other provisions of this Agreement and the Shareholders' Agreement.

6. Termination of Employment.

In the event of the termination of a Shareholder's employment with the Company for any reason whatsoever (except death), including without limitation disability, legal incapacity, retirement, voluntary or involuntary termination, or any other condition rendering Shareholder incapable of performing all duties for six consecutive months, said Shareholder or his or her legal representatives shall offer for sale, and the Company may purchase at its sole discretion some or all of the Shares then owned by said Shareholder at the Purchase Price as defined in Section 7 and upon payment terms and conditions set forth in Section 9. Such sale shall occur within sixty (60) days of Shareholder's termination.

7. Purchase Price.

With respect to any purchase of a portion of the Shares under Section 3 hereof, in the case of a proposed sale to a third party pursuant to a bona fide offer, Purchase Price shall be the lesser of (i) the proposed purchase price per share offered by such third party and (ii) the Appraised Value of the Shares as determined under Section 8 of this Agreement. With respect to any other purchase, Purchase Price shall be the Appraised Value of the Shares as determined under Section 8 of this Agreement.

8. Appraised Value.

The Appraised Value of each of the Shares shall be the value of the shares as mutually agreed upon from time to time by the Shareholders as set forth on Schedule A attached hereto and incorporated herein by reference, as said schedule may from time to time be amended by a writing signed by all the then parties hereto and attached hereto. If at such time as any notice to purchase or sell is given in accordance with the provisions of this Agreement, and the Appraised Value as set forth on Schedule A has not been amended during the twenty four (24) month period preceding the date of notice, then the Appraised Value of each Share shall be the fair market value thereof as determined by independent appraisers as hereinafter provided.

If the Appraised Value of each Share is to be determined by independent appraisers then the proposed purchaser shall promptly appoint one appraiser and the proposed seller (or his legal representative) shall thereupon appoint a second and the two appraisers shall thereupon appoint a third appraiser. Any unappointed appraiser or appraisers shall be appointed by the American Arbitration Association, Podunk, Pacifica, upon application of any party or appraiser. The three appraisers shall promptly proceed by majority vote to determine the current market value per Share. Appraisal costs shall be borne equally by proposed purchaser and seller.

9. Closing.

   For all purposes of this Agreement, any closing ("Closing") shall be held at a time and date not later than sixty (60) days after the exercise of the election to purchase the Shares sold. The Purchase Price of any Shares purchased pursuant to Section 3 of this Agreement shall, at the election of the Company or Purchasing Shareholder(s) as the case may be, be paid: (i) upon the terms and conditions as set forth in the Notice of Offer, if applicable, or (ii) in five (5) equal semi-annual installments commencing three months after the Closing (as defined below). The Purchase Price for any Shares purchased pursuant to any other Section of this Agreement shall be paid within thirty (30) days after the Closing. All Shares which the Company elects to purchase hereunder shall be tendered at the Closing to the Company by delivery of the certificate or certificates representing the Shares to be purchased, duly endorsed for transfer, in form satisfactory to the Company's counsel and such other papers, including warranties as may be reasonably required by said counsel. The Closing shall be held at an office of the Company designated by it.

10. No Dilution.

    The Company shall not issue any additional shares of capital stock nor any subscriptions, warrants, options or other rights for the issuance of any capital stock of the Company, without the prior written consent of all of the Shareholders.

11. Waiver; Disposition of Shares.

    From time to time the Shareholders, by unanimous written consent of the Shareholders at the time of said consent and the Company, may waive their respective rights, in advance, hereunder either generally or with respect to one or more specific transfers. No waiver by the Company or the Shareholder(s), in any one or more instances shall be deemed as a further or continuing waiver of any such term or condition contained herein except to the extent set forth therein.

12. Legend.

    In addition to any other legend required by law or included by the Company, the Company shall be entitled to imprint or type the following legend or any other legend it deems appropriate on each certificate representing Shares, allowing that the absence of such endorsement shall not relieve the parties hereto of their liability and responsibility hereunder:

THIS CERTIFICATE AND THE SHARES REPRESENTED HEREBY ARE SUBJECT TO RESTRICTIONS ON TRANSFER SET FORTH IN A RESTRICTED STOCK PURCHASE AGREEMENT DATED _____, 20____, AMONG THE SHAREHOLDERS AND THE COMPANY. THE COMPANY WILL FURNISH A COPY OF SAID RESTRICTIONS TO THE HOLDER OF THIS CERTIFICATE UPON WRITTEN REQUEST AND WITHOUT CHARGE THEREFORE.

13. Parties.
    This Agreement shall be binding upon the parties hereto, their respective heirs, representatives, successors and assigns and upon transferees of shares of the Company's stock as herein provided. Successor or additional holders of shares of the Company's stock may become parties to this Agreement by endorsing a schedule attached hereto in such form as the Company may from time to time determine, as set forth in Section 3 hereof or by executing a counterpart of this Agreement. A manually executed copy of this Agreement and of any Schedule or amendment shall be kept by the clerk of the Company.

14. Term.
    A. This Agreement shall terminate ("Termination") upon the occurrence of any of the following: (i) bankruptcy, receivership, or dissolution of the Company; (ii) cessation of the Company's business; (iii) the death of all Shareholders; or (iv) written agreement of all Shareholders then party hereto and the Company.
    B. Upon Termination, each Shareholder shall be entitled to surrender to the Company the certificate or certificates representing his Shares and the Company shall thereupon issue to him in lieu thereof a new certificate or certificates for an equal number of Shares without the legend set forth in Section 12 but with any other legend required by law or included by the Company.

15. Accounting Statements. The firm of certified public accountants regularly employed by the Company shall render quarterly accounting statements to all Shareholders with respect to the income of the Company.

16. Notices. All notices required by this agreement shall be sent by certified mail, return receipt requested, addressed to the Company at their principal offices at 747 Winding Road, Podunk, Pacifica 12345 and to each of the Shareholders, or their respective voluntary transferees, donees or involuntary transferees, at their respective addresses appearing on the records of the Company, or to such other address as may be designated from time to time by the party receiving such notice, with copies to: Mark Rahn Esq., at [Attorney's address].

17. Governing Law and Dispute Resolution
This agreement shall be construed under and governed by the laws of the state of Pacifica. Any conflicts shall be resolved by binding arbitration in [Podunk, Pacifica] under the rules and institutional supervision of the American Arbitration Association ("AAA"). Parties or witnesses may appear by telephone. Judgment upon the award(s) rendered by the arbitrator may be entered in any court of any country having jurisdiction thereof. The arbitral tribunal shall consist of one neutral arbitrator appointed by the AAA. The arbitrator shall award attorney's fees to the prevailing party.

18. Entire Agreement.
This Agreement represents the entire agreement of the parties and supersedes all prior agreements, negotiations and understandings, oral or written among the parties with respect to the subject matter hereof. No interpretation, change, waiver, termination or modification of any provision of this Agreement will be binding upon any party unless in writing and signed by all the then parties.

19. Severability.
If any general term or condition of this Agreement shall be invalid or unenforceable to any extent or in any application, then the remainder of this Agreement and such term or condition, except to such extent or application, shall not be affected thereby, and each and every term and condition hereof be valid and enforced to the fullest extent and in the broadest application permitted by law.

20. Further Documentation. The parties hereto agree to execute any and all necessary documents required to carry out the terms of this Agreement.

Executed this _____ day of _____, 20_____, as an instrument under seal in one or more counterparts, each of which shall constitute an original.

_____
Dana Darby

_____
Alex Johns

_____
Pat Ling

_____
Dusty Trayle

_____
Jean Zinter

Additional Shareholders
PERMITTED TRANSFEREE

_____

_____

_____

_____

CHAPTER 3

Financing a Game Development Venture

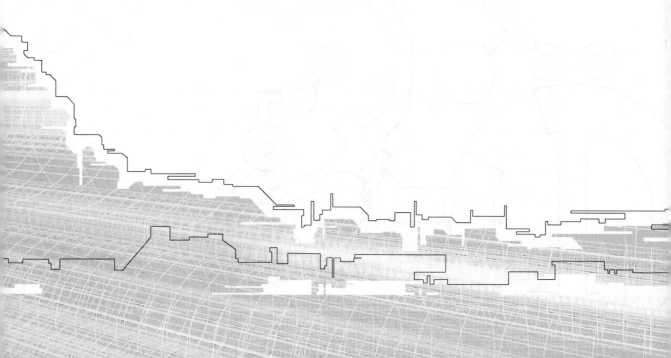

Financing in Action

After a couple of weeks working on the prototype, Dusty and Alex report to the group that most of Defunct's ex-artists and developers are still unemployed and not relishing the thought of relocating. They suggest that some of these folks might be interested in working on the pitch materials for free in exchange for the possibility of a good job in Podunk should Double D get off the ground. Dana, Pat, and Jean agree that this would be fantastic and would increase Double D's chances of getting work—since they would look like a company fully staffed by a team that had shipped product—but it also raised some financial and HR issues that Dana would need to talk over with counsel.

Meanwhile, the group started a time chart for its prototype and supporting documents that looked something like

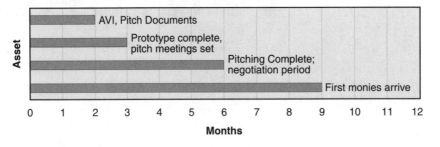

Pitch Build Timeline

Dana wanted to have the pitch ready so that she could set meetings for two upcoming big conferences: GDC and E3. As a new company, albeit one staffed by an old team, she knew their pitch needed to be airtight. She could rely on her cofounders to make a great playable prototype, and Jean and Alex could assemble an AVI file that would show some of the gameplay features that Dusty and company couldn't include in the playable.

She knew that the real decision about their game would be made by a committee they would never see and who might not speak English as a primary language, so her responsibility would be to assemble a sort of executive summary business plan for the game. She drew up a list of items for the document and the person responsible for completing that item:

- A one-sheet as the cover page, giving the vital statistics on the game (genre, platforms, release date, target demographic, two-sentence synopsis of game, competitor games); (Dana)

- The team bios (Dana)

- A stripped down design specification (Pat)

- A short technical specification (Dusty)

- A budget and schedule (Dana)

- "Screenshots" and representative art for every section of the document (Jean and Alex)

New staff or not, the group was recognizing that its initial $25K would probably need a boost to cover costs—software, travel to pitch meetings, rent, a network, and maybe even stipends—until a deal came through. A big staff would probably decrease the amount of time required to build the prototype and pitch materials, but it might mean getting an office, a real network, more software, and maybe even computers if everyone didn't have her own.

As Dana presented it, the group had two options: either forgo a fundraising and do everything by the bootstraps or scratch up some money and give away some of the company. Bootstrapping was a definite possibility, but would probably add a lot of time to their development schedule. "Furthermore," she noted, "we'll have to have some kind of office and network for a publisher to look at when they come around for due diligence." Raising money would take time and attorneys' fees and would probably mean giving up a chunk of the company, but it would give them breathing room and the ability to focus on the game.

It was decided that Dusty and Alex would talk to their old staffers to see if they wanted to come to work on Double D's prototype, with the understanding that they would be paid a small stipend until the company got a deal. Dana would come up with a budget based on the assumption that they would have a staff of 15 working in an office and that Double D wouldn't see a check for another 8 to 10 months.

She and Michael discussed Double D's funding options. Because the amount of money needed by the group was relatively small, friends and family seemed like a good option. An angel investor would be great, but no one in Double D knew any. Michael said that he knew of a few people who might be interested in funding Double D, but Dana would have to draft a good business plan to show them. Dana mentioned some of the game industry's financiers, but said that she would just as soon stay local and simple.

As she was leaving Michael's office, her mobile phone rang—it was Cokie Totenberg. Cokie had been an external producer on a Defunct project managed by Dana and was now in product development at the same publisher. They'd gotten along very well and had stayed in touch.

"I hear you've taken over Defunct."

"Bad news travels fast, huh."

"Only the worst. Is it true? I hear you've got everybody back together in your garage."

"I don't have a garage."

"Yeah, whatever. Anyway, I don't know if it's true or what, but in case it is, we've got a GBA shooter port that we're going to need done pretty soon. Are you interested?"

"Definitely not. Revenue? That sounds like a terrible idea."

"Good. Expect a call from us next week and make sure you can show a decent engine and set of tools."

"Oh. Um…right."

"And one day, your godfather will come to you with a request, and at that time, you are expected to honor your godfather's request."

Dana put her phone away and considered Cokie's offer. This put Double D in a strange position—the port would enable them to get up and running, but all of the software and tools they had created over the years would be gathering mold as the property of Defunct. Dana quickly called a close friend of hers, the CEO of another development studio, and got the phone number of Jamie Kells, their IP attorney.

Dana called Jamie and explained the situation to the attorney, who worked in Northern Pacifica. "Our old company just closed down. I don't think that the owners have any plans for the IP, since most of it is pretty useless without the people who created it—that's us, by the way. I don't know if they're in debt, or even if they're still in the country, but what we want is to buy all the rights to certain tools, and preferably to be able to pay it over time."

Jamie asked Dana if she had a good relationship with the owners of Defunct. "Yeah, very good." "Well, you can have me contact them first, or you could do it, or we could do it together. Let them know what you are interested in doing. If what you are saying is correct about the asset not having value to anyone else, they probably won't want an outrageous amount of money. You will need me or another lawyer to handle the transaction, not just because it's a pretty specialized contract but also because you'll need to do due diligence on the tools—does a publisher have any rights to them, for instance—and make sure that the company is legally able to enter into the transaction."

Jamie continued, "If they are in bankruptcy or about to enter it, you'll need to have your transaction blessed by the court to be sure that the bankruptcy court won't unwind the sale in the future." Dana fretted about her tight timeline, "These port people are going to be sniffing around in a couple of weeks." Jamie commented that odds were good that Defunct's owners would also be motivated to close the transaction quickly.

Dana and the rest of the founders decided on a price they could pay for the engine and the tools, and agreed that an installment plan would be best. They agreed too that they would be willing to borrow money from friends and family for the interim if Defunct insisted on a lump sum payment. Dana took Defunct's owners Malachi and Edward out for dinner, where they told her that they had decided to move to Hawaii to teach scuba diving and to an ashram in Oregon, respectively. Dana told them about what Double D was trying to get together, and they seemed genuinely enthusiastic and concerned for her health. Dana mentioned Double D's interest in buying the old IP from Defunct and the price that she could offer. Malachi and Edward said that they would think it over and call her in the morning.

The next day, Malachi called to say that he and Edward, as the sole shareholders of Defunct, would approve a sale of the IP to Double D for half of the cash Dana offered and 10 percent of Double D's equity. They would even give her first choice of the remaining office equipment. Dana ran this idea by her cofounders and Jamie and Michael, all of whom agreed it was a sound arrangement (pending due diligence). Michael warned Double D that research into Defunct's financial condition would be required to make sure that any sale wouldn't be undone later by a bankruptcy court.

INTRODUCTION

Given the choice between addressing financial strategy and snorting shards of glass, many game developers would have to pause. Unfortunately, development shops require active, constant financial oversight to thrive. This chapter addresses the three main financial issues developers face: raising money, handling a financial crisis, and selling the company.

A developer may want to raise money for start-up costs, including building pitch materials, but it may also pursue outside financing for an independent development or an R&D project. The process of raising money can be broken down into four questions:

- How much money do you need?
- Where do you get it?
- How do you persuade people to give it to you?
- What do you exchange for it?

The development business model is a difficult one, requiring developers to assume a lot of execution risk. Furthermore, payroll keeps burning even if a team isn't engaged on a project, which makes the end of every engagement pretty scary. Even when you've got a contract in place, getting paid can require some effort, not to mention your project can be terminated.

For these reasons, developers need to maintain a cash reserve big enough to buffer against harsh conditions. Even a well-managed company can hit the skids, so this chapter will cover both preventive measures and financial triage. There is also a discussion of winding your company down in a humane and civilized manner, should it become necessary.

If you manage your company well, and produce some great products, you may find yourself on the right side of a buyout offer. Should you accept it? If you do, what terms do you need to negotiate? This chapter will cover these topics and what else to expect during the sales process, including a sample letter of intent from a purchaser interested in buying a company.

HOW MUCH MONEY DO YOU NEED TO RAISE?

There is bad news, bad news, and good news about financing a start-up development shop. The bad news is that, unless your team has worked together before on a successful release, you are

The author would like to thank Li Reilly of Morrison & Foerster LLP (www.mofo.com) for her heroic assistance in preparing this chapter.

unlikely to get a publishing contract without a playable demo or prototype. The other bad news is that you can expect to spend $50K to $200K putting together something good enough to get a deal. The good news is that most of the "cost" of building this demo is labor, which is a lot easier to get on layaway than, say, manufacturing tools.

A start-up developer needs to figure its costs in two tiers:

- What it will cost to build a demo to get a deal
- What it will cost to make the entire game

> **TIP**
>
> Plan carefully. If you're smart, the work that goes into your demo/prototype can be used as the basis to build out the entire game, saving you time and money.

What You Will Need to Build to Get a Deal

Because of the skyrocketing cost of development and publishers' sensitivity to releasing games in the revenue quarter for which they are scheduled, unknown development teams—which can include an experienced group of developers working together for the first time—need to prove their ability to execute. The days of getting a publishing deal based on a design document are all but gone, and new teams will find it difficult to sway publishers and investors with a simple, non-playable demo.

> **NOTE**
>
> For purposes of this chapter, a demo will be defined as a sample of the game that is more graphically developed and less functionally/technologically developed. The demo will use animated mock-ups to show planned functionalities. A prototype will be defined as more technically oriented, using placeholder art to demonstrate functioning technology and gameplay. A "pitch build" is defined as whatever you build to shop around to publishers, whether a demo or a prototype.

Art usually takes less time than technology, but technology is likely to be more impressive to a publisher. This must be weighed against the talents available to you. Do you have financing and the money to hire complementary talent? Or are you working with what is available to you for free? If the latter, adjust your goals to your team: work on a prototype if you have a lot of technical talent; concentrate on a demo if you are art-heavy.

If you are building a demo, feel free to create animations that show features you plan to implement, but program in a baseline playability to allow a publisher to understand what the gameplay is like and what the fun factor is. Publishers have seen too many eye-popping features in demos that have no prayer of actually getting built into the game.

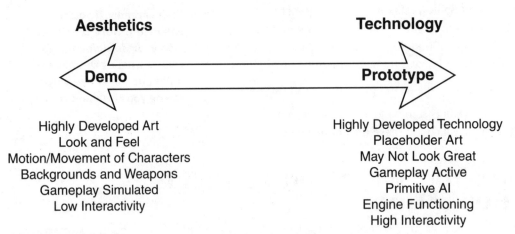

Demo vs. Prototype

Aesthetics   **Technology**

Demo   **Prototype**

Highly Developed Art   Highly Developed Technology
Look and Feel   Placeholder Art
Motion/Movement of Characters   May Not Look Great
Backgrounds and Weapons   Gameplay Active
Gameplay Simulated   Primitive AI
Low Interactivity   Engine Functioning
                                          High Interactivity

Figure 3.1

A startup team should look to the talents of its members in choosing to make a demo or prototype.

To organize yourself, draft a budget based on what everything would cost if you could pay for it. Example (with no bearing in financial reality):

Item	Cost	Total
Programmer × 2	(100/month × 6) × 2	1200
Designer	100/month × 2	200
Artist	100/month × 6	600
Office rent	50/month × 6	300
Office equipment and overhead		100
Computers and dev kits	20 × 4	80
Professional fees (lawyer, accountant)	100	100
TOTAL		**2580**

Of course, you may not have your full budget at your disposal—the point of this budget is so that you and your co-founders can point to each need and say, "Hey, my cousin Harry has a basement office in his pizzeria that never gets used. He'd give it to me for $400 a month, and we won't have to worry about feeding ourselves" and "I've got

TIP

Every member of your founding team should have 12 months' worth of expenses in the bank (or another way to feed himself for that time).

two decent workstations at my house that we can use, but we'll need to get a decent monitor for the art station," and so on. It's a strong possibility that none of you will be earning any income for around 12 months. However, it is perfectly reasonable to write up employment agreements with salaries, on the assumption that the company will essentially owe you this money until it can afford to pay it back.

How to Budget for a Product

The number one developer error cited by publishers, agents, and developers alike is underbudgeting the time and money a product's development requires. Understanding your budget for a project is somewhat simple in theory: who will you need, for how long, at what salary, and what equipment and outside technology will it require? Unfortunately, it takes years of experience to even start getting the "for how long" coefficient correct, let alone the "who will you need."

TIP

When pitching your project to publishers, keep in mind that they are evaluating you, not necessarily for the project you pitch, but for your suitability to develop other titles they need. (Example: you pitch an original IP fighting game; the publisher has recently purchased a boxing license; it declines your IP but offers you a work for hire developing its boxing license.) A big piece of that evaluation is whether you have a realistic understanding of a budget and timeline for a given set of features. A dramatically underbid project will raise flags for a publisher that you don't understand scope and that you will need additional financing mid-project.

If you are a developer, you are probably optimistic by nature; budgeting is a good time to get in touch with your darker side. Ask your technical and art leads to come up with the absolute most they could possibly imagine the product requiring, in duration and manpower. Factor in every last detail you can imagine, from per-employee phone use to taxes (don't forget taxes!). Then add in a profit margin, at least enough to let you pay everyone, keep the lights on, and quickly build up your cash

CAUTION

Developers have been known to get carried away with product love and spend their last dollar of margin to develop the very best game, figuring "we'll make it up in royalties." While that is a possibility, it is a dangerous risk to take with your company's life. As one seasoned executive put it: "No one misses what didn't go in."

reserve of a few months' *burn* (total monthly expenses). Then add a margin of error (most advocate between 20 percent for the more experienced and 35 percent for the less experienced).

$$\text{Budget} = [(\text{Time} \times \text{Salaries}) + \text{Equipment} + \text{Technology} + \text{Overhead}] \times$$
$$(1 + \text{profit margin}) \times (1 + \text{error margin})$$

Scalability

Your budget is based on certain assumptions: how long tasks will take, how many people will be needed to achieve them, and so on. When those assumptions need adjustment, your budget (along with the scope of your project) needs the flexibility to adjust along with them.

Example: Your original budget called for level 10 to have eight beasts created by an art team of five working with 21-inch monitors. You have four scalable elements in that assumption: number of levels in the game, number of beasts on the level, number of artists, and expense of technology. Depending on how far behind budget/schedule you are, you can make smaller (19-inch instead of 21-inch monitors, six beasts instead of eight) or larger (four artists, nine levels) adjustments.

> **CAUTION**
>
> This budget bears very little resemblance to an actual budget and is provided as a structural template, not an example of what a project's actual costs are.

Example of a budget structure

Developer's budget worksheet

Dev Team	Months	Involvement(1)	Salary/yr	Salary/mo	Costs
Lead Programmer	16	100%	$90,000	$7,500	$120,000
Programmer 2	16	100%	$70,000	$5,833	$93,333
Programmer 3	12	100%	$67,000	$5,583	$67,000
Programmer 4	5	100%	$64,000	$5,333	$26,667
Programmer 5	16	100%	$64,000	$5,333	$85,333
Programmer 6	13.6	100%	$62,000	$5,167	$70,267
Programmer 7	16	100%	$62,000	$5,167	$82,667
Programmer 8	12	75%	$57,000	$4,750	$42,750
Programmer 9	16	100%	$57,000	$4,750	$76,000
Programmer 10	16	100%	$57,000	$4,750	$76,000
Lead Artist	16	100%	$73,000	$6,083	$97,333
Artist 2	4	100%	$62,000	$5,167	$20,667
Artist 3	3	100%	$60,000	$5,000	$15,000

Dev Team	Months	Involvement(1)	Salary/yr	Salary/mo	Costs
Artist 4	3	50%	$57,000	$4,750	$7,125
Artist 5	8	100%	$57,000	$4,750	$38,000
Artist 6	10	100%	$55,000	$4,583	$45,833
Artist 7	10	100%	$52,000	$4,333	$43,333
Artist 8	12	100%	$52,000	$4,333	$52,000
Artist 9	12	100%	$52,000	$4,333	$52,000
Sound Effects					$200,000
Software/Hardware					$75,000
Sound engineer	1	75%	$50,000	$4,167	$3,125
Game designer 1	4	100%	$50,000	$4,167	$16,668
Game designer 2	6	50%	$50,000	$4,167	$12,501
Level designer	9	100%	$35,000	$2,917	$26,253
Producer	16	100%	$85,000	$7,083	$113,328
Line Producer	16	50%	$75,000	$7,083	$56,664
Total personnel costs					**$1,339,847**
Overhead					**20%**
Profit					**20%**
Total					**$2,906,725**
Rounded - final bid					**$3,000,000**

Note: This budget is radically simplified to provide a simple illustration of one method of budgeting a release. It does not include many required line items and should not be thought of as an accurate model of costs.

(1) Involvement reflects whether an employee is dedicated to one project or shared across one or more teams.

Special thanks to Tom Sloper for his help in drafting this sample

RAISING MONEY/FINANCING THE EARLY STAGE VENTURE

If you are a start-up, now that you know how much money you need to make your pitch build (or your full build, if you want to self-publish or try for the higher royalties of a finished game), it is time to raise it. Raising money for a company is never easy, and the high rate of failure for game developers doesn't make it much easier. On the other hand, the industry has the glow of expanding and generating profits all through the recent recession, which has given it some cachet in the public and investing audience. Furthermore, a game company is something that everyone with a console or a PC can relate to, which is always helpful when pitching.

This section will help you answer three core questions of financing your company:

- Who might fund you?
- What materials should you prepare to make your pitch?
- How do you take the investment into your company?

The practice of institutional equity financing is not currently common in the game development industry, but given the escalating cost of production and the rapid expansion of financing solutions and groups seeking to fund game development, it makes sense for developers to have a passing knowledge of the price of institutional money. This is discussed in the "Equity Investment Term Sheets" section.

Sources of Funding

Technically speaking, there are several sources of funding available for start-up companies, but practically speaking, an early-stage developer is only likely to shake fruit from one of four trees: friends and family, publishers, angel investors, or a game-focused financing entity.

Friends and Family

Professional investors all say that they don't bet on business plans or projects: they bet on people. Who knows you better than your friends and family? At the same time, remember that family and money mix only a little better than nitrogen and glycerine. The relative ease of raising money from people you know can be outweighed by the stress: If the company falls on hard times, will you feel like your friend looks at you funny if you buy a new sofa for your apartment? Will Uncle Mike get drunk at Thanksgiving and growl at you about where his money's going? Furthermore, it's hard enough to start a company and try to make it succeed without the added stress of knowing that the hopes of your loved ones are riding on you as well.

Advantages: They love you and want to help you; they are less likely to try to take over your company; if you hit hard times, they'll probably be more flexible about a workout (see the "Getting Into and Out of Trouble: Remedial Actions: Workouts" section later in this chapter).

> **TIP**
>
> If you decide to raise money from friends and family, do it by the books. Show them your plans, explain that it's quite probable they will never see their money again, discuss whether they want the investment structured as equity (ownership) or a loan, and have a lawyer dot the i's and cross the t's. Set expectations low and keep the transaction at arm's length.

Advantages/Disadvantages of Funding Sources

	Friends/Family	Publishing Deal	Angels	Financiers
Advantages	■ Easiest ■ Quick fundraising cycle ■ Less demanding ■ Probably won't take your company if you default	■ Won't own any of the company ■ Commitment to your product ■ Experienced advice	■ Quick fundraising cycle ■ Not as demanding as other fundraisers ■ Probably have business experience	■ Value-added investors ■ Can help with publisher relationship
Disadvantages	■ Can cause relationship stress ■ Not value-added investors	■ Publisher takes most of risk and profit ■ May be erratic 　–Early termination 　–Late milestone payments	■ May not have industry knowledge ■ Unless you know the angel, solicitation may violate securities laws	■ May cut into developer margins/require signifigant stake in development ■ Default can lead to losing your company

Figure 3.2

These are advantages and disadvantages commonly associated with different forms of capitalization; your experience may differ.

Disadvantages: The pressure! The guilt! If your company is having trouble, you'll want your family and friends to be a refuge from your business trouble, not a constant reminder of it. Also, most friends and family aren't what are known as "value-added investors," those investors with experience, knowledge, or contacts that can help the company as much as cash.

Publishers

Most start-up developers self-finance a pitch build to showcase their skills and use that to get a publishing deal (either developing that IP or another game that the publisher needs made). The publisher will fund the development of the game with a development advance (recoupable against royalties), payable in installments over the life of the development, which developers often use to keep the company's lights on and maintain a reasonable cash reserve. The publishing deal is covered in Chapter 6, "The Publishing Contract."

> **NOTE**
> Publishers generally don't want to hear that their milestone payments are covering your overhead—their idea is that the milestone payments should be going directly into the game costs. If you are in a financial position where you are using milestones to cover basic expenses, it may be best to keep that to yourself.

Advantages: Financial freedom (a publisher won't take a chunk of your company); publisher commitment (if someone at the publisher took a $4 to $8 million dollar bet on your company, you can be sure they'll see to it that marketing puts some muscle behind the release); publisher advice (if you get good external producers, they can be wise counselors).

Disadvantages: The publisher is taking on most of the risk, so it will take most of the reward (if any). Unlike other investments, which give the money to the company in one or two lump sums, which can earn interest, the development advance is paid over time and is contingent on performance of certain duties. Many developers speak of late milestone payments being the norm, and a constant battle to get paid taking time away from work on the game. If there is a hitch with a milestone, a developer can run into a cash crunch.

Angel Investors

Angel investors are wealthy individuals who like to find deserving young companies to support. The ideal angel is one with industry-specific experience and contacts who can advise the company as well as provide capital. Most angels have business experience (whether industry-specific or not) and can be a huge help in guiding new entrepreneurs through the hoops of running a company.

Advantages: Raising money from angels can be a relatively quick process, since there is only one person to deal with. Most angels are content to advise, but do not necessarily want to control the company, and generally do not demand as much ownership of the company as institutional investors like venture capitalists.

Disadvantages: Angels probably don't bring the same knowledge about the industry and development process as a publisher or game industry financier. Unless you know where to find them, you may be prohibited from soliciting them under the federal and state securities regulations (see the "Financing Vehicles: Regulation of Investments" section that follows).

Industry-Specific Financiers

As the game industry has matured, the risk (read: budget) of each development has increased and the financial industry has emerged with some models to address these risks. Investments have generally been in projects more than in companies. Two emerging models, both based on Hollywood film finance, are production companies and completion bonds.

Production Companies

Production companies position themselves between publishers and developers and function in a similar fashion to Hollywood film production companies. The production company solicits pitches for new games, usually new intellectual properties, and identifies a few promising projects. The production company funds the early stage development of those projects, terminating the projects that don't pan out and procuring financing and distribution for the projects that look most promising after prototype development. The production company is usually compensated with a share of the game's royalties, which will vary based on how it splits the cost of development with the publisher.

Advantages:

- Opportunity to get original IP developed.
- Intensive help and oversight by the production company.

Disadvantages:

- The developer probably won't see any royalties before the production company recoups its investment plus a premium.
- The developer may have to give up important IP rights to its games.
- Intensive oversight by the production company.
- The publisher may not put as much marketing muscle behind a release in which it has no other sunk costs.

Completion Bonding

Completion bonding is also known as film-style financing because it is a common financing method for film productions. How it usually works:

1. The developer, DevCo creates a special purpose entity, which we'll call GameCo.
2. GameCo contracts with the publisher to deliver *NewGame* on a specified date.
3. GameCo contracts with the bank for a loan to pay DevCo to do the actual game production. The loan is backed by the publisher's promise to pay the full amount of the loan to GameCo (who will then pay it to the Bank) on delivery of *NewGame*.

GameCo procures a *completion bond* from a specialized bonding company to insure the bank's loan against the risk of GameCo's not finishing the game. In other words, the completion bond is like an insurance policy that gets triggered if GameCo does not deliver the game. Without the bond, if GameCo did not deliver, the publisher would not pay GameCo, and the bank would lose its money. With the bond, GameCo gets the money from the bonder and repays the bank.

What's in it for the bonder? The bonder will charge a fee, from 2 to 10 percent of the game's budget. To manage its risk, it will aggressively investigate the project and the company, and will oversee the entire production. It may or may not require the developer to put up collateral for the bond.

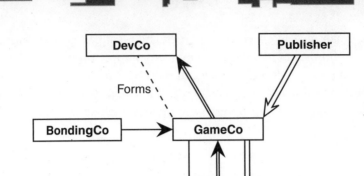

Proceeds from the completion bond if GameCo does not deliver game to Publisher

Bank releases milestone payments to GameCo, who pays DevCo, on Publisher approval

Publisher pays GameCo the full loan amount on delivery, which it releases to the bank

Figure 3.3

Completion bonding.

Advantages for developer:

- Payments are more likely to be on time because the bank, not the publisher, pays.
- The bonder can act to balance power between the publisher and the developer.
- A project that would not have been funded directly by the publisher may get a chance with a completion bond.

Disadvantages for developer:

- Expensive—even though the publisher will usually pay the bonding and loan fees, which range from 3 to 10 percent of the budget, these fees will probably be recouped from developer's royalties.
- Generally requires a prototype before a bonding company will issue a bond.
- The bonder may require the developer to put up collateral.
- The publisher may not put as much marketing muscle behind a release in which it has no other sunk costs.

Pitch Materials

When raising money, you need something concrete to show your goals, your talents, and your ability to execute a project. Pitch materials are the first project that potential investors see, and they judge your ability to execute a development project based on what they see in your pitch. Does it look completed? Are there typos in written material? Does it look as good as it possibly could (it should be in color and bound, with some kind of protective cover)? Is it well organized and clear? Is it thorough, or does it gloss over difficult sections or topics? Is it playable? Does it convey why someone will spend $25 to $60 on this game?

TIP

Many developers worry about having their ideas stolen during the pitch process. It may be difficult to get a prospective investor or publisher to sign an NDA protecting your confidentiality—their position is that there are only a few basic plots and most pitches are so similar to one another that they would be made too vulnerable by NDAs. You can obtain some measure of protection by documenting your presentation and mailing a copy to your attorney by certified mail and instructing her not to open it (clearly, you should consult with her first).

Business Plan

Writing a business plan is actually a great exercise for any company. It forces you to examine and quantify every one of your worst fears about the company, which has the effect of making them slightly less intimidating. It gets all of the founders discussing core strategies of the company. It vets problems that you might not have seen otherwise. It also sparks inspiration for problem solving in other areas.

Your business plan may need to be tailored to one of two purposes: a plan to raise money for the company as a whole, including all future projects; or a plan to raise money for a particular project or property development. Publishers generally do not need to see your company's business plan.

CAUTION

Remember to mark the business plan **CONFIDENTIAL AND PROPRIETARY** at the top of every page and © 200X [*Company name*]. All Rights Reserved.

The business plan should include long-range goals, but is likely to be anchored around a proposal for a particular game, whether a developer-originated IP, or some other IP to which the developer has acquired rights.

If you need a business plan to show to investors, you should plan to prepare a full document of around 20 to 40 pages, not including design documents. If it is for internal purposes, or if your potential investor requests "an executive summary," the document can be a few pages, plus team bios, design documents, and budgets.

Market

Describe the market, both for games in general and for the kind of game(s) you are looking to develop. Break the market down by genre and platform, and take into account worldwide sales. The industry is tracked by several entities, making it relatively easy to find this data on the Web. If you are looking toward licensing your technology or content, describe the market for those assets.

Product

In a sense, you have at least two products: game development services and the particular game you are trying to get funded. The most important product description for your game development services is in the section about your team, but the services you offer should be introduced in this section. Here is where you can describe your game briefly—the design document will bear it out more fully. If you plan to develop any proprietary technologies for licensing elsewhere, describe those as well. Discuss what differentiates your product and any sustainable competitive advantages you may have, including development tools.

For an original IP, describe any licensing plans including sequels, franchises, strategy guides and hint books, as well as other media.

Team

This is the most important part of your plan. List all of the members of your team, released games and sales of those games, genres, and platforms they have worked on, software they have worked with, and companies where they have worked. Give a history of the team as a whole in addition to each member specifically, in other words, how long the team has worked together, how many games they have released together, and so on.

Competition

Your competition falls into two categories, both of which should be discussed: competitors in the game development service business, and competitors for sales of the kind of game you are trying to make. Describe your competitors—both developers and games in the genre and on that platform competing for the same demographic. Remember to include internal development studios as well as external. If you do some digging around, you may be able to find out which major publishers have similar releases coming out around the time you believe your game would be completed. If you are developing a technology, describe other products on the market and in development, what their market share is, and how you plan to compete.

Costs

Insert a detailed budget for development of the game with notations on underlying assumptions. If you are pursuing investment in the company, not just in a game, break out company overhead and discuss expansion plans (like a second team), if any. Be somewhat realistic to maintain the credibility of your numbers.

Revenue

Take a deep breath, because this will feel like a shot in the dark. It is okay if your revenue numbers end up being wrong—what is important is that they are logical and you can defend them to a publisher or investor. For internal or investor purposes, you will be looking at company revenue from development advances and royalties. Revenue for the company is easy if you will be funding the game through a publisher: you will be receiving development advances in the

> **CAUTION**
>
> Federal and state securities laws have anti-fraud provisions preventing the use of misleading or inaccurate information to sell securities. This includes information found in a business plan, so be very accurate and conservative in your descriptions and have an attorney help draft and/or review the document before it is sent to potential investors.

amount of your product budget. Given that so few games actually show royalties every year, your wisest bet may be to note this fact and include data about the market in which you may, if you beat the odds, participate. Don't forget to include revenue from international markets.

Pre-Production Documents

Your pitch will need a set of pre-production documents. Keep two things in mind when drafting these presentation documents: (i) you will probably not have the opportunity to present them in person to many of the decision-makers; and (ii) they are your first opportunity to show a publisher how organized and thoughtful you are.

The greenlighting process for a game may go something like this: U.S. product development to U.S. sales and marketing to International sales and marketing, then back to U.S. executive committee.

Presentation is Key

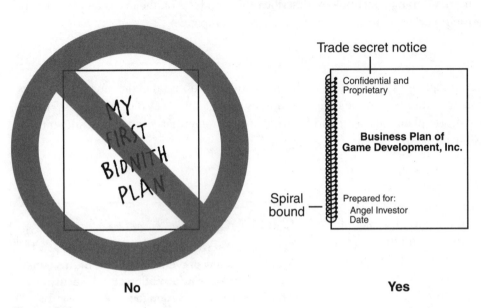

Figure 3.4

Books are indeed judged by their covers.

What does this mean for you? It means that your documents must be extremely terse and written in the publisher's language. If you excite someone in product development, give them documents that make it easy for them to get sales and marketing and international excited, too.

In addition to hard copies of the documents, provide your publisher with some kind of access to electronic copies of the pitch documents, perhaps on a password-protected Web site.

Your pitch documents should include:

- **Sell Sheet.** This is a one-page dossier on the game that helps sales and marketing do their jobs. Include your name and logo, genre, platforms, release date, target demographic, a two-paragraph synopsis of the game, unique selling point, and competitor games.
- **Team Bios.** Limit these bios to the vital statistics: names, released games and sales of those games, genres and platforms they have worked on, software they have worked with, and companies where they have worked. Give a history of the team as a whole

NOTE

Use as little text as possible and as much art as possible when drafting these documents. Only include information that will make a publisher's pupils dilate—remember that yours is one of hundreds and hundreds of submissions received.

in addition to each member specifically, that is, how long the team has worked together, how many games they have released together, and so on.

- **Design and Technical Specifications.** These should be stripped-down versions of your internal design and technical documents with enough specificity to show that you have thought through your execution plan.
- **Bible.** This document gives a visual tour of the product, with art showing the major characters and other visual elements like backgrounds, weapons, vehicles, and so forth.

Pitch Build

Some visual, at least modestly playable manifestation of your game is a requirement, especially for new teams and companies. A publisher is more likely to be impressed by technology than by art, but a more art-intensive demo has the advantage of taking less time to create.

Financing Vehicles

Once you have people willing to give your company cash, how do you take it in, and what do you give them in return? Your two options are equity and debt, discussed in the following sections.

Equity

Equity is ownership of the company. Equity in a corporation, LLC, and partnership are called stock, membership interests, and partnership interests, respectively. These are discussed more fully in Chapter 2, "First Steps."

This section will address the different terms involved in an equity financing. Note that these issues are more likely to come up in a later financing for more money: the first financing, often

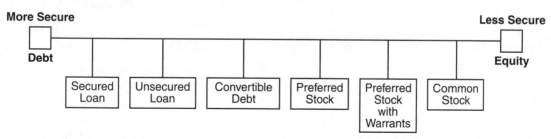

Figure 3.5

These are a few of the many flavors of securities.

called a *seed round,* is usually a small initial offering of common stock to insiders like friends and family or hands-off angel investors. As mentioned before, venture capitalists are unlikely to ever beat down a developer's door because generally the profits are not sufficient or predictable. However, as the development industry matures and different business models are explored by developers, the returns offered by those projects may be more interesting to investors.

Investors may have different needs from the founder-employees, and may require special *instruments* (types of investment). When an investor wants to share profits, but is not as interested in controlling the company, the company can issue different kinds or *classes* of equity that do not have the same voting rights as other classes. For instance, an LLC owner can be a *managing member* who has control over daily business and whose approval is required for certain actions, or a regular member, who may be more or less passive, depending on how the LLC operating agreement is written. A C-corporation may issue different classes of stock to investors that don't have the same voting rights as those held by founder-employees.

On the other hand, some investors want a *preferred return* (also called a *liquidation preference*), meaning that in case the business has to liquidate, the investor will be repaid before certain other equity investors. This can be achieved in a corporation by issuing preferred stock, which has certain rights by law and as written in the company's charter documents (see Chapter 2). Other entity types simply need to draft specific purchase agreements and other documents to achieve this end.

Equity Investment Term Sheets

Institutional investors usually want preferred stock because it receives a liquidation preference and it can be customized with a host of rights giving them more control over the company. The rights given to the investor will vary depending on the investor's investment objectives and relative bargaining power. These rights can be tailored by various agreements, such as a purchase agreement, investor rights agreement, or charter documents, to fit just about any needs. The investor's demands may differ based on the investor type, objectives, and sometimes even on geography (the West Coast – East Coast thing continues, to say nothing of U.S. versus Europe versus Asia). Your investor's wish list will be set out in an offer, also known as a non-binding *term sheet,* which may include any number of the following terms:

NOTE

Tax and securities law may make it necessary to create a separate class for investors.

TIP

As with a publishing contract, "price" is only one small issue and what looks like a great deal can be hollowed out by other terms of the contract. Get your lawyer involved ASAP in any investment discussion.

- **Type of Offering.** What is the amount and type (preferred stock? convertible preferred?) of securities being offered? For the first round of institutional financing, this may be called "Series A Convertible Preferred Stock" or "Series A Preferred."

- **Valuation/Capitalization of Company.** How much is your company worth, before and after financing? What percentage of the company is represented by the Series A investment? How many shares/options/other securities are outstanding? Sometimes the parties will attach a *cap table* that shows the breakdown of stock ownership before and after the round.

- **Dividends.** Dividends are cash distributions paid out to shareholders. Different classes of securities may have different rights to receive dividends. The Series A Preferred may or may not receive the same dividend payments as the common stock shareholders. The investor may ask for the right to receive a set annual dividend that is only payable if the company liquidates (if you're thinking this sounds a lot like an interest rate, you're right). Dividend rules are usually established in the incorporation documents.

- **Optional Redemption.** The investors will want the option to force the company at some point in the future to buy the investor's shares. The customary requested price equals the original purchase price of the shares plus any declared but unpaid dividends.

- **Conversion.** Investors who buy preferred stock often want the right to *voluntarily* convert, at any time, into shares of common stock (which has more upside potential) at some *conversion ratio*. The conversion ratio usually starts at 1 share of preferred for 1 share of common, but can be adjusted for dilution (see the following Anti-Dilution section).

- **Liquidation Preference.** In the event of a liquidation, winding up, or, in some cases, the sale of the company, preferred stock can grow big long fangs. A preferred investor can negotiate for the right to choose its compensation in a wind-up: it can elect to convert into common stock, or receive its original purchase price and then may even share any remaining proceeds pro rata with the common stock, among other possibilities.

- **Anti-Dilution.** If the company issues certain classes of stock at a price less than that of the investor's preferred ("cheap stock"), the investor's stock may have *anti-dilution protection*, which is a kind of purchase price protection. If shares of cheap stock are issued, normally that would dilute the value of the investor's stock. Same numerator, bigger denominator = diminished value. Anti-dilution protection adjusts the numerator to protect the investor's ownership proportion.

    There are various formulas for anti-dilution protection, with weird names like "full ratchet" or "weighted average." Beware of "full ratchet"—if triggered, the investor gets to buy the number of shares it could have purchased with its initial investment if the stock were sold at the cheap stock price. Think of it like retail returnables: Your mom buys you a full-price sweater at the Gap in December. It's too big, and you take it back (with the receipt) in January. Not only do you get to exchange it, now you can get the sweater in two other colors because it's on clearance sale. Good for you, not good for the Gap.

- **Board of Directors.** How many seats on the board will the investor be able to elect with its class of stock? How many directors can the common stockholders elect? Will the board have audit and compensation committees, and who will sit on them? These provisions will most likely appear in a voting agreement, a stockholders agreement, and/or the company by-laws.

- **Voting Rights.** The investors may want their stock to have special voting rights and approvals, such as the right to veto even an overall majority of the stockholders on certain key issues like amendments to charter documents; redemption or repurchase of any stock; large acquisitions by the company of stock or assets of another company; grants of exclusive rights to any intellectual property or exclusive distribution rights; payment of dividends; or a sale, merger, liquidation, or change of control transaction. Also known as *protective provisions*, these rights will be listed in the charter.

- **Information Rights.** This requires the company to deliver to the investor certain periodic financial statements and the right to inspect the books of the company. This would appear in the investor rights agreement or the purchase agreement.

- **Preemptive Rights.** Under this provision, if the company proposes to do another round of financing or otherwise issue more stock, with certain exceptions, the company must first offer such equity securities to the investor (and the founders, if they can negotiate this) on a pro rata basis (based on their initial investment). These rights can be waived, and sometimes a new investor will require such waiver. This right would appear in an investor rights agreement or a stockholders agreement.

- **Right of First Refusal/Tag-Along/Drag-Along.** This is a right of the investor's preferred stock to, at its election, purchase the founders' shares before they sell them to a third party (with certain exceptions, like family trusts, and so forth). The founders may get this right as well. A tag-along right is a way to give the investors some liquidity by allowing them to participate in a sale by the founders to a third party on a pro rata basis. In other words, if a third party agrees to buy 10 shares from a founder, and the Series A investors own half of the company, the Series A investors could elect to sell 5 of their shares and the founder would sell 5 of his shares to the third party. A drag-along right is where a majority of the shareholders, or a majority of the preferred, want to sell the company to a third party and can force the holdouts to sell their shares as well. These provisions will probably appear in an investor rights agreement or a stockholders agreement.

- **Expenses.** In many cases, the company is responsible for its own legal fees as well as those of the investors! And the investors' counsel does most of the drafting. In addition, the company may be responsible to the purchasers for consultant expenses (technology experts, accountants, and so forth) incurred in due diligence. This will appear in the stock purchase agreement.

- **Exclusivity.** The investors may ask for exclusivity for a certain period while they conduct due diligence and draft the appropriate documentation. This will be in the term sheet and will be one of the only binding provisions in it.

Not all of those terms will appear in a term sheet, and you should try to negotiate a lot of them away or at least make them more favorable. On the other hand, depending on the investment climate, you may be stuck with those terms.

Once you've got a signed term sheet (almost always non-binding), you are one step closer to getting financed. As long as no skeletons jump out of your company's closet during due diligence, most reputable investors will try to stick to the term sheet. Be aware that the deal is far from closed: many issues that were vague or ignored in the term sheet can be sticking points when your lawyers are negotiating the definitive documents with the other side.

NOTE

Demanding investors, particularly those interested in control of the company, must be scrutinized very carefully. First, your legal bills for creating new classes of equity and negotiating the terms can spiral. Second, a powerful outsider can make you feel like you're not quite in control of your destiny—and for most entrepreneurs, that's what makes the pain worthwhile. On the other hand, if you are working with a reputable and knowledgeable investor, you would hope that they would be working for the success of the company and your interests would be somewhat aligned.

Debt

There are two main differences between debt and equity: debt usually does not participate in the success or *upside* of a company, and it receives payment *priority* (is repaid before other claims) in case the company runs into bankruptcy. Debt is a great idea for family and friends and angel investors who are willing to extend unsecured loans.

There are basically two kinds of debt, *secured* and *unsecured*. Secured debt is backed by some kind of *collateral* (an asset, like a car) that the creditor can take or sell if the debtor cannot satisfy the loan (ever see *Repo Man?*). Your mortgage, for example, is secured by the home: if you default, the bank will take the home and sell it to satisfy the debt. Unsecured debt is not backed by an asset.

Because unsecured debt is riskier for the creditor, it usually carries higher interest rates than secured debt. However, any kind of debt will usually be "cheaper" for the company than equity: because it has payment priority and is less risky than equity, debt investors are satisfied with lower returns on their investments.

Depending on the risk/return objectives of a lender, some loans and debt instruments (sometimes called *notes*) may be issued with *warrants* (options to buy stock at a set price) or be convertible into equity upon a future event.

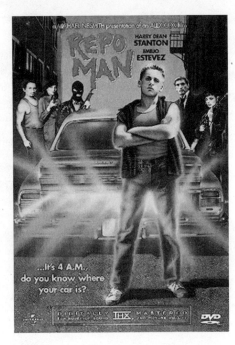

Figure 3.6

Here's someone you won't want to meet.

Because debt instruments are securities and securities are governed by federal law, be sure to work with an attorney when issuing debt instruments to comply with securities laws and other applicable laws.

Regulation of Investments

After the stock market crash of 1929 and the ensuing Great Depression, Congress and the states enacted laws regulating the sale of securities. *Securities* can include stocks, LLC interests, bonds, warrants, options, and other instruments issued by a company. The main federal laws are the Securities Act of 1933 and the Securities Exchange Act of 1934. Every state has its own laws regulating securities, called *Blue Sky laws* because they are designed to prevent unethical companies from promising and selling the blue sky above. Companies selling securities must comply with both the federal laws and the laws of any state where it will be offering or selling securities.

The goal of these laws is to ensure that purchasers receive enough accurate information to make an informed decision. The Securities and Exchange Commission ("SEC") requires that sellers of securities, known as *issuers*, register the sale, known as an *offering*, and provide a detailed prospectus containing all sorts of information about the issuer. This process is long and expensive (well into six figures), so the government created exemptions to these rules for companies raising smaller amounts of money.

In general, small offerings may qualify for an exemption if they are:

- Private offerings
- Limited offerings (less than $5,000,000)
- Only offered to qualified investors
- Only offered to investors residing in the same state as the company

> **NOTE**
> Even if your offering is exempt from registering with the SEC, you must still obey federal and state anti-fraud laws by avoiding making any untrue or misleading statements or omitting any material facts in connection with the sale. To minimize the risk of an SEC action and/or shareholders' suit, work with your lawyer throughout the process to be sure you comply.

Investments in a typical start-up game development company will most likely fall under an exemption, as it is likely to be selling securities to private investors or investment funds, and the amount of investment will be less than $5,000,000. But the penalties, such as fines and recission rights (paying back the investors' money), can be onerous, so work with a qualified corporate attorney to ensure your offering is exempt.

> **NOTE**
> While it won't be covered in depth here, note that you probably won't need to register stock offered to the company's employees, directors, general partners, and officers of a company; these offerings are generally exempt under Rule 701.

SELLING THE COMPANY

Selling your development company—most likely to a publisher interested in making you an internal studio—is the goal of many entrepreneurs. Other developers prize their independence and control more than the security and payday of selling the company. If you are a big enough star, you can negotiate a favorable price and maintain control.

If you are looking to sell your company, you may want to wait until you have at least two interested parties. Your leverage will be much greater. When choosing a buyer, look beyond the dollar signs to find: a company whose future you believe in (since you are likely to receive some compensation in stock); a company culture that values your staff; powerful distribution and marketing in your preferred platforms and genre(s); a buyer who is willing to allow your company autonomy, for instance, the ability to stay in your current location and to choose future development projects.

A publisher looks for a developer with a stable team and a track record of delivering hit games on time and on budget. The publisher is usually buying a team first and foremost, but it will pay a much higher price if there is valuable proprietary technology (like a great AI for war sims) and/or content (like a game franchise) attached.

While a sale can be full of more plot twists than a soap opera, it will usually follow this script:

1. Buyer and seller establish mutual interest and negotiate a *letter of intent,* a letter signed by both parties that sets out the basic terms of the sale. The letter of intent is usually valid for a short period of time, around 30 days, during which time the seller cannot shop the company around.

2. During the exclusivity period, the buyer performs a *due diligence* examination of the target company, looking into its financials, liabilities, making sure that it owns all of its intellectual property, and so on. At the same time, lawyers for both parties are assembling the contracts necessary for the sale.

3. If due diligence turns up unexpected liabilities (example: it turns out that the seller owes $50,000 in back taxes, or the seller does not have clear *title,* or ownership, to one of its intellectual properties), the parties will renegotiate terms of the purchase.
   The parties sign the documents and exchange property at a *closing.*

Due Diligence

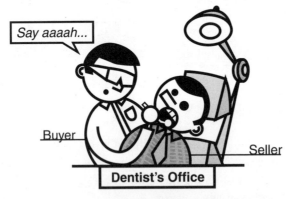

Figure 3.7

Due diligence: Too bad it doesn't come with laughing gas.

> **NOTE**
>
> Consider hiring an investment banker to represent you in your sale. These are companies who study the market for certain kinds of transactions in an industry and specialize in getting the best price at the best terms for a company. Naturally, you pay a commission for this representation, but it may pay for itself if you get a significantly higher premium.

Valuation

An old investment banking adage is that a company is worth whatever the highest bidder thinks it's worth. That said, there are a few benchmarks that publishers use when deciding how much to spend on a company. This section will discuss some of the ways that purchasers size you up, and how you can use that language to justify your own valuation. The biggest impact on your valuation will be the presence or absence of valuable content or technology rights, your team's experience, and your title history.

Comparables

One of the most important guidelines is what is being paid for comparable companies. Most publishers are public companies and report the price of their acquisitions. Find a company similar to yours in size, release history, genre- and platform-focus. The presence (or absence) of valuable proprietary technology or content will make the other company more or less comparable to yours.

If you can't find a similarly sized company that has sold recently, you can still extrapolate data from another sale to come up with a benchmark by using *multiples*, discussed in the next paragraph.

Multiples

If a comparable company (in terms of release history and intellectual property assets) has 75 employees and sold for $17,000,000, it is not outrageous to estimate your company's value at $260,000 per employee. If a comparable company sold 450,000 console units in the two years prior to sale, and your company has sold 500,000 console units in the past two years, it is not outrageous to think that your company should fetch a higher price. Of course, you cannot base your estimates on any one particular number, because a company's value is determined by so many other factors—future projects, R&D that may not be public, among others.

Another common multiple used in pricing development companies is based on earnings, meaning that your company is worth X to Y times its annual revenue.

IRR

Depending on whether an MBA is at the wheel, your purchaser may talk about IRR when justifying a price for your company. IRR means internal rate of return. Purchasers who think in these terms look at what kind of profit they need to make on their investment three, four, five years out—say 40 percent. Then they look at the cash flow your company is likely to throw off, based on your income statement for the previous years and any other relevant factors (like if you've got a great game based on a big movie coming up—your income will probably rise considerably). Now that they know how much money they will see each year, and what kind of a return on their investment they require, they can figure out how much they can pay for your company and still make their desired return.

Example: Company is likely to have cash flow of $10 in year one after purchase, $15 in year two, and $20 in year three, and would fetch $50 if sold at the end of year three. Purchaser wants a 40 percent return on its investment within three years. For every dollar that purchaser puts in, it expects to take out $1.40 at the end of year three. Purchaser prices the company as (Year 1 + Year 2 + Year 3 + 50)=1.4 * $XX. $XX=67.85. The purchaser is willing to buy the company for $67.85 now.

> **NOTE**
>
> This example is extremely simplified to sketch the idea of IRR and does not take into account basic principles of finance, like the time value of money.

NPV

NPV stands for "net present value." A dollar tomorrow is worth less than a dollar today. If I give you a dollar today, a bank will pay you interest all year for the privilege of using your money. If I give you that dollar next year, you lose out on the chance to earn the interest, and you also bear the risk that inflation has made that dollar even less valuable.

Net present value is a calculation that applies a *discount factor* to let you figure out what a dollar tomorrow or 10 years from now would be worth in today's dollars. It is a way of calculating the value of future payments in terms of what they are worth today. A company can be thought of as a machine that cranks out a cash payment once a year—profits in year one, profits in year two, and so on. If you can project your profits for the next 5 to 10 years, you can apply a *discount factor* (a financial formula based on the interest rate and time period) to each year's profit, tally them up, add the discounted value of the sales price at the end of the five or ten years and you get the value of the machine today.

Example:

Assume:

Interest rate = 10%

	Year 1	Year 2	Year 3	Year 4	Year 5	Sale Price @ end of Year 5	Total Present Value
Expected Profit	$10	$10	$10	$10	$10	$100	
Present Value	$9.09	$8.26	$7.51	$6.83	$6.20	$62.09	**$99.98**

Letter of Intent

Before settling into the meat of the letter of intent ("LOI"), decide on a time frame. How long do you want the purchaser to have an exclusive option to buy the company? What is your target sale date? Be careful that all of your commitments to the purchaser have deadlines, or the due diligence/closing process can drag on for months and then collapse. Furthermore, how binding do you want your LOI to be? Do you want an agreement that, barring any unforeseen issues coming up in due diligence, the purchaser is obligated to complete the purchase? If so, the LOI needs to be renamed "Binding Short Form Purchase Agreement."

The letter of intent should cover the headline issues such as:

- What are they buying? The purchase can be structured as a sale of the assets or as a sale of the stock. In an asset sale, the purchaser usually buys all of the target's assets except cash, and leaves the liabilities behind. These assets are subsumed into the purchaser entity. The target then uses the proceeds from the sale to satisfy its debts and distributes the rest to the owners. A sale of assets generally benefits the buyer—it can escape the target's liabilities (like federal and state income taxes, payroll withholding taxes and legal actions) and gains tax bonuses. In a stock sale, the acquiror purchases all of the target's stock, meaning that the acquiror steps into the shoes of the target entity (Devco, Inc.) and the acquiror takes over all of the assets and liabilities of the target. Note that the structure of an acquisition is often dictated by tax considerations for the acquiror and the selling shareholders.

- Most acquirors hedge against surprise liabilities by requiring the seller to make certain representations and warranties about the financial condition of the company, and retaining the right to reduce future payments by the amount of any surprise liabilities.

- Is the purchaser buying all of the company, or only some? Keep in mind that a 51 percent share of a company is usually worth more than 51 percent of the assets: a premium will likely be paid for control. Some would argue that it never makes sense to sell only 51 percent of your company on the theory that if you

CAUTION

In choosing to structure a deal as a stock transaction, the seller should be aware that the sale of stock in a closely held corporation falls under the umbrella of federal securities laws. This places a greater burden on the seller in a stock transaction to fully disclose all material information about the company. Failure to do so exposes the seller to the risk of securities anti-fraud rules. Also, if the target shareholders are receiving stock of the acquiror, the acquiror is making an offering and therefore must comply with securities regulations and/or exemption criteria.

give away the milk, nobody buys the cow (in other words, you're giving away all of the control of the company for only some of its cash value).

■ What is the price, and how/when will it be paid? The three main currencies are cash, acquiror stock, and assumption of debt (in other words, if you owe a $100,000 electricity bill, the acquiror will pay it and consider that part of the purchase price). The precise mix is a subject of intense negotiation: $35,000,000 in stock is a lot different from $35,000,000 in cash. Will all of the compensation change hands at the closing, or will the purchase price be paid in installments? Keep in mind that $35,000,000 in a lump sum is worth a lot more than $7,000,000 every year for the next five years and not just because of the time value of the money—this is a volatile business and publishers go under, too. Are there contingencies/bonuses? For example, if the company ships its next product on time, it receives $1,000,000.

■ What happens to the status quo at the company? Will all the employees remain? Will they receive the same or better compensation and incentives? Will the office remain where it is? Where will the company fit into the reporting structure of the acquiror?

■ Key men. Employment agreements, non-competes and non-solicits (for example, no-poaching rules) will need to be negotiated for key executives. It is likely that key employees will be required to stick around for a certain amount of time, or risk losing stock options or other compensation.

Due Diligence

After the LOI is signed (though they may start the financial/valuation diligence before it's signed), the acquiror does its due diligence on the target company, the equivalent of kicking the company's tires. The acquiror (or its attorneys, more likely) will comb over your financial records, dig through your contracts, read any of your corporate (or LLC or partnership) documents, and poke and prod wherever necessary to get a solid understanding of your company's position. One of the most important portions of the due diligence is the intellectual property audit, in which the acquiror researches what you own, the conditions and terms of any licenses, and any problems with your title (ownership) to the property (like an independent contractor who worked on your license without signing an assignment of invention agreement).

> **NOTE**
> You will need to have an NDA, reviewed by your attorney, signed and in place before the due diligence process begins.

Purchase Agreement

The purchase agreement contains the terms of the LOI, but adds in a lot of representations and warranties, conditions to closing, and post-closing covenants as well as other provisions that will flesh out the terms of the LOI. If significant problems came up during due diligence, they will be addressed here. The purchase agreement will also make reference to several other documents that are likely to be included as exhibits, such as the key executives' employment agreements with the acquiror, the target's outstanding publishing agreements, the target's original shareholders' agreement, an escrow agreement (if some shares are put into escrow for purposes of a future purchase price adjustment), and many more.

Special note on the employment agreements: these are sometimes left until the 11th hour because both sides think that they have an "understanding" as to the employment arrangements. On the contrary, employment arrangements deal with more personal issues (what's my title, who do I report to, how do my new stock options vest?), and they are often the subject of the most heated negotiations. If you are a founder or key employee, make sure everyone is on the same page about your arrangement; otherwise, you may get accused of holding up the deal and may feel pressure to cave in on important issues.

GETTING INTO AND OUT OF TROUBLE

Most developers experience nail-biting episodes of financial stress at some time or another, often frequently. Underbudgeting a release, finding another project for a team that's wrapping up, and not getting paid on time are the three most common causes of financial trouble. While developers can't necessarily control these realities, there are certain measures they can take to buffer against them.

Preventive Measures

- Be realistic about your budget and schedule. When creating the budget and schedule for your release, hire a designated pessimist to question your assumptions. Add in twice as much fudge factor as you think you'll need. While it seems impossible that your project could possibly cost more/take longer than you've accounted for, somehow, falling behind is the rule and not the exception in the business.
- Make your budget and schedule scalable. Be humble and assume that you won't be able to accomplish everything in your plan within the time and budget allocated. Prioritize and benchmark the development so that at regular intervals you can compare your progress to where it needs to be and scale back features and scope as needed.
- Plan for your publisher to pay you late. Whether due to your tardiness on a milestone, or theirs in paying you, money usually does not arrive when it's supposed to. Keep at least

two milestones in the bank or a few months' of burn. This requires a lot of discipline, both in terms of keeping a lid on project scope and avoiding the illusion of comfort that a swollen cash reserve can create. Don't be fooled—it's called a reserve because you'll need it at some point.

- Finding new projects. As a general rule, companies start beating the pavement for work once a team hits alpha on its current project. Start earlier if you're less established or trying to get an assignment on a new platform.

- Staffing up. Payroll is a developer's most worrisome expense; if you doubt your ability to keep enough work coming to have everyone on a project, consider hiring contractors (see Chapter 4, "Human Resources") instead.

Remedial Actions

The faster you recognize and address problems, the more leverage and credibility you will have with your creditors. Before planning your strategy, first make a spreadsheet of all outstanding creditors, what they are owed, for which assets, how overdue you are, with amounts more than 60 days put in red, and estimates of amounts that will be coming due in the next two months. This can be a difficult, scary job, but keep a few things in mind: (i) the fact that your company is having trouble does not make you a failure or a bad business owner; (ii) your company's best chance for survival depends on your grabbing the situation by the throat; (iii) having everything in black and white can put a floor on your anxiety—at least you know it's no worse; and (iv) you set the tone for the company's morale, so you have to keep a positive attitude.

Prioritize Your Creditors

If you have a limited amount of capital to go around, you want to get as much time per dollar spent as possible. Look at your creditor list and try to prioritize in order of whose cooperation is mission-critical. Once you have this list, take a look at the mission-critical creditors (employees and landlord, for example) and start figuring out how much cash you have and will have over the next

> **TIP**
>
> Remember that one of your options is partial payment, so think about a reduced payment that might be acceptable to those creditors.

few months to allocate among these debts and the debts that will come due in the next few months. Now you know what your cash shortfall is for the next few months, and you can start looking for options to meet it.

A Developer's Sleepless Night

Figure 3.8

Sleep tight.

Core creditors can include:

- IRS and State Taxing Authorities
- Landlord
- Computer/Equipment Lessors
- Utilities
- Employees

Options

Once you know what your shortfall is, you have five basic options: going to your creditors to negotiate a different payment plan that will help you through the rough patch, known as a *workout*; going to your publisher for more money; going to your investors for more money; filing Chapter 11 bankruptcy, which stalls creditors while you try to get the company on its feet; or closing up shop, which may or may not include filing Chapter 7 bankruptcy. Because a development company's

> **CAUTION**
>
> Any party who has personally guaranteed any of the company's debts (including the lease) and any general partners should consult their own attorneys to assess their exposure to the company's liabilities.

main creditors are usually employees, Chapter 11 is generally not much help with keeping the company going and will not be discussed at length.

Any changes to your obligations or the status of your relationships with third parties need to be adequately documented and structured with your attorney's help, or you could end up down a deeper hole, shovel in hands, wondering how you got there.

Workouts

A workout is a renegotiation of the amount or payment schedule of your debts that usually occurs directly between you and the creditor. Before approaching any creditors with a proposal, you'll need a credible budget for the next few months. While some creditors may be willing to restructure your debt based on a good relationship, others will want to see some indication that you won't come back in the same situation at the end of three months. Be conservative in your estimates, and don't allocate every last dollar to creditors—keep a reserve to be sure you can fulfill your workout commitments. Creditors value predictability almost as much as cash: many would probably prefer to have you pay 30 cents on the dollar for three months and make the payments on time than pay 40 cents and be late again. Be sure that you and the creditor document any changes in your obligations in a signed writing. Your attorney will tell you if you need a simple letter or something more formal like a *settlement and release* (for example, if a creditor agrees to take a $3,000 lump sum payment in settlement of a $5,000 debt) which legally establishes that the creditor is accepting your payment in full satisfaction of the debt and relinquishes any other rights against you, or is accepting a revised payment schedule and will not later sue you for breach under the original terms of the debt.

Publisher Assistance

First, don't count on your publisher's stepping up to loan you money. While it is entirely possible that they will, there may be any number of reasons why they won't. If your original champion has left the company, whomever inherited your project may not be inclined to extend the company any further than its current commitment. Other problems with a scheduled release may arise that make it more logical for a publisher to let a project drop than invest more money, so if you give them the opportunity to get out of a contract for free (by breaching your agreement to deliver milestones), they might take it. Don't forget: publishers run into cash flow problems, too.

That said, if you are in a squeeze, don't linger in denial until the last minute and then ask for help. A popular delusion when a schedule starts to slip is that the shortfall will get made up later: odds are, your project will be late, and you will have to cover more months of burn than you'd originally budgeted.

When you start missing milestones, talk with your publisher about options should the situation persist. If a publisher gives you more money to complete the project, it is likely that it will need some kind of compensation for this, possibly in the form of a lower royalty. A better choice for both parties may be to review the milestone schedule and reduce the scope of the project. With a modified milestone schedule, the publisher can meet its revenue projections, and you will have the benefit of delivering a project on time.

Investor Assistance

Company investors, including friends and family, may be willing to either lend the company money or to exchange a cash infusion for another piece of the company. If you need the cash right away and there is not enough time to fully negotiate a stock purchase, a *bridge loan* may be in order: it's basically a short term loan (usually unsecured) that will convert into equity upon the occurrence of a milestone event or a future round of financing. Investors might prefer this where the company is on the verge of insolvency (remember debt gets paid before equity).

Chapter 11

Chapter 11 is like a workout, but generally used when the company's debts (and number of creditors) are more significant and complex. Under Chapter 11 of the bankruptcy code, a company's debts can be "reorganized" while continuing operations. Various committees (of creditors, equity holders, and others) may be appointed to oversee the reorganization, and the reorganization plan is submitted to the bankruptcy court for its blessing. The aim of Chapter 11 reorganization is to dispose of obligations under *pre-petition* debts and make a fresh start for the company. Note that a company that is on its last leg can't file for Chapter 11 reorganization just to avoid dealing with creditors (see discussion of Chapter 7 bankruptcy in the next section).

Closing up Shop

You will be remembered as much for how you close a company down as for how you ran it. If you wait until the last minute and tell your employees on a Friday not to come back on Monday, you are hurling a karmic boomerang that will eventually come back right between your eyes. Of course, developer employees tend to be a very bright bunch and can sense when the company is in trouble, but they will appreciate the respect of some kind of warning and/or severance.

Closing down can be done without filing for Chapter 7 bankruptcy, and even has some benefits. However, it requires a dedicated and disciplined management team to acknowledge that the company needs to close down and then stick around to perform the clean-up.

How do you know it's time to close? This varies from situation to situation. One suggested benchmark would be when you get down to liabilities plus three weeks' severance for your employees.

CHAPTER 7 VERSUS DIY

The choice between filing Chapter 7 and liquidating your company yourself (without the bankruptcy court—but you should still have an attorney's help) will depend on the assets to liquidate (for example, if they need an expert to sell them correctly—as is likely if most of your salable assets are intellectual property); how motivated your creditors are to work with you; and whether management can handle sticking around to deal with the wreckage.

Chapter 7 bankruptcy is a liquidation proceeding. It does *not* discharge the company's debts, but limited liability generally bars the creditor from coming after any owners or executives for satisfaction of the debt. Like Chapter 11, Chapter 7 bankruptcy can be voluntary or involuntary. Either the company or one of its creditors may file a bankruptcy *petition* under Chapter 7, usually when there are competing claims to limited assets and it is clear that the company cannot satisfy or work out all of its debts and continue operation. Once the petition is filed with the bankruptcy court by or against the company, there is an *automatic stay*, which is like an injunction that, with certain exceptions, stops creditors from taking the company's stuff back or suing it outside the bankruptcy court. Then the court appoints a bankruptcy trustee to liquidate assets, return equipment, and deal with creditors. Operations of the company cease except to the extent necessary to preserve the value of the company's assets.

> **NOTE**
>
> According to special rules regarding the treatment of intellectual property licenses where the licensor is in bankruptcy, a licensee may choose to continue to use the IP even after bankruptcy is filed. Consult with a bankruptcy attorney to analyze this issue.

> **CAUTION**
>
> Outside of bankruptcy, you may find an angry creditor suing the officers as well as the corporation to collect his debt. This is usually little more than a nuisance thanks to limited liability, but any individuals named will have to appear and defend in the lawsuit, or a judgment will be entered against them. Also there may be directors and/or officers liability if the creditors claim breach of fiduciary duties (that is, management did not handle the assets prudently, or engaged in other shenanigans). You may be indemnified by the company, but without D&O (directors and officers) insurance, an indemnity isn't worth much.

If you choose to do it yourself ("DIY"), you become, in effect, the bankruptcy trustee and take on all of those tasks. You will be responsible for liquidating the company's assets and halting operations. Creditors will have a right to recover their claims from the assets of the corporation (not from the owners or managers personally if they are in a limited liability entity, see Chapter 2, "First Steps"), but once the corporation has no assets, any creditor lawsuits are probably moot.

Advantages of Chapter 7

The bankruptcy trustee has special powers under the Bankruptcy Code to maximize the sale value of company assets, including the ability to sell leases (for below-market rents, for example) despite anti-assignment provisions and to sell other assets that would otherwise be restricted by creditors' claims.

The automatic stay freezes creditors' abilities to take actions to get satisfaction for their debts. This can free up cash for the trustee to pay the most pressing needs like taxes, employees, and debts guaranteed by individuals.

The trustee and his lawyers will be in charge of most of the paperwork (less work for you).

Disadvantages of Chapter 7

Assuming you have the option of voluntarily entering Chapter 7 (as opposed to being dragged in by a petition to the Bankruptcy Court), the following are disadvantages of filing for Chapter 7 Bankruptcy:

- The bankruptcy trustee will probably lack industry-specific knowledge, so he is unlikely to get top dollar for saleable assets.
- Insiders may be prohibited from buying technology, intellectual property, or projects in development, which are usually the most valuable assets in a development company.
- The trustee will generally be paid before anyone else.
- Unlike a DIY, where management has latitude in deciding whom to pay, the bankruptcy trustee must repay claims according to priorities set out in the Bankruptcy Code.
- If you repaid certain insider creditors before entering bankruptcy, a trustee has the power to unwind those transactions if they are found to be legally fraudulent or preferences.
- Bankruptcy can be as slow as water torture, and about as pleasant.

> **TIP**
>
> It is possible to blend DIY and bankruptcy: management can liquidate as many assets as possible and then file bankruptcy to take care of the rest.

Advantages of a DIY

■ Because you built the assets, you are probably best suited to sell them: you know the market, can explain the asset to potential purchasers, and have more motivation to get the best price than a bankruptcy trustee. Furthermore, outside of bankruptcy, you can sell assets to insiders—who may be uniquely positioned to take advantage of assets like proprietary technology—at fair prices.

■ Outside of bankruptcy, you control who gets paid with the available funds. This can be a big deal when management or investors are exposed to debt they've guaranteed.

■ You can take advantage of opportunities that might slip in the bankruptcy delay, such as subletting a below-market rental.

■ Payments you make to creditors before filing for bankruptcy generally cannot be undone by the bankruptcy trustee.

Disadvantages of a DIY

■ Spending time with the wind up will delay your moving on.

■ You will probably have to coordinate your activities with your creditors and lessors. And if you truly do not have enough cash to go around, you will spend a lot of energy worrying and haggling with creditors.

■ If, despite your best efforts to "work out" your debts, your company nevertheless subsequently ends up in bankruptcy, some payments to creditors made immediately before bankruptcy may have to be returned to the *debtor's estate* (the pool of assets remaining with the bankrupt company). This is due to the rule of *preference*: the court does not want you paying off your friends and then freezing everyone else out with a bankruptcy filing; they want the assets distributed pro rata in accordance with the bankruptcy rules.

■ You will have a lot of people expecting you to "do the right thing" (see next section).

■ Your latitude in deciding who gets paid may result in a spurned creditor (or even an equity holder) suing you as an individual to try to recover. Despite corporate limitations of liability, such a suit would nevertheless be a nuisance and a stressor.

How to Liquidate Your Company

If you decide to do some or all of the wind-up yourself, remember three things:

■ The board of directors of an insolvent company owes its duty of loyalty to the creditors, not the owners.

■ Creditors are paid before equity holders.

■ Under certain circumstances management can legally pay some creditors and not others.

Chapter 7 vs. Self-Liquidation

	Self-Liquidation	Chapter 7
Who Liquidates	Company owners and employees sell assets and negotiate payoff with creditors. Limited liability protects owners.	Company files, court appoints a Chapter 7 bankruptcy trustee to sell assets and pay creditors. Trustee fees paid first. Limited liability protects owners.
Advantages	■ Know assets and market well; will get best price ■ More control over who gets paid ■ Can act quickly ■ Pre-bankruptcy payments usually not unwound by trustee	■ Has special authority to get around creditor restrictions, like ability to sublet ■ Creditors less likely to sue company individuals ■ Creditors usually frozen, freeing up cash for vital needs
Disadvantages	■ Time-consuming, may not be compensated ■ Will likely have to coordinate with creditors ■ May be sued by disgruntled creditors	■ May pay trustee from sale of assets ■ Trustee probably can't get top dollar for assets ■ Insiders may not be allowed to buy assets ■ Company has little control over payment priority ■ Slow ■ May unwind pre-bankruptcy insider transactions

Figure 3.9

Some advantages and disadvantages to Chapter 7 liquidation.

First, create a schedule of the company's assets. Assets may include intellectual property, developments in progress, licenses, below-market leases that may be assigned (check the lease for restrictions on assigning or subletting), or anything else that can be sold. Assets may also include any prepaid expenses like security deposits and taxes. You may be able to access this cash by terminating or assigning your lease, or contacting the taxing authority and filing dissolution forms.

Dissolving a Business Entity

These are some of the steps that may be required to officially dissolve your business:

- Vote for dissolution.

- Surrender your Certificate of Authority to transact business.

- Notify your secretary of state of the dissolution of your business. This may take the form of Articles of Dissolution and/or a Notice of Intent to Dissolve.

- Notify your secretary of state that you are discontinuing the use of an assumed or trade name.

- File the appropriate forms with the IRS.

- Determine whether you will need to file IRS forms at a later date.

- Obtain and file a good-standing certificate with your state tax authority.

- Publish notice of your business's intent to dissolve.

- Contact your commercial insurance agent, notify him/her of the dissolution and determine the best protection against third-party lawsuits that may arise after your dissolve.

- Pay debts.

- Determine whether state statutes require that you notify creditors or the public of your dissolution.

- File an additional notice with your secretary of state stating that all debts have been paid and all assets have been distributed.

- Determine the statutory time limits for third parties to bring suit against you and plan accordingly.

- Collect your remaining assets, and sell or donate property that you are not going to distribute to owners or creditors.

If any assets are collateral for secured debts (where the creditor can take an asset and sell it if the debtor cannot repay the loan), those can't be sold without the permission of the creditor, and should be listed separately. An example of a secured loan is a car loan, which is secured by the car.

Next, create a list of the company's liabilities and creditors, separating out debts for which officers or individuals within the company are personally liable. These may include property and equipment leases, credit cards, and trade accounts where the contract is in the name of an individual or an individual has guaranteed the debt. Don't forget about taxes: officers, directors and those with check signing authority may be personally liable by law for unpaid employment taxes or sales taxes of the business.

As a rule of thumb, you will want to pay debts in the following priority: taxes, employees and vendors critical to the wind up, debts for which individuals are guarantors or otherwise liable, landlord, and all other debts.

Once you start selling assets, mind a few guidelines:

- Get fair market value, albeit liquidation value, for all assets sold (especially if sold to insiders). The business's assets belong essentially to the creditors: management cannot give the assets away or sell them for less than their value.
- Keep records of the assets' condition, receipts of payments and your efforts to sell them in case there is a later accusation of mismanagement or self-dealing in the sale of assets (proving reasonableness of your efforts will help prevent an unwinding of any transactions).
- Arrange for final tax returns and issuance of W-2's to employees.
- Back up financial and other vital data now on computers so that the records remain available despite what happens to the computers.
- Keep copies of paper records.

SUMMARY

The cycles of feast and famine make managing a developer's finances quite a challenge. Once a development shop is up and running, it still must worry about getting paid on time, reining in cost overruns, and finding its next project. Getting started is even tougher: a start-up developer usually needs a small team of people prepared to work for free long enough to build an impressive set of pitch materials and then be able to feed themselves until a development advance arrives.

Developers have a few main financing options, ranging from friends and family to bootstrapping off of development milestones, to angel or professional investors. Each option has advantages and disadvantages that need to be weighed in light of the developer's unique situation.

If all goes well over the course of a developer's business, it may seek to sell the company, most likely to a publisher. A developer will need to assess the financial health of the acquiror and the terms of the acquisition, not just the price.

Most developers experience some brush with financial danger over the life of the company. These dangers are somewhat predictable and a developer can take measures to insulate itself, such as making all budgets and schedules scalable to guard against overruns and maintaining a healthy cash reserve. Perhaps the most important part of financial management is keeping a current, accurate picture of the company's health; the temptation can be great to ignore warning signs and concentrate on the game production. Problems addressed early on have more options: publisher or investor assistance, creditor workouts, and so forth.

If the company is forced to close down, a developer may or may not have the option of winding its affairs up on its own or electing Chapter 7 liquidation. Both scenarios have advantages and disadvantages, though many find Chapter 7 attractive because it allows the company's owners and managers to move on immediately and let a bankruptcy trustee take care of the clean-up. Treat your employees and creditors (including publishers) fairly; this is still a small industry, and you will be remembered for how you closed down as much as for how you operated.

Stock Purchase Letter of Intent

[LETTERHEAD OF ACQUIROR]

Dear [*CEO of target company*]:

This letter sets forth the preliminary agreement of terms under which Acquiror, Inc. ("Acquiror") will purchase all of the issued and outstanding shares of stock of Target Development, Inc. ("Target"):

1. Purchase and Sale: Acquiror will purchase all of Target's issued and outstanding shares of stock, which consists of _____ common stock, _____ Series A Preferred Stock and _____.

2. Purchase Price: Acquiror will pay Target a total of [$_____], [$_____], in cash, [$_____], in Acquiror common stock or [$_____], assumption of Target debts (collectively, the "Purchase Price").

3. Payment Terms: The payment described in paragraph 2 herein shall be payable as follows:
   a. [$_____] shall be paid in cash on the date of closing of the transactions contemplated by this agreement (the "Closing");
   b. [$_____] shall be payable in shares of Acquiror's $.01 par value common stock ("Common Stock") valued at a price per share equal to the average per share value for the five (5) consecutive trading days immediately preceding the closing, such shares to be transferred at the Closing; and
   c. [$_____] shall be payable in cash upon the delivery of a [Game title] gold master if and only if such delivery occurs on or before [gold master milestone date]. [Target shareholders may want this escrowed and not just a promise to pay.]

4. Employment Issues: Certain key Target employees shall negotiate and sign employment agreements to remain with Target for _____ months following acquisition as a condition of sale. Such key employees will be required to sign any and all documents necessary containing covenants not to compete of reasonable duration following the purchase and covering the scope of Acquiror's business.

5. Due Diligence: Due diligence must be completed prior to the signing of a definitive agreement. Acquiror, its employees, accountants, attorneys and other agents shall immediately have the right to inspect all of the books, records and assets of Target. Target agrees to cooperate in any manner whatsoever with this inspection. Target shall

direct all of its employees, accountants, attorneys and other agents to comply with any and all of Acquiror's requests for information. Acquiror retains the absolute right to terminate the transaction and negotiations for any reason whatsoever in the sole discretion of Acquiror, until the definitive agreement is signed.

6. Confidentiality: The parties shall execute a non-disclosure agreement stating, *inter alia,* that all information gained by either party concerning the other as a result of this transaction shall be treated as confidential and proprietary information and shall be used only for the purpose of evaluating the desirability of this transaction. Acquiror may disclose any information regarding Target to its lenders and agents, but in all other respects, shall abide by any and all previously executed confidentiality agreements. Additionally, neither Acquiror nor Target shall disclose the existence of this letter and the possibility of an Agreement to anyone—including but not limited to Acquiror or Target employees—without the consent of the other party, except as required for the purposes of complying with due diligence covenants.

7. Proposed Timeline for Closing: The proposed timeline in entering into this contemplated purchase is as follows:
   a. Execution of the letter of intent [LOI date]
   b. Due diligence list supplied to Target [date plus one week]
   c. Delivery of first draft of purchase and sale agreement ("P&S Agreement") [LOI date plus two weeks]
   d. Due diligence complete [LOI date plus three weeks]
   e. P&S Agreement execution and Closing [LOI date plus four weeks]

8. Exclusive Dealing. Until the earlier to occur of the Closing or [LOI date plus four weeks], Target shall not, nor shall it permit any of its officers, directors, agents, representatives or affiliates to directly or indirectly participate, encourage, or initiate any negotiations or discussions with any entity or individual other than Acquiror concerning the sale of Target, or any of its products, except in the ordinary course of business.

9. Broker: Acquiror and Target agree that there is no broker or agent claiming a fee in this transaction. Target shall be solely responsible to pay any fees to third parties related to this transaction retained by it and Acquiror shall be solely responsible to pay any fees to third parties related to this transaction retained by it. Each party shall indemnify and hold each other harmless from any claims for failure to pay any fees.

10. Contingencies: The Purchase Price is contingent upon: (i) results of Acquiror's due diligence; (ii) Acquiror obtaining successful financing prior to the signing of the P&S Agreement; and (iii) any other factors which, in Acquiror's sole discretion, mandate an adjustment to the purchase price offered in this letter.

11. Operations Prior to Closing: Target will not cause or permit Target or any of its employees to take any actions that may negatively impact the value of Target. Target shall continue to operate its business consistent with past practices, through the date of closing, including but not limited to, diligently pursuing its development activities for its products.

12. Expenses: The parties shall each pay their own expenses incurred in connection with negotiating and executing this contract, whether or not the transaction is consummated.

13. Legal Effect: This letter is a non-binding expression of the parties' intentions and does not create any binding legal obligations, other than as set forth in Paragraphs 6 and 8. Both parties recognize the terms of this letter may change during the course of Acquiror's investigations and neither party shall be bound by its terms except as set forth in Paragraphs 6 and 8 absent the negotiation, execution and delivery of more formal and definitive agreement which will contain customary representations and warranties by the parties and be subject to review by both parties' attorneys. Please indicate your acceptance and approval of the foregoing proposal and statement of our intentions, by executing and returning a copy of this letter.

Sincerely,

ACQUIROR SOFTWARE, INC.

_____

By:
DULY AUTHORIZED

Agreed and Accepted this _____ day of _____, _____

TARGET ENTERTAINMENT, INC.

_____

By:
Title:
DULY AUTHORIZED

CHAPTER 4

STAFFING UP

Staffing Up in Action

Dusty and Alex's pitches to former Defunct employees, which had gone well to begin with, got significantly more traction when they told their former staffers that they could be getting paid quite a bit sooner. Everyone wanted Double D up and running. Revenue from the port would enable them to put an office and a network together, lease a bunch of machines and the software they'd need, and have some leftover cushioning to pay people for work on the prototype. Defunct's office administrator had found another job already, but she gave Dana lots of advice on what it took to run the HR side of a game company, including the name of the lawyer Defunct had used for all of its HR work: Robin Canigget. Even though Robin was more expensive by the hour than Michael, Dana figured that the work would be done more quickly and with greater expertise about the issues peculiar to a game company.

Despite the excitement and the prospect of solvency without fundraising, Dana insisted that the founders sit down to work out a budget and staffing plan before any further discussions with prospective employees. After they figured out what resources they'd need for the port and what would be needed to have a pitch build ready in four months, they came up with salary allocations. At first, they'd wanted to bring everyone in as an independent contractor for the duration of the port, but Dana knew from her talk with Robin that most of their workers would probably fail a legal test of whether they were independent contractors or employees. "Except QA, since they'll be short term. We can get QA in as contractors."

She suggested that they hire everyone else as employees and adjust the salaries downward to reflect the additional expenses and taxes of employment. Given the precarious position of the company, they agreed that Double D couldn't afford benefits until they got a long-term contract. Again it was decided that Dana would handle the details: employment agreements, setting up rudimentary policies and an employee handbook, and making sure that every employee understood Double D's position and had an accurate understanding of the company's insecurity. As Dana put it: "I don't want anybody coming here who couldn't handle being unemployed in six months."

Robin came up with a basic template for Double D's employment and independent contractor agreements (see end of this chapter).

INTRODUCTION

In a development house, your people are your core asset. They are also a primary source of legal difficulty. Hiring a staff is not just about buying computers and writing checks. There's payroll, benefits, insurance, state and federal laws, intellectual property, and confidentiality to worry about. This chapter will help you learn how to take care of your employees while protecting yourself against the volatilities inherent in all HR relationships, as well as providing a few pointers on avoiding common morale killers.

In this chapter you will learn:

- How to see things from your employees' point of view. Most people who start game companies have spent years honing their game production skills, but maybe haven't had as much experience with the science of managing human beings toward a goal.
- How to employ people without putting your company at risk. Employment and termination disputes are fertile ground for lawsuits. This section will give the bulleted list of do's and dont's.
- How to use and interpret state and federal laws. Employment relations and the workplace are heavily regulated, through laws like Title VII's anti-discrimination provisions and the Internal Revenue Code, as well as by state and local laws. We will highlight the most important federal laws and touch on some notable state variations.
- What you should include in an employment agreement. The employment agreement, a document that clarifies what is expected from the employer as well as employee, can be both sword and shield for an employer. This section outlines the major terms to be contained in such an agreement, and gives an example at the end of the chapter.
- How to hire contract employees. Independent contractors can be a great way to manage resources efficiently,

CAUTION

The law surrounding human resources is deep and complex, and state laws vary widely. It is absolutely essential that you consult with a local attorney (for every office, if you hire employees in more than one state or country) before hiring anyone.

The author would like to thank Myra Packman of Meiselman, Denlea, Packman, and Eberz P.C. (www.mdpelaw.com) for her assistance with preparing this chapter.

but employers need a solid contract with the contractor to prevent intellectual property ownership disputes, and must take precautions against a contractor's being reclassified as an employee (resulting in a tax hit to the employer).

■ How to avoid lawsuits. This section will detail the precautions you can take against discrimination and/or wrongful termination suits.

SEE THINGS FROM YOUR EMPLOYEES' POINT OF VIEW

Managing the legal issues surrounding workers should be addressed within the context of managing people. Development is a knowledge-based industry, knowledge that is in the heads of employees, so success is far more contingent on managerial skills than in many other industries.

Challenges Peculiar to the Industry

Managing morale at a game development company is a full-throttle challenge for several reasons:

■ It is a creative venture that answers to corporate demands.
■ Milestone deadlines, often requiring round-the-clock work, can create an atmosphere of intense pressure.
■ Frequently, the employees are very young.
■ Work and personal boundaries tend to blur and can add a layer of complexity.
■ The work is full of interdependencies (e.g. programming can't do its job until the assets from art are completed) and very communication-intensive.
■ Because manpower to actually build the games is so expensive, there is almost never much of a managerial layer, leaving more management responsibility in fewer hands (hands that are usually full with other responsibilities).
■ Many development houses experience periodic "do-or-die" financial straits, leading to significant employee anxiety.

The most common problems that developer CEOs cite are

■ Facilitating communication between groups
■ Keeping an eye on morale before flare-ups
■ Managing the overlap between boss and friend
■ Staffing up without risking layoffs

Good Management Practices

Every manager must find the style that works with a given group of employees, but there are certain constants:

Communicate

Short weekly status meetings among individual teams, team leaders, and the entire staff were cited by many developers as key to staying on schedule and maintaining a sense of cohesion. Another trick to good communication: clear e-mail protocols. See the contrast between disciplined and undisciplined e-mail in this exchange between Jim and Micky.

GOOD E-MAIL

To: Necessary Person(s) Only
Re: Art Schedule Revision
Micky,
Looks like we were optimistic. Please get
me the revised asset production schedule
we discussed in the meeting for level 4 by
Friday.
Thanks,
Jim

To: Jim
Re: Asset Pdxn Schedule-Delay to
Monday
CC: Phil
Jim,
I'll try for Friday, but can guarantee
Monday.
p

BAD E-MAIL

To: Entire Art Team
Re: RE: RE: FWD: FWD [6] bowling?
Micky,
Can you handle that thing we talked
about in the meeting yesterday?
Sooner=better.
Thanks,
Jim

No Reply

Define Expectations

Defining expectations is key to accountability, the bedrock of an ordered workplace. How can someone do a job correctly if she doesn't know precisely what that job is? And how can you discipline someone if you haven't communicated his responsibilities in a permanent, fixed medium? Roles, responsibilities, and consequences must be clearly articulated, publicized, and *enforced* (the latter making "the difference between a clubhouse and a company," as one CEO put it). This means having a central organization chart for the company, available to employees, as well as organization charts for every major project outlining resource allocation (especially important where two or more teams will be sharing), roles and responsibilities, and reporting structure.

Respond

Technically, this fits under the category of communication, but it is important enough to merit a separate heading. Employees complain about management, no matter how great the company. It's a fact of work; I'm sure even the angels have beers and talk smack about management. Good management understands this, doesn't take it personally, and takes steps to prevent normal healthy whining from spiraling into a morale problem.

When there is an unpleasant flavor in the air at a company and workers are displeased, the temptation is to want to put your head down, be silent and ride the problem out, especially if the displeasure is due to management action (or inaction). Management can feel resentful of employees, believing that the stresses and efforts of managing the company go unnoticed. This is the worst strategy, as it allows the spiral to continue. Two good defenses against a poisonous atmosphere:

- Have a complaint valve. Create a structure through which employees may comfortably raise concerns. This structure can be the boss, another person, an internal board, or even a suggestion box—the core requirement is that the employees feel uninhibited with the process or person and that the complaints receive acknowledgment, if not solution or explanation, from management.
- Be visible. Where possible, leave doors open. Humans process much information visually, men more so than women, and developers exponentially so. A visual representation of management's availability and openness goes a long way toward preventing employee alienation.

See-Joe Fridays

Joe Minton of Cyberlore Studios has lunch every Friday in the company lounge at a set time for what is now known as "See-Joe Friday." Employees know that he will be there every week with no other purpose than to answer questions, field concerns, or just catch up on personal events.

EMPLOY PEOPLE WITHOUT GETTING SUED OR SCREWED

1. Have an experienced local attorney review your personnel policies and develop the related contracts such as employment agreements, NDA and invention assignment agreements, and so forth. Labor law is convoluted, doubly so where it concerns creation of intellectual property, and you need an experienced attorney to be sure you follow all federal and state regulations.
2. Have all employees sign an employment agreement.
3. All employees should be employed on an at-will basis.
4. Be sure all contracts have adequate assignment of invention, non-disclosure, and non-compete (where applicable) language.
5. Independent contractors. Don't try to pass off employees as independent contractors, or you'll end up with a painful tax problem or, worse, being legally responsible for the "contractor's" actions as an agent of the company. Follow the rules in the "Independent Contractors" section in this chapter to determine whether the contractor passes the legal tests. If so... Never let a contractor start work without all applicable agreements, including a basic service contract, an NDA, an assignment of invention, and a non-compete clause where applicable.
6. Develop an employee handbook, to be given to everyone, explaining policies on discrimination, harassment, computer privacy, confidential information, salary, and other operating policies.
7. Document every complaint. Discrimination or harassment complaints require extra documentation (see the "Avoiding Lawsuits" section).
8. Remember that employers can be held responsible for damage caused by employees' acts, for example, if an employee hits a pedestrian while the employee is on his way to Staples to get more printer paper for the company, the employer is liable for the accident.
9. Get insurance. See "Rainy Days and Harassment Suits Always Get Me Down" sidebar.

CAUTION

More dangerous is the employer's responsibility for an employee's misappropriation of another's intellectual property. Example: your music director samples an obscure chunk of music for the soundtrack, without clearing the sample or informing the company. The company is nonetheless subject to suit by the original composer.

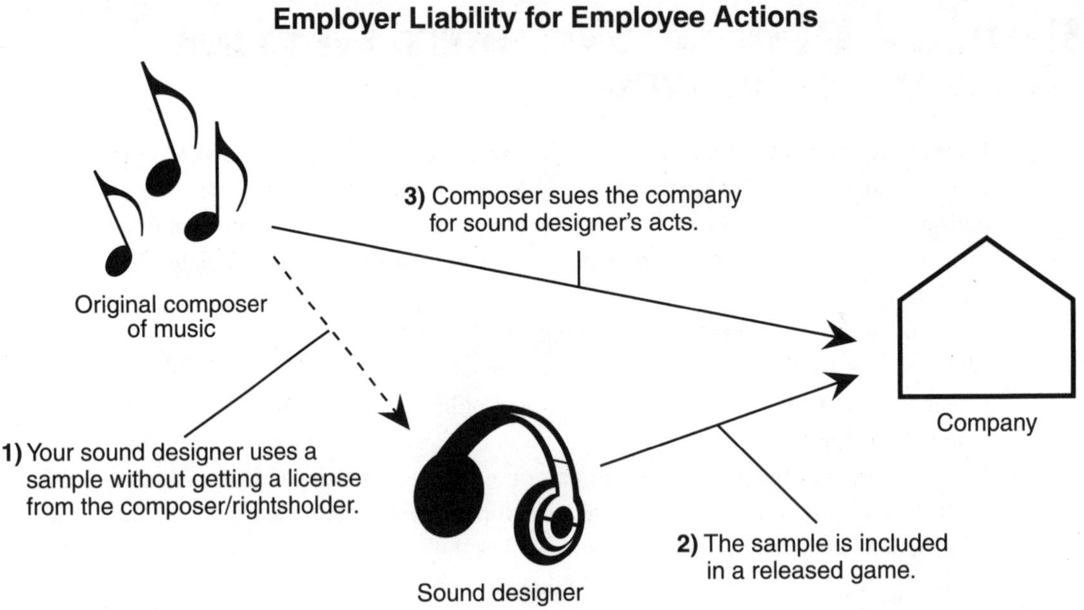

Employer Liability for Employee Actions

Original composer of music

3) Composer sues the company for sound designer's acts.

1) Your sound designer uses a sample without getting a license from the composer/rightsholder.

Company

2) The sample is included in a released game.

Sound designer

Figure 4.1

The employer may be liable for infringing activities of its employees whether or not it knew of the infringement.

Why Have an Employee Handbook?

- It provides legal protection for the employer in a discrimination litigation by showing that efforts were made to educate the employees and provide channels for airing complaints.
- Providing a FAQ eases HR administration.
- Rules are more likely to be followed if publicly stated and standardized.

CAUTION

An employee handbook can be used against a company if it is not carefully drafted. Two main dangers: 1. That it will be construed as creating a contract between the employee and the company; and 2. That an employer will be held liable for not following the policies (e.g. termination) to the letter.

TIP

Include two disclaimers at the beginning and end of the book that sound something like this:

"Employer reserves the right to alter, delete, add to, or revise any and all policies contained herein without notice. This handbook is not a contract of employment and does not create any obligation whatsoever between Company and worker."

What to Include in an Employee Handbook

This is a partial list. Employee handbooks need to be reviewed by your attorney and customized for every workplace and office. It may even make sense to have a different handbook for executives than you do for other employees.

- **At-will status acceptance**: If your state allows, include a statement confirming the "at-will" status of employment.
- **Anti-discrimination and harassment policy**: A statement of the anti-discrimination and workplace harassment policies. Make it clear that you expect all employees, whatever their rank, to comply with this policy. Include the name and contact information of at least two people to whom complaints may be filed formally or informally, how long an employee should expect to wait for a response, possible penalties for breach of the policy, an anti-retaliation provision (i.e. that a worker won't be penalized later for having filed a complaint), and a notice that filing false claims may result in termination.
- **E-mail and computer use**: Note that e-mail must not contain any illegal, libelous, or offensive statements, that office e-mail is for business purposes, not for personal use; that all e-mail is company property and the company has the right to access e-mail sent to or from every computer, including deleted e-mail; that the company reserves the right to monitor employees' computers and their usage, and that violation of the e-mail policy may result in discipline or termination.
- **Drugs, alcohol, and smoking**: State the company's policy concerning smoking, drugs and alcohol in the workplace.
- **Violence**: A statement of policy against workplace violence.
- **Technology use**: A statement on the use of technology in the workplace. Clearly set forth whether employees may make personal use of telephones, word-processing systems, computer games, facsimile machines, copiers, employer Internet connections or other office technology either during or after work hours. Remember that if you ask people to work more than a 40-hour week, it will be difficult for them to accomplish their errands without some leniency in this regard.
- **Plan benefits**. Don't detail the plan benefits, merely state that they exist and refer to the policy documents for detail.
- **Vacations and holidays**: How is vacation time earned and spent (e.g. scheduling)? What paid holidays are included?
- **Sick days and other absences**: State policies on sick time, jury duty leave, witness leave, voting time off, and so forth. Your local counsel will be able to tell you if there are state laws regulating these policies.
- **Medical leave**: State medical leave policy. State laws and/or FMLA (see the "State and Federal Regulations: Family Medical Leave Act" section) may apply and must be complied with; the FMLA requires adopting a specific policy in your handbook explaining

how FMLA leave is coordinated with other paid time-off policies such as sick leave and vacation time.

- **Reviews**: What are the review periods? Perhaps show the employee appraisal form so that workers understand the criteria on which they are being judged.

- **Discipline**: Employers will want to be careful not to box themselves in here by creating requirements that they may wish to disregard (for example, a verbal and a written warning before termination). A good idea is to state a general policy and note that the employer reserves the right to amend this policy without further notice based on the nature of the offense.

- **Termination**: Explain the employee's right to accrued vacation time or other compensation upon termination.

> **CAUTION**
>
> **You must must must have a local attorney (for every office location) review your handbook for compliance with state and federal laws.**

Every employee should receive a copy of the handbook and sign a written acknowledgment that they have received, read, and understood the handbook (which acknowledgment will go into the employee's file). This acknowledgment can be very useful in later disputes by showing that employees were on notice of policies and expectations.

> **CAUTION**
>
> **Review the handbook at least annually and make any necessary amendments; a handbook containing outdated information and/or policies can be a weapon against you. Example: if the discrimination go-to person no longer works at the company, an employee could (rightly) argue that the company was not doing its utmost to protect against infractions. Be sure that any updates and amendments have written confirmation of receipt by employees.**

STATE AND FEDERAL REGULATIONS

It is vital that an employer contact local counsel for every one of its offices, as state laws vary widely and federal laws change.

Title VII of the Civil Rights Act of 1964

Title VII of the Civil Rights Act of 1964 applies to businesses with 15 or more employees and protects against discrimination based on race, color, religion, sex (including pregnancy or childbirth), or national origin. It does not protect independent contractors. Title VII protects *potential employees* as well as current ones, meaning that employers must adhere to anti-discrimination rules in their employment solicitation and application procedures.

To prevail in a discrimination case, the plaintiff must prove that the employer *intentionally* discriminated on the basis of race, religion, sex, or national origin. He can prove this by showing that:

> **CAUTION**
>
> **Beware pre-employment discrimination, a.k.a. What can and can't be asked during the interview. See discussion in the Applications and Interviews section later in this chapter.**

1. The employee is a member of a protected class.
2. He sought and was denied an available position or benefit for which he was qualified. The employer has a legal defense to such discrimination if it can provide evidence of legitimate, non-discriminatory grounds for its decision.

A plaintiff can also prevail by showing *disparate impact* of employer's policies. The discrimination here can be *unintentional*: what is important is proving that the policy, practice, or rule affected different groups disproportionately in a statistically significant way. Again, an employer has a legal defense to the disparate impact of its policies if the practice at issue is:

1. Job-related
2. A business necessity (beyond inconvenience or annoyance)

Even if the employee proves that discrimination did occur, an employer has certain *statutory* defenses under Title VII:

- Bona Fide Occupational Qualification. An employer who discriminates based on a bona fide occupational qualification ("bona fide" meaning not based on assumptions, stereotypes, or preferences of co-workers) reasonably necessary to the normal operation of business may avoid liability by showing a reasonable basis for believing that a certain class would not be able to perform the job at issue. This defense is not available for discrimination based on race or color.
- Bona Fide Seniority/Merit Procedures. An employer will not be liable for discrimination where the business has an established seniority or merit system in place that is not intentionally discriminatory, and the alleged discrimination is consistent with that bona fide system. A plaintiff may overcome this defense by proving the system has a discriminatory *intent* (not just impact) or illegal purpose.

Sexual Harassment

Title VII also protects against sexual harassment in the workplace. There are two forms of harassment:

- *Quid Pro Quo*, literally "this for that," where a person is punished in any way for refusing a superior's sexual advances.
- *Hostile Environment*, where a hostile workplace environment is created by the physical or verbal sexual conduct of others in the workplace, not just superiors.

CAUTION

Employers are strictly liable for *quid pro quo* harassment by their employees, whether or not the employer knew of the harassment. An employer will be liable for *hostile environment* harassment if it knew or *should have known* of the harassment and failed to take remedial action.

Sexual Harrassment

Quid Pro Quo
A person is punished for refusing a superior's sexual advances.

Company is liable whether or not it knew of the harassment.

Figure 4.2

Quid pro quo harassment is a nightmare for all involved.

Come to Hawaii with me or you're fired.

Hostile Environment

Creation of a hostile work environment by physical or verbal conduct of others in the workplace.

Vicki—you don't mind if I put this Jenna Jameson poster up here, do you?

Well, Harry, yes, I do.

*Oh come on, you'll get used to it. Say, you kind of look like her, Jenna, I mean. Are you busy Friday night? Want to get busy with me? Ha ha, hey, it was just a **little** pinch, and you've got such a **big** butt...*

Figure 4.3

Sensitivity training could have taught Harry that the office is probably not the most appropriate venue for his poster.

Employers face two primary difficulties in protecting themselves from harassment claims:

1. Monitoring. While it is impossible for an employer to be everywhere at all times, the law nevertheless holds that employer responsible for what happens in its workplace. Remember the liability distinction: An employer is liable no matter what for *quid pro quo* harassment, but only for *hostile environment* harassment where the employer knew or should have known.

2. One person's hostile environment is another's happy workplace. Many smooth, functional workplaces are rife with what look like hallmarks of the hostile environment but are actually indicators of strong morale. Provocative banter, for instance, is an exceedingly common feature of many functional workplaces, particularly those with a high concentration of young people. As one young woman said of this: "How else do you expect me to stay awake during the meetings?" The best way to handle this ambiguity is to provide several channels of communication for employees to communicate discomfort, including *asking* employees if they ever feel uncomfortable as part of annual reviews and documenting their responses.

Company-wide training is an employer's best response to the challenges of keeping a workplace harassment-free. Draft your policy, make sure it is disseminated to everyone in the company, conduct periodic sensitivity training, and be sure that the policies and procedures you set up are followed to the letter, especially with regards to documentation.

Age Discrimination

The Age Discrimination in Employment Act (ADEA) is a federal law applying to businesses with interstate commerce and 20 or more employees that protects those forty and older from discrimination. It does not apply to independent contractors.

An employer may be found in violation of the ADEA if the plaintiff shows that he was either denied employment or benefits of employment because of his age, or that he was fired and replaced by a significantly younger person. The employer can avoid all liability by showing that it had a legitimate, nondiscriminatory basis for its decision. The employee would then have to prove that such basis was a *pretext* for discrimination.

Disability Discrimination

The Americans with Disabilities Act ("ADA") is a federal law applying to businesses with 15 or more employees who work at least 20 calendar weeks per year. It protects those with physical and emotional disabilities from discrimination and requires employers to make reasonable accommodations to employees' disabilities. This is one of the most expensive and difficult laws with which to comply. Disabilities are defined as a mental or physical impairment that substantially limits one or more of a person's major life activities. Disabilities may include: infertility, alcohol addiction, and panic disorder, but the ADA does not protect those addicted to illegal drugs or legal drugs acquired illegally (for example, Oxycodone). It does not apply to independent contractors.

Employers are required to make *reasonable accommodations* so that the employee can perform her job unless such accommodations would be an *undue hardship* for the employer. "Reasonable accommodation" is still a hazily-defined term, but the following are suggested in the Act:

- Making work facilities accessible
- Modifying job or schedule
- Acquiring or modifying equipment or devices
- Modifying exams, training material, or policies
- Providing interpreters

"Undue hardship" is defined as anything requiring significant difficulty or expense compared against the:

- Nature and cost of the accommodation required
- Financial resources of the facility, number of people employed at the facility, and the impact on resources—financial and otherwise, at the facility
- Financial resources of the company and size of the business
- Type of business employer conducts with respect to composition, structure, and function of the workforce, geographic distribution, and relationship of facility to company

Legal Defenses: The employer avoids liability by showing that it had a legitimate, nondiscriminatory basis for its decision. The employee would then have to prove that such basis was a *pretext* for discrimination.

CAUTION

Note that allowing absences is a common requirement, which means giving the job back to the employee after his absence. Game developers are most likely to encounter this law in relation to repetitive stress injuries and emotional/substance abuse disorders. A recent Supreme Court decision noted that not all RSI can be considered a disability, only those restricting a person's ability to carry out required life activities, such as household chores.

CAUTION

Even if a company is exempt from the federal laws due to its small size, it may be subject to state restrictions.

Do's and Don'ts

The following guidelines can help you adhere to the anti-discrimination statutes. Be sure to check with your local counsel for additional guidelines necessary to comply with applicable state laws.

Solicitation (Want Ads)

DON'T include any express or implied statements of preference or requirement based on sex, age, national origin, religion, color, or race. This means that employers should not post ads looking for "A few good men to program a AAA title," or seeking "Artist for anime illustrations, Japanese a plus," or any reference to youth.

DO include bona fide occupational requirements such as,. "Candidate must be fluent in Japanese," if advertising for a position as a Japanese market consultant.

DO include a tagline stating that the company is an equal opportunity employer that does not discriminate based on color, race, religion, sex, nationality, disability, or age.

Applications and Interviews

A good rule of thumb for employers: Avoid topics that would identify the applicant as a member of a class protected under Title VII.

DON'T ask about an applicant's:

- Sex, marital status (including questions about applicant's maiden name or whether she prefers Miss, Ms., or Mrs), family, or intentions to start a family.
- Age, birth date, dates of education. *Exception:* To comply with other laws, for example, child labor or employment of minors (an important exception for developers, as there is a high incidence of employees under the age of 18). You should ask questions about age, birth date, and dates of education in order to comply with state and federal laws regarding child labor or employment of minors. Remember, in game development there are many underage employees. You must know the laws that apply to their employment and adhere to them.
- Nationality, citizenship status. Once an employer determines that any employee is qualified to work, it should then extend an offer conditioned on employee's production of a complete *INS I-9* form within 7 days. It is illegal for an employer to *knowingly* hire an individual not authorized to work in the U.S.

- Religion, what religious holidays applicant intends to observe, and so forth.
- Disabilities and/or medical conditions, height, weight, hair/eye color. *Exception:* An employer may describe the job requirements and ask the employee if he has any physical conditions that would impinge on his or her ability to perform the job.

How Federal Discrimination Statutes Are Enforced

Before anyone can file a lawsuit under any of the Title VII (anti-discrimination) laws, she must first try to redress her grievance through the Equal Employment Opportunity Commission. Anyone wishing to sue under Title VII must acquire a *right to sue* letter before he may file suit. The EEOC is a federal administrative agency that functions a bit like a mediator in that it tries to bring the parties to an amicable resolution without resorting to litigation.

The EEOC Process:

1. Someone believing he has a Title VII discrimination claim files a *charge of discrimination* with the EEOC, stating his case.
2. The EEOC then investigates, sending a copy of the employee's charge to the employer and asking it to respond in writing, including any relevant documents. (Employers will note that this is where the documentation of communications with the employee comes in handy.)
3. After reviewing the charge and the employer's response, the EEOC either:
   a. Finds reasonable grounds to believe the employer violated the law and begins informal mediation; or
   b. Finds no reasonable grounds to believe the employer violated the law. The employee can then sue in civil court by requesting a *right-to-sue* letter from the EEOC, which gives the employee 90 days to file suit against the employer; or
   c. Doesn't quite get around to the investigation within the time limit, in which case the employee may also request a *right-to-sue* letter and take the employer to civil court.
4. If the EEOC finds reasonable grounds and cannot come to a resolution with the employer, it may sue the employer on behalf of the employee and anyone else who has filed a charge.

See the Avoiding Lawsuits section of this chapter for preventive measures.

Other Important Federal Laws

Congress has passed several other laws regulating the workplace, among them:

Family and Medical Leave Act

The Family and Medical Leave Act ("FMLA") provides employees the opportunity to take time off of work for family and health reasons without losing their employment. It applies to business-es with 50 or more full-time employees (California requires employers with fewer than 50 employ-

Does Employee Have the Right to Sue Employer in Civil Court?

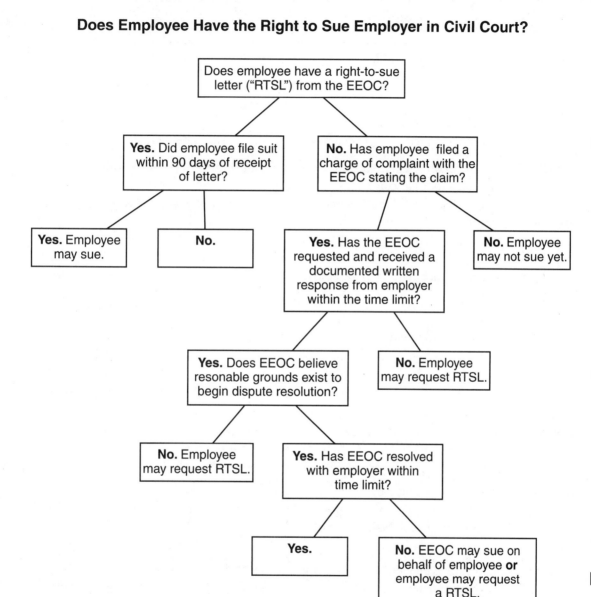

Figure 4.4

Employees usually must work with the EEOC before suing an employer for discrimination.

ees to grant family and medical leave). Eligible employees (those who have worked for the employer for at least 12 months or at least 1,250 hours per year) receive up to 12 weeks of unpaid leave per year in connection with the following:

- The birth of a child
- The placement of an adopted/foster child with the employee
- Care of a child, parent, or spouse
- A health condition rendering the employee unable to perform his/her job

The employer must restore the employee to the same or an equivalent position (with respect to benefits, pay, stature, and other conditions of employment) following expiration of the leave. *Exception:* If the employee is a "key" employee, i.e. among the top 10 percent of salary earners at the company and substantial harm to the company would result from his reinstatement, the employer does not have to restore the employee to his prior position. The employer must notify the employee of its intention to deny job restoration immediately upon determination that reinstatement would cause such harm and give the employee a reasonable amount of time to return to work from leave.

Fair Labor Standards Act

The Fair Labor Standards Act protects wage workers by regulating minimum wage, overtime, and child labor practices. It applies to all businesses engaged in interstate commerce (your state's legislation may extend the protections to all businesses, regardless of whether they engage in interstate business). It only protects non-salaried employees and children. It does not apply to independent contractors. Employers may not pay a non-exempt (see below for exemptions) employee less than the federal minimum wage ($5.15 as of March 2003) per hour worked and 1.5 times that wage for all time worked in excess of forty hours per workweek.

Minors: The FLSA regulates the use of minors (those under 18). Many of the rules have to do with the hours that minors can work and the kind of work they can do. See sidebar: "Hiring Kids" for a complete guide to the child labor experience.

Exempt Employees: Some employees are exempt from the FLSA, meaning that an employer is not required to pay them overtime. Employees must have certain responsibilities that they fulfill on an unsupervised basis to qualify as exempt. Exempt positions usually include executive, administrative, professional/salaried workers, and salespeople/commission workers.

CAUTION

While many computer programmers are considered administrative employees, the Department of Labor has decreed that those solely performing debugging work or translating narrative into code are not exempt.

Hiring Kids

Game development is a young business to begin with, and its labor force tends to be directed at a very young age. This is an extremely democratic, merit-based business, and many companies elect to make use of skilled and enthusiastic minors, whether as artists, programmers, testers, or interns.

Two rules to follow:

1. Have a legal guardian co-sign all documents. A minor employee and his legal guardian must sign, at the very least, an NDA and an assignment of all IP, if not a full employment agreement.

2. Observe the FLSA laws. The FLSA has two sets of rules for office work, one for 16-17-year-olds, who may be employed for unlimited hours in any occupation, and another for 14- and 15-year-olds, who may work outside of school hours, between the hours of 7 a.m. and 7 p.m. (9 p.m. during the summer) in certain jobs for up to:

   3 hours on a school day

   18 hours in a school week

   8 hours on a non-school day

   40 hours in a non-school week

Note that many states further regulate the hours that workers under age 18 may work, so check with your State Department of Labor.

Worker's Compensation

These statutes regulate businesses' insuring against worker injury sustained on the job, and the remedies and recoveries available to those injured workers. Workers are entitled to benefits regardless of blame (though a worker will not receive benefits if he was intoxicated, violating safety codes, or committing a crime when injured), but the benefits are generally limited to medical treatment, lost wages, and vocational rehabilitation. Except in rare cases, a worker

NOTE

Developers should note that repetitive stress injury might be considered a workplace injury if it would not have occurred but for the job requirements, as may emotional illnesses brought on by workplace stress.

cannot sue the employer if the worker has received worker's compensation benefits. This means workers do not get pain and suffering and other categories of damages available in a civil suit. Independent contractors are not covered by worker's compensation.

If an employee is injured on the job, he tells the company and the company files a report with its worker's compensation insurer, who then investigates and administers the claim.

An employer will obtain the worker's compensation insurance in one of three ways, depending on state regulations: self-insuring (also known as "Russian Roulette," in which the employer is obliged to maintain a sufficient cash reserve to cover claims); buying into a state-administered insurance pool; or buying insurance from a private company.

Caveat: If insurance is not obtained in strict adherence to state law, employers face penalties ranging from fines to temporary shutdowns to exposure to tort litigation by the employee.

ANATOMY OF AN EMPLOYMENT AGREEMENT—INCLUDING STOCK COMPENSATION

Every person who performs any work for the company should sign an employment agreement before beginning work. Failure to do so may give rise to trouble ranging from ambiguity to litigation. The primary dangers of allowing employees to work without signing an employment agreement are:

- *Termination*. Absent a written agreement, an employee may claim that management made oral promises of employment for a certain duration. Furthermore, having an employee's duties clearly enumerated in writing helps employers defend themselves against wrongful termination suits (or the threats thereof).
- *Ownership of Intellectual Property*. Without the *assignment* provision in an employment agreement, which states

TIP

Many employers, particularly small companies, have a hard time imagining any of their employees going to the expense and effort of taking them to court, and can become lackadaisical about these agreements. What is more common is the *strike suit*, where an ex-employee's attorney (quite possibly working on *contingency*, in which the attorney is paid a percentage of any settlement or other monies received) threatens suit to extract a quick settlement from a company eager to avoid the expense and hassle of litigation, regardless of the merits of the claim. The tighter your HR agreements, the fewer potential grounds for suit, the lower the probability that an attorney will put time into the case on contingency.

that the employee assigns (gives over) all intellectual property rights to any creations made while in the employer's employ, the employee could lay claim to whatever work product he creates.

- *Adherence to non-disclosure and non-compete agreements.* Without a signed NDA or non-compete agreement, an employer will have a hard time preventing an ex-employee from sharing inside information or setting up a competing shop using information learned while at the company.

Rainy Days and Harassment Suits Always Get Me Down, or Why Buy Insurance

As mentioned in Chapter 2, "First Steps," you need to find a good insurance broker and figure out what kind of insurance you should carry. Your state probably mandates that you carry certain kinds of insurance, like worker's compensation and disability, which are already pretty pricey. There are several other kinds of insurance that you should consider, particularly if your business has 15 or more employees (which usually brings you under more regulations), including, but by no means limited to:

- **Employment Practices Liability Insurance.** This will protect you from lawsuits filed by employees or ex-employees for things like harassment.

- **Liability for employee acts.** If your employees frequently travel around in cars on business errands, you may want to consider some kind of insurance to protect your company in case of an accident.

- **Intellectual property defense.** This insurance covers your costs of defense against infringement claims.

The key concept to understand about insurance is that it isn't just to cover the cost of any awards against you, it is to cover your costs of *defending* against claims. Plenty of employees try to shake down their employers, and the cost of defending against such suits can be astronomical.

A solid employment agreement should include the following:

- *Commencement date.*
- *Title and reporting structure.* If applicable, state the employee's title and the title(s) of the person(s) to whom the employee will report. See sidebar on "Organization Charts" for a primer on creating a coherent organization. Note: the exercise of analyzing and elucidating the employee's duties and reporting structure carries the additional benefit of promoting logical organization charts and forcing management to take a somewhat global look at the company structure.
- *Duties and Responsibilities.* Lay out the employee's duties and responsibilities with enough specificity that you can terminate someone for failing to meet the enumerated duties, but with enough flexibility that you can add to and/or modify the description as the employee grows within the company. Always include language to the effect that "Company reserves the right to modify these duties and responsibilities in good faith as required."
- *Schedule.* To comply with federal and state wage and labor laws, hourly employees should have a regular schedule (see the Fair Labor Standards Act section in this chapter).
- *Location.* This is important if the company has more than one office or if the employee will be telecommuting. It may not be in the employer's interest to specify location because it may give the employee grounds for wrongful termination if the employer requires the employee to move to a different location to continue employment.
- *Term and termination.* Every contract should be clearly stated to be "at-will," meaning that either party may terminate for any reason and without a required notice period. The employer will still need to observe termination protocols and take care to follow the laws of its state (see the Avoiding Lawsuits section later in this chapter). To preserve its ability to terminate at any time, with or without cause, an employer should take care not to make any statements in e-mail or person that could be interpreted as promises of employment for a given duration. As long as the employment agreement carries an *integration clause* (stating that the written agreement contains the entirety of the agreement between the parties and can only be modified in writing signed by both parties), the employer should be protected against any claims arising from casual statements, but caution is always the better part of valor in such matters.

If the employee successfully negotiates for a term of employment, he becomes a *term* employee. Consequences of termination for a term employee vary according to *why* the employee is terminated, whether *for cause* or *without cause*. In other words, a term employee has a guarantee of employment so long as he does not give the employer cause—which will be defined in the contract (usually theft, gross incompetence, or something of equal gravity). If the employer terminates him for any reason other than the contractually defined causes, the employee will receive certain compensation defined in the contract (ranging from a few months' salary to the rest of the contract). This right is often subject to the ex-employee's *duty to mitigate*, which means that the employee must look for comparable employment, which, if attained, would terminate the ex-employer's duties to pay out the balance of the contract.

Other terms that need to go in the employment agreement include:

Compensation

A compensation package can have several components, the most common being salary, benefits, and incentive compensation (bonus, profit-sharing, royalty participation, and so forth).

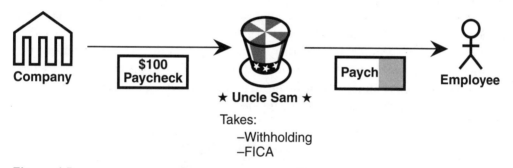

Figure 4.5

Compensating employees is more complicated than writing a check.

Salary

State explicitly the employee's annual salary, how it shall be paid (for example, in accordance with the company's payroll practices), and that it will be subject to all income and withholding taxes. The company will prefer not to specify raises or compensation review periods, but an employee will want some language regarding pay review periods (every six months, for example) and a clear articulation of benchmarks by which compensation decisions are made.

Benefits

There are three major categories of benefits:

Plan benefits like health, dental, retirement, stock options/profit participation. The agreement should not provide details of coverage under the plans, but should state that the employee will participate on the same basis as other employees in x, y, and z plans, according to the terms and conditions contained in the plan documents, and that such documents are subject to modification.

For stock option plans, the agreement must state that any option grants are made subject to the rules of the company's option plan and that any stock or options are subject to a *vesting* schedule. Otherwise, an employee who leaves before all of his or her equity interests have vested may argue that the equity was not subject to vesting and that he deserves the full amount of equity.

Time benefits like vacation, personal days, sick leave. These benefits should be stated explicitly, perhaps four personal days per year, ten vacation days, and so forth, as well as policies for extended absences.

"Other" benefits like a car allowance, expense account, computer for home, cell phone, and other such "perks." An employer will want to provide enough specificity here to prevent exorbitant spending (set a ceiling on monthly car expenses) and give guidelines where needed, especially regarding expense account spending and entertaining, as well as providing that the company is the actual owner of any items and may require their return at any time at the company's sole discretion. The employer will also want some flexibility to modify, so that if a benefit becomes unnecessary, or another is needed, it may change the package.

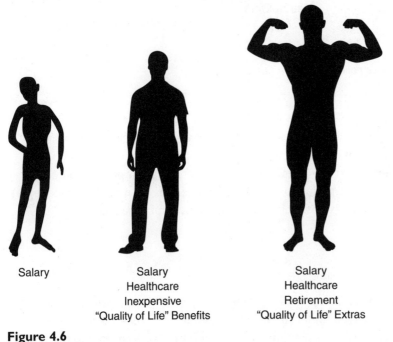

Salary	Salary	Salary
	Healthcare	Healthcare
	Inexpensive	Retirement
	"Quality of Life" Benefits	"Quality of Life" Extras

Figure 4.6

Let your benefit plan match your company's financial health.

The Quick and Dirty on Benefits

There are three things to know about benefits:

1. They're expensive, often adding between 20 and 30 percent to an employee's salary package.

2. They're expected. Employees get very emotional about benefits, seeing them as a direct index of how an employer values the health and welfare of its people.

3. They're complicated. Not only are the *plans* themselves complex and difficult to administer, there are many laws governing provision of benefits. Employers must be careful to have their benefit plans checked for compliance with discrimination laws. Many small businesses elect to outsource benefit administration to a broker. Shop around with different solution providers, and see what kinds of packages you can get (health and 401(k) administration, for instance).

With a bit of creativity, you can add a lot of value to your package without costing the company an arm and a leg. The two main value-adds you can leverage:

1. The company's increased purchasing power means you can offer your employees lower group rates for optional insurance such as life, disability, auto, vision, and dental, or negotiated rates with local merchants like a health club or even a massage therapist.

2. The company can use its administrative resources to help employees take advantage of somewhat confusing, paperwork-intensive benefits.

Health Insurance

This is a must. Variables that can increase or decrease the cost: HMO (health maintenance organization) vs. PPO (preferred provider organization); dental; vision; employer covering all of premium or only a portion; employer paying for all, part, or none of employee's family premium.

NOTE

Your organization will likely have to offer continuation of health coverage to departing employees for 18 months under **COBRA** laws, but you may bill the employee for 102% of the cost of his coverage.

TIP

You may be able to help your employees set up medical spending accounts, which will allow them to pay for any unreimbursed medical expenses from pre-tax dollars.

Retirement Plans

Since more people under 40 believe in aliens than that social security will be around for them to collect, retirement plans are a hot button. The small employer's three big concerns are:

1. Keeping administrative costs low.
2. Maintaining flexibility about how much and whether to match or contribute to the employee's plan. There are several types of tax-advantaged plans to help your employees contribute pre-tax dollars to a retirement account, summarized in the table at the end of this chapter.
3. Availability of vesting. Unfortunately, the more flexible plans designed for small businesses do not allow for vesting of retirement plans, so when an employee leaves, he takes everything with him. Some businesses respond to this problem by waiting a certain amount of time (one or two years) before enrolling an employee in the retirement plan program, but this can lead to bitter feelings by the employee.

> **TIP**
>
> Take a look at the availability of a *cafeteria* (Section 125) plan for your business. Cafeteria plans help you maximize your benefit dollars by allowing employees to choose their own benefits (like you choose your food in a cafeteria), funded with some mix of your money and withheld salary. While they can be difficult to administer and must meet legal hurdles, the result is tax-advantaged for you (no FICA) and for them, since they pay with pre-tax dollars.

Performance-Based Compensation

If the company awards bonuses, it will often be from a *bonus pool,* a fund—usually taken from royalties—set aside in accounting for division among the employees. The company should state whether the bonus is entirely at the employer's discretion or whether it is calculated by a standard metric (for example, 2 percent of the bonus pool). Generally speaking, an employer will want to be as nonspecific as possible so as to avoid committing itself to a plan that it later wishes to modify. The employee may wish for a set of guidelines to know how performance correlates to bonus.

Other Key Terms of the Employment Agreement

Verification of Immigration Status

Federal laws strictly regulate the employment of immigrants; all employees need to fill out an I-9 form attesting to and providing adequate documentation (U.S. passport, work visa, or "green card") of legal U.S. work status.

Sharing the Wealth: Four Methods of Performance-Based Compensation

Performance-based compensation is almost a given in technology-based companies. While equity has fallen somewhat out of favor ("so much paperwork, so little return," as one CEO put it), consider the four main varieties of "thanks, good job," in order of administrative complexity (lowest to highest):

1. Bonuses. Bonuses are the most common salary supplement. Rather than wait until the end of the year, when employees can easily compare bonuses, you may want to give them out at the time of a particular achievement. The pros are that this method can be dramatically different from year to year and employee to employee, and it reflects achievement most closely. On the other hand, bonuses can cause strife among employees and can create an emphasis on appearances over substance.

2. Royalty Pools. Royalty pools set aside a certain percentage of royalties from a given game (or from all royalties, as preferred) for distribution among employees. This is another very flexible plan. Administrative hassles are low; employees are compensated for the projects they work on; there can be a "vesting" effect if employees must still be employed to draw from the royalty pool. Then again, not many projects actually return royalties, so you may end up paying cash bonuses to reward employees.

3. Profit-sharing plans. Profit-sharing plans include both immediate cash payout plans and deferral plans. A payout plan pays cash to eligible employees at the end of a stated period of time, typically at the end of the company's fiscal year. A deferral plan can take many forms. The company could make deposits on behalf of employees into their IRA or 401(k) plans. Deferral plans can have tax advantages for employees. Profit-sharing plans are more like retirement plans, have high administrative costs, and don't really reflect performance since the percentage is set as a percentage of salary and all employees generally receive the same percentage.

4. Ownership. Some employers grant employees actual ownership in the form of stock options or shares. This is low cost, and it allows employees to participate in the company upside. However, there are high administrative costs, and additional shareholders can create legal headaches.

Termination

Where the term of employment is *at will*, meaning that either party can terminate the relationship at any time for any reason by providing notice to the other, an employer generally has only to notify the employee and to be within the basic principles outlined in the Avoiding Lawsuits section of this chapter.

Ownership of Intellectual Property

A development house's main product is intellectual property ("IP"). Every day, employees come to work to create new IP in the form of copyrights, trademarks, and trade secrets (and rarely, patents). See Chapter 5, a Primer on "Intellectual Property," for more discussion of these. Unlike most other forms of property, however, Congress has legislated a set of rights that accompany that work of creation, even if someone else is paying you to do it. A company's intellectual property maintenance program has two major functions:

- Laying the legal paper trail to make sure that it actually owns IP created by its employees.
- Making sure that the company controls and receives all benefits deriving from that IP.

Works Made for Hire

Copyright law generally accords "authorship" of a copyrightable work to the employer where the creation is the work product of an employee acting within the scope of employment, hence the term work made for hire. However, disputes can arise surrounding the definitions of "employee" and "scope of employment" that may lead to the intellectual property creation failing the work for hire test and ownership being granted to the person who "created" it.

The legal test of whether a work qualifies as a work made for hire will look to:

- **Control.** Did the employer direct and supervise the creation of the work?
- **Initiative.** Who initiated the creation of the work?
- **Pay.** Did the employee receive compensation of an amount and kind commensurate with creating such a work?
- **Time.** How much time was spent on the work?
- **Resources.** Did the employer own or pay for the tools, including location and support personnel, used to create the work?

Assignment of Inventions

An employer will want language in the employment agreement clearly stating that all works of authorship and any intellectual property created during employment are works made for hire and that to the extent the employee retains any rights in any such works, the employee irrevocably assigns such rights to the company with no further consideration (compensation). This language acts as a catch-all for any rights an employee may have in any work created during employment that may not qualify for treatment as a work made for hire. The language consists of a present assignment ("I hereby assign," not "I agree that I will assign") of all intellectual property rights to any results of employee's work during employment. See Exhibit B in the appendices to this chapter.

Figure 4.7

Treat your employees right!

Treat your employees like gold, for gold is what they make.

NOTE

Some states allow a company to claim all of an employee's work, whether or not created during work hours, using the employer's equipment or proprietary information, or relating to employer's business. Other states, California and Washington included, prohibit employer's from laying claim to work created on the employee's own time, without use of the employer's materials or proprietary data, and unrelated to the employer's business.

CAUTION

To prevent claims of prior invention and to ensure compliance with the assignment provision, employers will want to require that the employee identify any pre-existing inventions at the time the agreement is signed and to agree to disclose any and all inventions during the term of employment as well as for a certain amount of time post-employment (six months to one year is reasonable). This obligation allows the employer to "vet" any inventions, in other words, to review them to see if the company believes it has any valid ownership claims.

Employee Files

Every employee should have a confidential file—electronic is nice, but since it will have several original signed documents, hard copy is wise. What goes in there:

1. Resume and application

2. Original and updated job description

3. Performance evaluations (signed by employee). See form at the end of this chapter.

4. Signed receipt for employee handbook

5. W-4 (IRS form for payroll withholding and taxes)

6. Form I-9 (certifying that the employee may work in the U.S.)

7. All benefit paperwork, i.e. 401(k) documents

8. Documentation of any disciplinary action

CAUTION

Personnel files contain sensitive data and must be kept under lock and key (physical and/or electronic) and shown only on a "need-to-see" basis. Particularly sensitive documents—such as those having to do with health or harassment issues—should be kept separately. Many states regulate the maintenance of personnel files, so check with your local counsel for every office to be sure you are compliant.

NOTE

Employees are entitled to a copy of all documents that they sign.

TIP

Standardize your forms. At the very least, create simple templates for performance reviews (see example at the end of this chapter) and disciplinary actions. Disciplinary actions should note: name of employee; date of incident and date of document; name of all parties to whom the issue has been communicated and other co-workers involved in the action; what happened; actions being taken.

Non-Disclosure Agreement, AKA the NDA

This is sometimes a separate agreement, attached as an appendix to the employment agreement. This language protects the company from any employee leaking *proprietary* information or using such proprietary information. The NDA will not extend to use of any information publicly available or publicly known. The restrictions can last anywhere from four years to indefinitely. Highlights include:

- *Definition of proprietary information.* Usually defined as all trade secrets and other information gained during employment and not generally known in the employer's industry, including any information about the business, employees, product, customers, business practices, or potential customers.

- *Equitable Relief.* Equitable relief is a kind of non-monetary legal compensation, generally forcing the losing party to do (*specific performance*) or refrain from doing (*injunctive relief*) certain things. Most NDAs include language stating that *damages*, money, may not be sufficient and that equitable relief may be sought by the employer. Example: An employee leaves an employer and uses the employer's confidential marketing list to contact potential customers. In addition to suing the former employee for money lost due to the employee's actions, the company will sue for an injunction prohibiting the employee from conducting any business resulting from the offending use of the company's confidential information.

Non-Compete

One challenge facing employers in an industry as IP-intensive as game development is that employees walk out the door every night with the company's most valuable assets. Fortunately, they usually come back the next day, but employers are powerless to "take back" a departing employee's knowledge. What employers *can* do is put a temporary restriction on a departing employee's ability to use that knowledge in a manner competitive with the original employer.

An employer can restrict an employee from competing with the company during the term of employment. Some states, most notably California, restrict a company's ability to enforce a non-compete clause *after* the employee leaves. Other states allow enforcement of reasonable (for example, time-limited or geographically relevant) post-employment restrictions on competition. Generally, an employer will want to prevent the employee from taking any employment with or providing services for a competitor, owning an interest in, operating, or preparing to operate a competing venture for at least one year, more if this was a key employee. If the employee is not an at-will employee and is leaving before the expiration of the employment term, the non-compete will often be in force for the duration of the original term *plus* some additional period of

Figure 4.8

Your company's most valuable asset goes home every night.

> **NOTE**
>
> There is a gray area concerning the definition of "operating." If an employee leaves the company, takes a job as a barista for two years and spends his nights coding a project that he sells the first day his restriction is lifted, has he been "competing" during those two years? If your employment agreement restricts that employee's ability to prepare to compete, then such activities *are* prohibited. A further complication, however, is the legal enforceability of such restrictions; some states and courts will not allow what they see as excessively restrictive post-employment covenants.

time. Because game development is highly virtual and pays little attention to geographic boundaries, a world-wide restriction is reasonable.

Non-Solicit

Closely related to the non-compete clause, a non-solicit provision prohibits a departing employee from recruiting, employing, or inciting the departure of any other employees for a period of time, usually one year.

Integration

The *integration* clause protects both parties from later claims that the document does not reflect oral or other promises made by the opposing side. This clause states that the written document reflects the entire agreement between the parties, in other words, there are no promises or conditions influencing the relationship that are not reflected in the written document.

Arbitration

Arbitration is an alternative to litigation (where the parties go to trial). Arbitration may be much quicker and cheaper, taking place in front of one to three people, usually experienced attorneys, who review the evidence and rule on the case. An arbitration clause may be to the benefit of both the employer and employee, since exorbitant legal expenses will not deter a party from seeking redress; some feel that employees gain leverage from the threat of costly litigation and the exposure of a court trial, not to mention the natural sympathy between jurors and another working person. In some states, however, there are no rules of evidence to protect a party; furthermore, parties may lose the right to appeal an arbitrator's decision. See the Arbitration section in Chapter 6 for further discussion of this clause.

INDEPENDENT CONTRACTORS

Everybody loves independent contractors. They can be cost saving because the company won't have to pay benefits, worker's compensation insurance, social security, Medicare, or unemployment tax. Using independent contractors can also help a company manage *burn* (monthly cash outflow) between projects.

There are two major risks to manage when using independent contractors:

- Preventing the contractor from being reclassified by the IRS as an employee (resulting in a major tax hit)
- Assuring adequate control of intellectual property and proprietary information

Successful Use of the Independent Contractor, Part One: Is the Worker an Employee or an Independent Contractor?

The IRS uses two main principles in classifying workers: independent contractors will generally:

- Have control over the outcome of the work and ownership of the tools to create it; AND
- Offer and provide services to more than one company.

A court determining a worker's status will apply a test looking to the following factors:

Independent Contractor or Employee?

Factor	More likely to be classified as employee if	More likely to be classified as independent contractor if
Employer supervision and control of work product	Employer has high degree of supervision and control	Worker is largely unsupervised and controls work product
Kind of occupation	Unskilled position	Highly skilled worker
Permanence and duration of employment	Long-term and open-ended	Short-term with a clear end date
Social security taxes	Employer pays	Worker pays
Retirement and Health benefits	Employer provides	Worker provides
Ownership of facilities and equipment used in work	Employer-owned	Worker-owned
Is the work performed by worker integral to the company's business	Yes	No
How payment is calculated	Hourly/time based	Per job/work-based
Worker's opportunity for profit/loss?	Low	High
Skill, initiative, judgment required for successful performance of work	Low	High
Worker receives sick leave or vacation time	Yes	No
Parties have a written agreement stipulating that worker is an independent contractor	No	Yes

To get the gestalt of what the IRS is looking at, keep in mind that a major goal of the law distinguishing between employees and independent contractors is to prevent the exploitation of workers by companies looking to avoid paying the taxes, insurance, and benefits attached to employee status. The law is looking to establish that any persons classified as independent contractors do so voluntarily as part of a scheme to offer services to several entities, with adequate negotiating leverage to make the decision to be an independent contractor from preference and not necessity.

Successful Use of the Independent Contractor, Part Two: The Contract

While a written agreement will not necessarily protect a company from the reclassification of independent contractors, it is a necessary part of any independent contractor relationship.

The independent contractor agreement should be signed before the contractor begins work and should detail:

- The work to be performed.
- The reporting relationship.
- That the contractor will be working without supervision, on his own schedule, and has the option of working at the company office or not, and may use the company equipment or not, as the contractor prefers.
- Responsibility and any personnel reporting to the independent contractor.
- Milestones and time frame for completion of work.
- Fees and timing of payments (which should be tied to successful milestone completion).
- Provision of resources and equipment for completion of work.
- Where work is to be performed.
- Reimbursable expenses.
- That the work is to be done on an independent contractor basis, and that the contractor will be responsible for paying all taxes, insurance, and benefits.
- Representation and warranty that no work submitted by the contractor will violate the rights of any third party (e.g. intellectual property right infringement).

Successful Use of the Independent Contractor, Part Three: Intellectual Property and Information Control Concerns

A company has three basic nightmare scenarios:

1. The independent contractor claims intellectual property ownership of the work product.

2. The independent contractor uses confidential information gleaned during the engagement in a subsequent product.
3. The independent contractor contributes infringing content (someone else's code or art) and the infringed property owner proceeds to sue the company.

To guard against an independent contractor retaining any ownership rights in the product, the parties must sign an agreement setting forth the relationship of the parties and containing language that:

- Defines the "work product" and any interim deliverables. Defines the work product broadly as including but not limited to all inventions, artworks, trademarks, copyrights, patents, and know-how created during the engagement.
- Catalogs pre-existing property. If the contractor will be using a pre-existing IP, such as an engine or a tool set, these need to be named and described with specificity. Furthermore, the contractor must grant the company a license to use that IP. Whenever pre-existing IP is incorporated into the work product, the company will want an irrevocable, non-exclusive, permanent, sub-licensable, royalty-free license to use the contractor's IP so that the company will not have to negotiate with the contractor every time it sells or changes the work product.

> **NOTE**
> A company's license to the pre-existing property is only for the particular manifestation created for the company, i.e. the company can't break out the engine and sub-license it to someone else. It can only be sublicensed as part of the game.

- Sets up invention disclosure parameters. The contractor should promptly and fully disclose all intellectual property created during the engagement and as a result of work performed during the engagement.
- Assigns all IP to the client. The company will want to own all intellectual property created by a contractor as a work made for hire. The contractor should irrevocably assign to the company all rights that do not qualify as a work made for hire. The contractor should also agree to execute all documents and provide any other assistance required to establish the client's ownership.
- No Contest. Contractor should agree not to contest ownership of the IP.

To maintain good information hygiene, the independent contractor agreement should prohibit the contractor from disclosing confidential information to any third parties. The agreement should also:

- Define confidential information broadly, including information given to the client by third parties.
- State that the contractor has no existing conflict of interest and will not accept any engagement giving rise to such conflict during the course of work for the company.

To guard against being the unwitting recipient of work violating a third party's rights (stolen code or artwork that could be deemed to defame an existing person—an ex-girlfriend, for example), the agreement should contain:

- Contractor's representations that no element of the work product will contain any materials that infringe a third party's rights; and
- Contractor's agreement to *indemnify* and hold the company harmless against any claims, losses, etc. resulting from a breach of the contractor's representation. In other words, if the contractor provides artwork that turns out to have been stolen from a third party, the contractor will be liable for attorney's fees or settlement costs, the costs of swapping out the artwork, and so on.

AVOIDING LAWSUITS

The two most common sources of worker lawsuits are wrongful termination and discrimination.

Before addressing preventive measures specific to each category, there are a few general cautions that are worth a pound of cure:

- Hire smart. Trust your intuition. Remember that, beyond an employee's skills, workplace chemistry is the bedrock of good morale.
- Learn how to interview. Learn about what you can and can't say when trying to learn about a prospective employee. With all of the laws to follow regarding interview, getting information about a prospective employee has been likened to drinking a glass of water with your hands behind your back.
- Check references. First, actually make the calls. You'd be shocked, simply *shocked*, at how many Mr. Hydes get hired because management was too harassed to call the references. Second, listen carefully: many ex-employers are wary of the retribution a negative reference can bring, so, as with stock analysts, you have to listen between the lines—lack of enthusiasm can be an indicator that there's something the reference would like to say but won't.
- Conduct standard periodic performance reviews and keep written records.
- Consider instituting a probation period for new hires, even if they are at-will employees. A probation period with reviews after 1, 2, and 3 months communicates to new hires that their status with the company is still undetermined.
- Get it in writing: Every worker should sign:
  - An Employment/Independent Contractor Agreement
  - Reviews
  - Complaints

Discrimination

Note regarding state regulations. Some expand the federal acts to all businesses regardless of number of employees. States vary on who is considered a protected class, for example, some states protect homosexuals from discrimination on the basis of sexual orientation, but others do not.

In a harassment/discrimination litigation, an employer wants to be able to prove it exercised its best efforts to prevent any poor behavior by employees. The following efforts will bolster an employer's argument that it did all it could to prevent the situation:

1. **Policy guide.** Every employer should give new employees a policy guide outlining prohibited actions and clearly stating where to report any violations, the procedures that the employees must follow, that such reports shall be free from retribution (anti-retaliation clause), and so on. The employee should sign an acknowledgment that he has received, read, and understood the document. See sidebar: "Employee Handbook."

2. **Training.** Management and employees should receive sensitivity training. Lower level management is particularly important in preventing harassment, as they *see* the employees on a day-to-day basis and are likely to be the first to notice any problems. Moreover, an employee is most likely to make his or her first complaint to an immediate supervisor. Management should receive training in:
   - The nuts and bolts of harassment and discrimination law
   - Company procedures for handling complaints and potentially volatile situations
   - How to recognize potential harassment/discrimination situations *before* they receive a complaint

3. **Open communication lines.** The best prevention for sexual harassment or any kind of discrimination litigation is a short line between the offended party and upper management. Publicly designate a "go-to" person for any complaints, and clearly communicate that consultations with the go-to will be confidential.

4. **Reinforcement.** Many employers elect to have periodic (annual or bi-annual) "training" lunches where a lecturer educates employees about what constitutes harassment and discrimination, and what to do should such a situation arise in their workplace.

5. **Documentation.** An employer then wants to be able to prove that it took all available steps to address and remedy the problem.
   - Follow the steps outlined in the corporate harassment policy.
   - All complaint communication must be documented
   - After addressing a complaint, the company will want to receive some signed documentation from the complainant that the measures taken by the company were effective and satisfactory. This will reduce the likelihood of a subsequent lawsuit alleging insufficient measures.

How to Fire Someone Politely and Effectively

Do not fear the axe. A wise man once said: "It's not the people you fire who make your life miserable; it's the ones you don't." Nothing is worse for morale than lack of consequences for those employees who make everyone else's job harder. It is wise to keep careful documentation of poor performance for two reasons: (i) in case of a wrongful termination suit, you need to be able to prove that the employee's performance was the cause of termination; and (ii) to minimize your unemployment insurance tax rates. Employees terminated for poor performance generally do not receive unemployment benefits, but those who are laid off do. In most states, a company will pay into a state's unemployment insurance fund through a tax on payroll, and the state will require higher tax rates from companies whose employees have drawn unemployment benefits. Minimize the number of employees receiving unemployment benefits and you'll minimize your unemployment insurance payments.

Conduct performance reviews every 6 to 12 months, have the employee sign them, and keep them in a personnel file. Any complaints against the employee must be documented, signed by the employee to prove that the issue was brought to the employee's attention, and kept in the personnel file.

While term employees can only be terminated for the reasons and on the conditions enumerated in their individual contracts (see the Anatomy of an Employment Agreement section), at-will employees can be terminated at any time for any reason.

An ex-employee may claim exception to this rule by arguing that he was *wrongfully discharged* for any of the following three reasons:

1. Employee and employer had an *implied contract*. Even without a written contract, courts have ruled that an implied contract to fire only for cause exists where employer behavior created a reasonable expectation in the employee. Factors leading to the existence of an implied contract include: a long term of employment; the employer stated that it would not terminate at employee's level without cause; the employee was assured that employment would continue with good performance; the employee had received raises, promotions, and other signs of employer approval; the employee had been told that he had performed well and had never been criticized or warned.
2. Employer violated the *implied covenant of good faith and fair dealing*. This hallowed covenant has been deemed by courts to exist in the background of almost every contract, essentially giving courts a reason to prevent one party from utterly exploiting another. Hence, employers should beware firing an at will employee the day before he receives the royalty bonus unless the employer can firmly establish that the employee is being terminated for good cause.

3. Employee was terminated for a reason violating public policy. Most employers' moral compasses will help them avoid this trap, but some examples of invalid reasons to terminate an at-will employee include: refusing to assist employer to break laws or engage in deceptive practices; whistle-blowing; and filing a worker's comp claim.

> **CAUTION**
>
> When a high-level executive is terminated, or anyone receives a severance package, be sure to get something in writing acknowledging the position of the parties as well as a release of employer liability. You don't want to pay a generous severance package and then be sued three months later for wrongful termination.

Organization Charts

Man may be born free, but he elects the comfort of society's chains. I have found this a helpful principle—that structure is a preferred evil—in organizing young, creative companies. "Flat" organizations (so-called because there is little or no hierarchy) were the vogue result of a realization that the collaborative approach often creates happier employees and faster development times. However, such structures are more chaos-prone for the simple reason that *no one knows where to take a problem for the authority to solve it.* On the other hand, a structure with too many layers can bog down processes and alienate knowledge (usually held by the workers) from decision-making. The goal is to give fertile minds the room to roam, contribute, and problem-solve while providing a support skeleton that is informed and able to listen for and identify trouble, intervening quickly where needed.

Creating an organization chart becomes even more important when your organization has more than one project in motion at a time. There are three main philosophies of organizing your personnel:

1. Pure Project: In a pure project organization, people are grouped into teams by project, instead of function. A programmer reports to the project lead, and not to a Technical Director or other functional head. Advantages: Total focus on a project, strong team identity, minimized red tape, maximized flexibility. Disadvantages: Competition between teams can get out of hand; specialized knowledge can fail to get transferred to the institution (example: team 2 doesn't understand team 1's technology and tools); renegade managers can

turn the company into fiefdoms; resource allocation can be inefficient (example: art staff lying fallow while waiting for next project).

2. Functional: Personnel report to a functional head, so programmers would report to a Technical Director. Duties for new projects would be added to and divided among function groups (like the technical department) by the function head, who would also serve as the project manager for a given function. Advantages: Stability, cohesion, common pool of knowledge within a department, coherent career paths. Disadvantages: Competition for resources, communication not as fluid among project contributors, not quite the same goal fervor.

3. Matrix. The matrix format combines the project and function forms by having personnel report to more than one supervisor. Employees are organized on a permanent basis into functional groups and report to function heads, but "seconded" (dedicated) to project teams for a given project for whatever duration is required (which may not be the entire life of the project). One way to imagine the matrix is to see the functional group as the employee's family, and the project team as its peer group. Employees spend more time with their peers, but their primary identification is as a member of the family, and it is to the head of that family that they go with any problems. Benefits: project emphasis, strong access to all of company resources, institutionalization of technology and knowledge, continuity after projects end. Disadvantages: Disputes can arise between functional heads and project managers over resources and authority, with employees caught in the middle; major problems can arise when a project gets shut down.

SUMMARY

Employees bring creativity and energy to a company as well as legal complexity and liability exposure. A human resources lawyer is essential to protecting your business interests, and you should consult her as early as possible to set up policies and contracts. Some key points to remember:

■ You are vulnerable to wrongful termination and discrimination suits and must take aggressive measures to protect your company.

■ The byword of employment law is "document" (verb form). Example of use in a sentence: "Document! Document! Document!"

- In addition to the federal labor laws and those of the company's home state, your company may be subject to employment laws of different states. Example: you have more than one office. Consult local counsel and be mindful of the different state and federal laws that may apply to your company.
- Develop policies early on regarding harassment, discrimination, computer use, salaries, confidential information, and other aspects of operation. Write these up in a handbook and have every employee sign a receipt that he has received, read, and understood it.
- Every employee should be on an "at will basis" and should sign an employment agreement before starting work.
- Get clear title to all IP by having employees and independent contractors sign confidentiality/assignment of invention agreements.
- Don't pretend your employees are independent contractors.
- Talk to a good insurance broker about applicable coverage.
- Put some thought into your organizational structure, both as it is and how you want it to be in three years. Draw up an organization chart that fits that vision.

A comparison of major retirement options and their key features, compiled by the Pension and Welfare Benefits Administration

Key Advantage

SEP-IRA	Easy to set up and maintain.
Payroll Deduction IRA	Easy to set up and maintain.
SIMPLE-IRA	Salary reduction plan with little administrative paperwork.
401(k)	Permits employee to contribute more than in other options.
Profit Sharing	Permits employer to create large account balances for employees.
Defined Benefit	Provides a fixed, pre-established benefit for employees.
Money Purchase Plan	Permits employer to make a larger contribution than through other Defined Contribution Plans.

Employers Who Can Provide This Option

SEP-IRA	Any business that does not currently maintain any other retirement plan.
Payroll Deduction IRA	Any business with one or more employees.
SIMPLE-IRA	Any business with 100 or fewer employees that does not currently maintain any other retirement plan.
401(k)	Any business with one or more employees.
Profit Sharing	Any business with one or more employees.
Defined Benefit	Any business with one or more employees.
Money Purchase Plan	Any business with one or more employees.

Employer's Responsibilities

SEP-IRA	Set up plan by completing IRS Form 5305-SEP. No employer tax filing required.
Payroll Deduction IRA	Set up arrangements for employees to make payroll deduction contributions. Transmit contributions for employees to funding vehicle. No employer tax filing required.

SIMPLE-IRA	Set up by completing IRS F5304-SIMPLE or 5305-SIMPLE. No employer tax filing required. Bank or financial institution does most of the paperwork.
401(k)	There is no model form to establish a plan. Advice from a financial institution or employee benefit advisor would be necessary. Annual filing of IRS Form 5500 required. Also requires special testing to ensure plan does not discriminate in favor of highly compensated employees.
Profit Sharing	There is no model form to establish a plan. Advice from a financial institution or employee benefit advisor would be necessary. Annual filing of IRS Form 5500 is required.
Defined Benefit	There is no model form to establish a plan. Advice from a financial institution or employee benefit advisor would be necessary. Annual filing of IRS Form 5500. Actuary must determine funding obligations.
Money Purchase Plan	There is no model form to establish a plan. Advice from a financial institution or employee benefit advisor would be necessary. Annual filing of IRS Form 5500 is required.

Funding Responsibility

SEP-IRA	Employer contributions only.
Payroll Deduction IRA	Employee contributions remitted through payroll deduction.
SIMPLE-IRA	Employee salary reduction contributions and/or employer contributions.
401(k)	Employee salary reduction contributions and/or employer contributions.
Profit Sharing	Employer contribution level can be determined year to year.
Defined Benefit	Primarily employer; may require or permit employee contributions.
Money Purchase Plan	Employer contributions only.

Maximum Annual Contribution Per Participant

SEP-IRA	Up to 15% of compensation or maximum of $24,000 (indexed).
Payroll Deduction IRA	$2,000

SIMPLE-IRA	*Employee*: $6,000 per year (indexed). *Employer*: Either match employee contributions $ for $ up to 3% of compensation (can be reduced to as low as 1% in any 2 out of 5 yrs.) or contribute 2% of each eligible employee's compensation, up to $3,200
401(k)	*Employee*: $10,000 (indexed). *Employer/Employee combined*: Up to a maximum of 15% of compensation or a maximum of $30,000.
Profit Sharing	Up to a maximum of 15% of salary or a maximum of $30,000.
Defined Benefit	Per plan terms, employer may permit or require employee contribution.
Money Purchase Plan	Up to a maximum of 25% of salary or a maximum of $30,000.

Minimum Employee Coverage Requirements

SEP-IRA	Must be offered to all employees who are at least 21 years of age, employed by the business for 3 of last 5 years and earned at least $400 in a year.
Payroll Deduction IRA	Should be made available to all employees.
SIMPLE-IRA	Must be offered to all employees who have earned at least $5,000 in previous 2 years.
401(k)	Must be offered to all employees at least 21 years of age who worked at least 1,000 hours in previous year.
Profit Sharing	Must be offered to all employees at least 21 years of age who worked at least 1,000 hours in previous year.
Defined Benefit	Must be offered to all employees at least 21 years of age who worked at least 1,000 hours in previous year.
Money Purchase Plan	Must be offered to all employees at least 21 years of age who worked at least 1,000 hours in previous year.

Withdrawals, Loans & Payments

SEP-IRA	Withdrawals at anytime; subject to current federal income taxes and a possible 10% penalty if the participant is under age 59 1/2.
Payroll Deduction IRA	Withdrawals at anytime; subject to current federal income taxes and a possible 10% penalty if the participant is under age 59 1/2.

SIMPLE-IRA	Withdrawals at any time. If employee is under age 59 1/2, may be subject to a 25% penalty if taken within the first 2 years of participation and a possible 10% penalty if taken afterwards.
401(k)	Cannot take withdrawals until a specified event, such as reaching 59 1/2, death, separation from service or other event as identified in plan. May permit loans and hardship withdrawals. Withdrawals may be subject to a possible 10% penalty if participant is under age 59 1/2.
Profit Sharing	May permit loans and hardship withdrawals. Hardship withdrawals may be subject to a possible 10% penalty if participant is under age 59 1/2. Payment of benefits generally at retirement.
Defined Benefit	Payment of benefits generally at retirement, may offer participant loans.
Money Purchase Plan	Payment of benefits generally at retirement, may offer participant loans.

Vesting

SEP-IRA	Immediate 100%
Payroll Deduction IRA	Immediate 100%
SIMPLE-IRA	Employee and employer contributions vested 100% immediately.
401(k)	Employee contributions vested immediately. Employer contributions may vest over time according to plan terms.
Profit Sharing	May vest over time according to plan terms.
Defined Benefit	May vest over time according to plan terms.
Money Purchase Plan	May vest over time according to plan terms.

Contributor's Options

SEP-IRA	Employer can decide whether or not to make contribution year to year.
Payroll Deduction IRA	Employee can decide how much to contribute at any time.
SIMPLE-IRA	Employee can decide how much to contribute. Employer must make matching contributions or contribute 2% of each employee's salary up to the set maximum.

401(k)	Employee makes contribution as set by plan option. The employer may match.
Profit Sharing	Employer makes contribution as set by plan terms.
Defined Benefit	Employer makes contributions as set by plan terms.
Money Purchase Plan	Employer makes contribution as set by plan terms.

EMPLOYMENT AGREEMENT

This employment agreement (the "Agreement") is entered into this ___ day of _____, 200__ by and between Double D Development, Inc., a California corporation ("Company"), and [employee's name], the undersigned individual ("Employee") (each a "Party," collectively the "Parties").

Whereas, Company and Employee desire to enter into this Agreement setting forth the terms and conditions of Employee's employment with the Company as [Job title].

NOW, THEREFORE, in consideration of the mutual covenants and agreements hereinafter set forth, the Company and Employee agree as follows:

1. Employment.
   a. Term. Employment is at will.
   b. Duties and Responsibilities. Employee will be reporting to [direct supervisor] for performance of the following duties:
      i. _____
      ii. _____
      iii. _____

2. Compensation.
   a. Base Salary. Employee will be paid a base salary ("Base Salary") at the annual rate of $_____ payable in biweekly installments consistent with Company's payroll practices.
   b. Pay. Employee shall receive all compensation in accord with the relevant Company policies in effect, as changed from time to time, including normal payroll practices, and shall be subject to all applicable employment and withholding taxes.
   c. Benefit Plans. Employee shall be entitled to participate in the Company's [medical, dental, vision, retirement] plan(s).
   d. Vacation. Employee shall be entitled to _____ (____) weeks of vacation each year of full employment, exclusive of legal holidays, as long as the scheduling of Employee's vacation does not interfere with the Company's normal business operations.
   e. Bonus. Company may, at its sole discretion, award employee an annual bonus based on employee performance and financial position of Company.

3. Intellectual Property
   a. Ownership. Company and Employee expressly agree that that Company is the exclusive owner of all rights and title to the copyright, trademark, patent and moral rights to any and all work that Employee assists in, creates, collaborates

on or otherwise contributes to, including but not limited to all ideas, processes, trademarks, service marks, inventions, designs, technologies, computer hardware or software, original works of authorship, formulas, discoveries, patents, copyrights, copyrightable works products, marketing and business ideas, and all improvements, know-how, data, rights, and claims related to the foregoing that, whether or not patentable ("Work") during the term of this Agreement and any extensions. Company shall also be the exclusive owner of all right, title and interest in and to any rights in any Work that either: (1) relates to the Company's current or contemplated business or activities; (2) relates to Company's actual or anticipated research or development; (3) results from any previous Work; (4) uses Company's equipment, supplies, facilities or trade secrets; (5) results from or is suggested by any Company endeavor; or (6) results from Employee access to any of Company's intellectual property, including memoranda, notes, records, drawings, sketches, models, maps, customer lists, research results, data, formulae, specifications, inventions, processes, equipment, non-public information received by Company from third parties, or other materials (collectively, "Proprietary Information").

b. <u>Assignment</u>. Where applicable, all Work shall be a word made for hire as defined by Section 101 of the United State Copyright Act. To the extent that any Work produced pursuant to this Agreement does not so qualify, Employee hereby irrevocably assigns and sells to Company, its successors and assigns the following: a) the entire right, title and interest in and to the copyrights, trademarks, patents, and other rights in any such Work and any rights in and to any works based upon, derived from, or incorporating any such Work ("Derivative Work"); b) all existing registrations or copyright applications relating to any such Work or Derivative Work, and any renewals or extensions thereof; c) the exclusive right to obtain, register and renew the copyrights, trademarks, or patents in any such Work or Derivative Work; d) all income, royalties, damages, claims and payments now or hereafter due or payable with respect to any such Work and Derivative Work; and e) all causes of action in law or equity, past and future, for infringements or violation of any of the rights in any such Work or Derivative Work, and any recoveries resulting thereof.

c. <u>Moral Rights</u>. Employee also hereby waives in writing any moral or other rights that he has under state or federal laws, or under the laws of any foreign jurisdiction, which would give him any rights to constrain or prevent the use of any Work or Derivative, or which would entitle him to receive additional Compensation from Company.

d. <u>Further Documents</u>. Employee agrees to execute all documents, including without limitation copyright assignments and applications, and to perform all acts that

Company may reasonably request in order to assist Company in perfecting its rights in and to any Work, and Derivative Work anywhere in the world.

4. <u>Proprietary and Confidential Information</u>. Employee has executed and agreed to the non-disclosure, non-compete agreement attached as Appendix A [omitted from this sample].

5. <u>Exclusive Employment</u>. During employment with the Company, Employee will not do anything to compete with the Company's present or contemplated business, nor will he plan or organize any competitive business activity. Employee will not enter into any agreement which conflicts with his duties or obligations to the Company. Employee will not during his employment or within one (1) year after it ends, without the Company's express written consent, directly or indirectly, solicit or encourage any employee, agent, independent contractor, supplier, customer, consultant on any other person or company to terminate or alter a relationship with the Company.

6. <u>Assignment and Transfer</u>. Employee's rights and obligations under this Agreement shall not be transferable by assignment or otherwise, and any purported assignment, transfer or delegation thereof shall be void. This Agreement shall inure to the benefit of, and be binding upon and enforceable by any purchaser of substantially all of Company's assets, any corporate successor to Company or any assignee thereof.

7. <u>No Inconsistent Obligations</u>. Employee is aware of no obligations, legal or otherwise, inconsistent with the terms of this Agreement or with his undertaking employment with the Company. Employee will not disclose to the Company, or use, or induce the Company to use any proprietary information or trade secrets of others. Employee represents and warrants that he or she has returned all property and confidential information belonging to all prior employers.

8. <u>Representations and Warranties</u>. Employee represents and warrants to the Employer that (i) Employee is not a party to or subject to any outstanding contract, agreement or order whereby Employee is prohibited from entering into this Agreement or performing the services or which would interfere with or prevent Employee's employment with the Employer or performance of the services, and (ii) Employee does not intend to use, and shall not use, any confidential information or materials belonging to any former employer or other person in connection with Employee's employment with the Employer or performance of the services.

9. <u>Miscellaneous</u>.
   a. <u>Governing Law and Dispute Resolution</u>. This Agreement shall be governed by and construed in accordance with the laws of the State of [Company's state of organization]. Any controversy, claim or dispute arising out of or relating to this

Agreement or the employment relationship, either during the existence of the employment relationship or afterwards, between the Parties hereto shall be settled by arbitration in [Company's home city] before a single arbitrator. Such arbitration shall be conducted in accordance with the then prevailing commercial arbitration rules of the American Arbitration Association. Such decisions and awards rendered by the arbitrator shall be final and conclusive and may be entered in any court having jurisdiction thereof. The arbitrator shall not have the right to award punitive damages, consequential damages, lost profits or speculative damages to either party. The parties shall keep confidential the existence of the claim, controversy or disputes from third parties (other than the arbitrator), and the determination thereof, unless otherwise required by law or necessary for the business of the Company. The arbitrator(s) shall be required to follow applicable law.

b. <u>Entire Agreement</u>. This document contains the entire agreement and understanding between the parties hereto and supersedes any prior or contemporaneous written or oral agreements, representations and warranties between them respecting the subject matter hereof.

c. <u>Amendment</u>. This Agreement may be amended only by a writing signed by Employee and by a duly authorized representative of the Company.

d. <u>Severability</u>. If any term, provision, covenant or condition of this Agreement, or the application thereof to any person, place or circumstance, shall be held to be invalid, unenforceable or void, the remainder of this Agreement and such term, provision, covenant or condition as applied to other persons, places and circumstances shall remain in in full force and effect.

e. <u>Construction</u>. The headings and captions of this Agreement are provided for convenience only and are intended to have no effect in construing or interpreting this Agreement. The language in all parts of this Agreement shall be in all cases construed according to its fair meaning and not strictly for or against the Company or Employee.

f. <u>Rights Cumulative</u>. The rights and remedies provided by this Agreement are cumulative, and the exercise of any right or remedy by either party hereto (or by its successor), whether pursuant to this Agreement, to any other agreement, or to law, shall not preclude or waive its right to exercise any or all other rights and remedies.

g. <u>Nonwaiver</u>. No failure or neglect of either party hereto in any instance to exercise any right, power or privilege hereunder or under law shall constitute a waiver of any other right, power or privilege or of the same right, power or privilege in any other instance. All waivers by either party hereto must be contained in a written instrument signed by the party to be charged and, in the case of the

Company, by an officer of the Company (other than Employee) or other person duly authorized by the Company.

h. <u>Remedy for Breach; Attorneys' Fees</u>. The parties hereto agree that, in the event of breach or threatened breach of any covenants of Employee, the damage or imminent damage to the value and the goodwill of the Company's business shall be inestimable, and that therefore any remedy at law or in damages shall be inadequate. Accordingly, the parties hereto agree that the Company shall be entitled to injunctive relief against Employee in the event of any breach or threatened breach of any of such provisions by Employee, in addition to any other relief (including damages) available to the Company under this Agreement or under law. The prevailing party in any action instituted pursuant to this Agreement shall be entitled to recover from the other party its reasonable attorneys' fees and other expenses incurred in such action.

i. <u>Notices</u>. Any notice, request, consent or approval required or permitted to be given under this Agreement or pursuant to law shall be sufficient if in writing, and if and when sent by certified or registered mail, with postage prepaid, to Employee's residence (as noted in the Company's records), or to the Company's principal office, as the case may be.

j. <u>Assistance in Litigation</u>. Employee shall, during and after termination of employment, upon reasonable notice, furnish such information and proper assistance to the Company as may reasonably be required by the Company in connection with any litigation in which it or any of its subsidiaries or affiliates is, or may become a party; provided, however, that such assistance following termination shall be furnished at mutually agreeable times and for mutually agreeable compensation.

k. <u>Counterparts</u>. This Agreement may be executed in two or more counterparts, each of which shall be deemed an original, but all of which together shall constitute one and the same instrument.

IN WITNESS WHEREOF, the parties hereto have duly executed this Agreement as of the date set forth below.

[Employee]   Double D Development, Inc.

By: _____   By: _____

Name: _____   Name: _____

Title: _____   Title: _____

Date: _____   Date: _____

WORK FOR HIRE AGREEMENT

This consulting agreement ("Agreement") is entered into this [day] of [Month], 200_ by and between Double D Development, Inc. ("Company"), a California corporation; and John Q. Programmer ("Contractor").

RECITALS:
  a. Company desires to hire Contractor for a limited duration as an independent contractor to perform artificial intelligence software development services for the game based on the intellectual property currently known as "*Newgame*" (the "Property"); and
  b. Contractor desires to provide such services to Company as an independent contractor.

NOW, therefore, in consideration of the mutual covenants and promises contained herein, the receipt and sufficiency of which are hereby acknowledged, Company and Contractor hereby agree to the following:

1. Term. This Agreement will remain in effect for the term of Contractor's engagement by Company, currently contracted to be through _____, 200__ ("Term").

2. Services. Contractor will perform the works detailed in Exhibit A of this agreement (the "Work") on the schedule following the specifications set forth in same Exhibit.

3. Consideration. $_____ be paid as follows: 10% due on execution of this agreement, _____% due on satisfactory completion of Milestone One, ____ % due on satisfactory completion of Milestone Two [etc.].

4. Independent Contractor. Consultant shall not for any purpose be deemed to be an employee of Company by performance of his obligations under, and during the term of, this Agreement, and shall be at all times an independent contractor. Consultant shall have no authority to act on behalf of or to bind Company in any manner whatsoever. Company shall be under no obligation to Contractor to (a) withhold any monies payable to Contractor hereunder for any taxes, insurance, social security payments or other contributions or (b) provide Subcontractor with worker's compensation, disability or other similar insurance coverage.

5. Intellectual Property.
  a. Contractor acknowledges that Company is the exclusive owner of all rights and title to the copyright, trademark, moral and other rights to the Property.
  b. Company and Contractor expressly agree that Company shall own all right, title, and interest in and to Contractor's Work and any other work which Contractor

assists in, creates, or collaborates on during the Term and shall, where applicable, be a work for hire as such term is defined by Section 101 of the United States Copyright Act, for Company as copyright owner. To the extent that any Work produced pursuant to this Agreement does not qualify as a work made for hire as defined by Section 101 of the United States Copyright Act, Contractor hereby irrevocably assigns and transfers to Company as copyright owner, its successors and assigns the following: a) the entire right, title and interest in and to the copyrights, trademarks and other rights in any such Work and any rights in and to any works based upon, derived from, or incorporating any such Work ("Derivative Work"); b) any existing registrations or copyright applications relating to any such Work or Derivative Work, and any renewals or extensions thereof; c) the exclusive right to obtain, register and renew the copyrights or copyright protection in any such Work or Derivative Work; d) all income, royalties, damages, claims and payments now or hereafter due or payable with respect to any such Work and Derivative Work; and e) all causes of action in law or equity, past and future, for infringements or violation of any of the rights in any such Work or Derivative Work, and any recoveries resulting thereof.

c. Contractor hereby waives in writing any moral or other rights that he has under state or federal laws, or under the laws of any foreign jurisdiction, which would give him any rights to complain of or prevent the use of any Work or Derivative, or which would entitle him to receive additional Compensation from Company.

d. Contractor agrees to execute all documents, including without limitation copyright assignments and applications, and to perform all acts that Company may reasonably request in order to assist Company in perfecting its rights in and to any Work and Derivative Work anywhere in the world

6. <u>Proprietary and Confidential Information, Assignment of Inventions</u>. Contractor has executed and agreed to the non-disclosure, non-compete and assignment of inventions agreement attached as Exhibit B.

7. <u>Governing Law and Dispute Resolution</u>. This Agreement shall be governed by and construed in accordance with the laws of the state of [Company's home state]. In the event of a dispute concerning this Agreement, no inference will be drawn based on authorship of the Agreement, and any and all disputes related to this Agreement will be resolved by a single arbitrator appointed by the American Arbitration Association and sitting in [Company's home city]. The Arbitrator's decision shall be binding and may be entered in any court of competent jurisdiction.

8. <u>Entire Agreement</u>. This document contains the entire agreement and understanding between the parties hereto and supersedes any prior or contemporaneous written or

oral agreements, representations and warranties between them respecting the subject matter hereof.

9. <u>Amendment</u>. This Agreement may be amended only by a writing signed by Contractor and by a duly authorized representative of Company.

10. <u>Severability</u>. If any term, provision, covenant or condition of this Agreement, or the application thereof to any person, place or circumstance, shall be held to be invalid, unenforceable or void, the remainder of this Agreement and such term, provision, covenant or condition as applied to other persons, places and circumstances shall remain in full force and effect.

11. <u>Nonwaiver</u>. No failure or neglect of either party hereto in any instance to exercise any right, power or privilege hereunder or under law shall constitute a waiver of any other right, power or privilege or of the same right, power or privilege in any other instance. All waivers by either party hereto must be contained in a written instrument signed by the party to be charged and, in the case of Company, by an officer of Company (other than Contractor) or other person duly authorized by Company.

12. <u>Survival of Restrictive Covenants</u>. The covenants contained in this Agreement (including Exhibit B) concerning intellectual property rights, use of proprietary information, and competition shall be construed as independent of any other provision hereof and shall survive the termination or expiration of the Agreement.

13. <u>Remedy for Breach; Attorneys' Fees</u>. The parties hereto agree that, in the event of breach or threatened breach of any covenants of Contractor, the damage or imminent damage to the value and the goodwill of Company's business shall be inestimable, and that therefore any remedy at law or in damages shall be inadequate. Accordingly, the parties hereto agree that Company shall be entitled to injunctive relief against Contractor in the event of any breach or threatened breach of any of such provisions by Contractor, in addition to any other relief (including damages) available to Company under this Agreement or under law. The prevailing party in any action instituted pursuant to this Agreement shall be entitled to recover from the other party its reasonable attorneys' fees and other expenses incurred in such action.

14. <u>Notices</u>. Any notice, request, consent or approval required or permitted to be given under this Agreement or pursuant to law shall be sufficient if in writing, and if and when sent by certified or registered mail, with postage prepaid, to Contractor's residence (as noted in Company's records), or to Company's principal office, as the case may be.

15. <u>Counterparts</u>. This Agreement may be executed in two or more counterparts, each of which shall be deemed an original, but all of which together shall constitute one and the same instrument.

IN WITNESS WHEREOF, the parties hereto have duly executed this Agreement as of the date set forth below.

[Contractor Name]   Double D Development, Inc.

By: _____   By: _____

Name: _____   Name: _____

Title: _____   Title: _____

Date: _____   Date: _____

SAMPLE

Exhibit A

Milestone_____   Due Date_____

[Detailed milestone description]_____   [Date]_____

[Detailed milestone description]_____   [Date]_____

Exhibit B

CONFIDENTIALITY AND ASSIGNMENT OF INVENTIONS AGREEMENT

I understand that Double D Development, Inc. ("Company") has developed and used and will be developing and using confidential information in connection with its business, including, but not limited to, information relating to the development of interactive entertainment products such as product development and distribution plans, sources of content, licensing and royalty arrangements, profits, sales, pricing policies, operational methods, technical processes business plans and methods, plans for future developments and other information which is not readily available to the public.

I understand that this information is valuable, that Company has expended and will expend significant resources toward its development and that the Confidential Information constitutes trade secrets of Company.

During my engagement by Company, I will come in contact with such Confidential Information. I will adhere to all of Company's policies and procedures regarding the protection of such information.

In consideration of my engagement by Company and the consideration to be paid to me for my services, I agree to the following:

1. I agree that during and after my term of engagement with Company:
   (a) I will keep secret all Confidential Information and not reveal or disclose it to anyone outside of Company, except with Company's prior written consent;
   (b) I will not make use of any of such Confidential Information for my own purposes or the benefit of anyone other than Company; and
   (c) I will deliver promptly to Company, upon the termination of my engagement and at any time Company may so request, all software, data, memoranda, notes, records and other documents (and all copies thereof) constituting or relating to such Confidential Information which I may then possess.

2. All work which I create in connection with my employment shall be considered to be "works made for hire" under the U.S. Copyright Act, 17 U.S.C. §§\x11101 et seq. In the event a work is not construed to be a work made for hire, I hereby irrevocably assign to Company any and all right, title, and interests I may have in any trade secrets, trademarks, copyrightable subject matter, developments, designs, inventions, improvements, or proprietary information which I have made or conceived, or may make or conceive, either alone or with others and either on or off Company's premises:
   (a) During my engagement with the Company;
   (b) With the use of the time, materials or facilities of Company;

(c) Relating to any product, service or activity of Company of which I have knowledge; or,

(d) Suggested by or resulting from any work performed by me for Company (the "Developments").

I agree that I have no proprietary interest in any Developments, including any patent, copyright, trademark and trade secret rights. Any and all programs, inventions and other works of authorship developed by me while performing services for Company are created for and owned exclusively by Company. I agree not to register, file or obtain any patent, copyright or trademark covering any of Developments in my own name. I agree to execute any further documents necessary to establish, perfect, protect, and enforce Company's rights in the Developments, including but not limited to ownership of any patents, copyrights or trademarks.

3. I understand that this Agreement shall be governed by and construed in accordance with the laws of the State of California.

AGREED TO AND ACCEPTED:

Name: _____

Signature: _____

Date:_____

EMPLOYEE REVIEW FORM

Date: _____

Employee: _____   Reviewed by: _____

A. Highlight achievements since last performance period:
   1. _____
   2. _____
   3. _____
   4. _____

B. Employee strengths:
   1. _____
   2. _____
   3. _____
   4. _____

C. Problems since last performance period:
   1. _____
   2. _____
   3. _____
   4. _____

D. Employee weaknesses:
   1. _____
   2. _____
   3. _____
   4. _____

E. How has employee functioned in team context?
   1. _____
   2. _____
   3. _____
   4. _____

F. Does employee require warnings? If yes, state.
   1. _____
   2. _____
   3. _____
   4. _____

G. Rate Employee on the Following:

	Average	Excellent	Above Satisfactory	Satisfactory	Below Average	Unsatisfactory
Attitude						
Initiative						
Reliability						
Work quality						
Work capacity						
Skills						
Team Work						
Organization skills						
Decision-making						

H. Other comments: _____

_____

_____

_____

_____

_____

SAMPLE

CHAPTER 5

A Primer on Intellectual Property

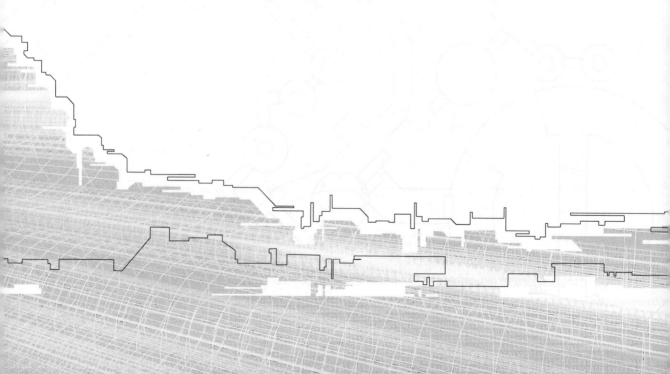

Intellectual Property in Action

The mood at Double D is almost giddy. The port contract came through, which helped put a security deposit and first and last month's rent down on an ugly, windowless office outside of town. The network is still being tweaked, but the hardware and software work, and the team gets along as smoothly as ever.

Dana has been project managing the port half-time, drafting and assembling the documents for the pitch build, and trying to make sure the office is run like a real grown-up workplace. She's quite pleased with the fact that everyone has an employment agreement—containing an NDA, non-compete, and assignment of invention—and a handbook.

She is vaguely aware of a missing component in their grown-up workplace: a system for protecting the intellectual property they create. Their HR attorney Robin put a confidentiality policy in the handbook specifying measures like where and when to put confidentiality and copyright notices on work, and now Dana needs to figure out what else the company can do to protect itself.

Double D's office building has electronic keypad access all day, meaning that no one can get in without the access code or an escort. Dusty set up a security system for the FTP site and installed access-restriction software on the network. Dana called an all-hands meeting to explain the company's trade secret protection plan, and why each of the measures was so important. She also emphasized the employee's role in protecting the company by not discussing work outside the office and leaving confidential material in the office under lock and key.

Next she turned to the original IP being created for the pitch, which needed to be protected before she started showing it all over the West Coast. Dana researched as much as she could about software protection on the Web so that she could be extra-efficient with their IP attorney Jamie. She e-mailed Jamie a two paragraph description of the projects the company is working on and a list of questions in advance of their phone meeting.

Jamie tells Dana that Double D should mark anything that would be valuable to competitors with a confidential and proprietary legend as well as copyright notices, and that she should put together federal copyright registrations for the pitch document, .AVI files, and prototype (which will protect the source code and any audio-visual elements of the prototype), as well as any music they create. The pitch document and prototype should be registered with the special trade secret registration process, which will preserve the material's confidentiality and trade secret status, and Dana may want to consider trade secret registrations for other assets. As soon as Double D comes up with a name for their game, Jamie continues, it should be trade-marked. They should also consider trademarking any other major characters they develop. "Most companies trademark their name and logo." Jamie noted, "If you have a logo, I'm not sure I want to know what it looks like, but consider getting it protected if you haven't already."

ithout proprietary technology and/or content, a development company is a code facto-
ry. While game development requires creativity and will therefore never become a com-
modity product, a developer with a unique competitive advantage (such as a great proprietary
technology) is more likely to escape the yoke of constantly scrambling for customers of its team's
time. Furthermore, creating scalable, reusable, modular technologies enables your company to
leverage its proprietary assets to reduce development time of subsequent projects.

Most people working in a technology-intensive industry like game development are sensitive to
the business imperative of intellectual property rights to their work product. This chapter will
also alert you to other areas of your business that need protection, such as your enterprise name
and logo.

Many developers balance the need to protect their investment against what they see as a core
ethic of programming—enabling innovation through the sharing of information. There is a significant movement lobbying against software patents, as many are seen as overbroad and unfairly
restricting competition. This chapter presents and explains the law of protecting software with
trade secrets, copyright, and patents, and leaves it to the reader to determine which is the right
choice for his company.

Enforcing intellectual property is usually a joint effort between owners and publishers/distribu-
tors. International registration and enforcement poses unique, unavoidable problems: the game
industry, like the film and television industry, relies on worldwide release revenue to support production costs. This chapter will review the laws of different countries and the best way to safe-
guard your property abroad (including how to figure out if it's worth the cost). Unfortunately,
not every country operates with the same protective zeal as the U.S., so we'll review some piracy
and gray market precautions.

This chapter is broken into two main sections, "IP 101" and "Protecting Your Assets." There are
four main categories of intellectual property:

- **Trade secrets.** Trade secret law protects confidential business information and processes
  that create a competitive advantage. Trade secrets can protect assets like program structure, processes, business documents, and contract terms.

The author would like to thank Jeff Carton of Meiselman, Denlea, Packman, and Eberz P.C.
(www.mdpelaw.com) for his assistance with preparing this chapter.

- **Copyrights.** Copyrights protect the tangible, fixed expression of an idea. Copyrights protect everything from works of art to software. Most software is protected by copyright, either alone or in conjunction with other protections.
- **Trademarks/Service marks.** Trademarks protect brands in a range of properties, from a company's name and logo to the name and appearance of characters in its games. While not directly pertinent to code, trademarks are an important category of rights for game developers.
- **Patents.** Patents are the nuclear weaponry of intellectual property rights: very powerful, expensive to develop, subject to significant regulation, and considered by many to be rather ridiculous and dangerous. Because patents give so many rights, the qualifying bar is very high. Currently, many companies find they can achieve satisfactory protection for their software and technology through copyrights and trade secrets, making patents optional in the game developer's arsenal.

The section "IP 101" will introduce them, review what they are, how to qualify for and obtain the protection, enforcing rights, strengths and weaknesses of each category, and assets that can be protected under a given category.

The section "Protecting Your Assets" will review methods of maintaining the value of your property, including: (i) legends and notices, which alert the world to the protected status of the material; (ii) ways to enforce your rights against infringers; (iii) how to protect your property abroad; and (iv) gaining clear ownership of IP produced by your employees and contractors.

IP 101

Intellectual property is one of the United States' main exports—evidence, some would say, that the government achieved its goals in enacting the laws that protect such property.

Congress created laws governing intellectual property that create four major classes: trade secrets, copyrights, trademarks, and patents.

The animating principles behind these laws is threefold:

To encourage innovation by allowing a creator to control and reap the rewards of a creation;

To grant few monopolies in intellectual property, which stifle innovation; and

To protect consumers from brand confusion, where one party's goods are confusingly similar to another's.

Table 5.1 IP Categories and Basic Facts

	Trade Secret	Trademark or Service Mark	Copyright	Utility Patent
What is Protected	Processes, concepts, ideas, software, documents, contract terms, more.	Words, names or symbols, character design.	Computer software, audiovisual elements, music, art, more.	Ideas and concepts made tangible.
Requirements	Valuable to competitors, not generally known, secrecy.	Identifies source of goods.	Originality.	Novel and unobvious.
How rights are acquired	Maintenance of secrecy.	Minimal rights acquired by use; federal protection through USPTO registration, which requires use or intent to use.	Minimal rights acquired at time of creation; registration through Copyright Office recommended to prove ownership, required to sue for infringement.	Registration with USPTO.

Table 5.1 IP Categories and Basic Facts

	Trade Secret	Trademark or Service Mark	Copyright	Utility Patent
Term of Protection	So long as secrecy preserved.	Unregistered marks have minimal protection as long as used. Federally-registered marks: 10 years with right to renew for 10 year terms in perpetuity if mark in use.	Owned by person: life of author + 70 years. Owned by company: lesser of 95 years from the date of publication or 120 years from the date of creation.	20 years from filing.
Infringement	Disclosure or use by party with duty not to disclose or use.	Using mark that creates likelihood of confusion as to source of goods.	Duplication or substantially similar work.	Making, using, selling a device coming within the scope of any patent claim.

The following is a discussion of United States intellectual property law. Protecting your property abroad is discussed in the section "Protecting Your Assets: Enforcement: International Considerations."

Trade Secrets

Trade secrets give companies a legal right to the secrecy of certain kinds of information. This offers an alternative or supplement for a company that either (i) prefers not to pursue other forms of protection for any number of reasons (cost, disclosure requirements, time and energy) or (ii) fears that the information would not qualify for other forms of protection. For example: copyrights cannot protect ideas and processes; trade secrets can.

Trade secrets protect the confidential information a business collects and creates to enable it to compete. The classic legal example of a trade secret is the formula for Coca-Cola. In game development, trade secrets can run the gamut from source code to contract terms or design documents.

Trade secrets can be combined with other protections like copyrights or patents to offer the maximum level of protection. For example, source code can be registered for a copyright and maintained as a trade secret.

Only certain people have a legal duty to maintain your trade secrets. If a competitor overhears one of your employees chatting to another about a trade secret and the competitor then exploits that information, you have recourse against your employee, but probably not against the competitor who has no obligation to maintain confidentiality of your trade secrets if legally acquired. This reality leads to two requirements of any good trade secret protection program:

- Creating that legal duty wherever necessary through the use of agreements.
- Establishing systems of physically protecting the trade secret information.

Trade secret law varies from state to state and country to country, so local counsel is required. A discussion of protecting trade secrets abroad follows in the "Protecting Your Assets: Enforcement: International Considerations" section.

What Is a Trade Secret

A trade secret is any information like a formula, compilation, program, method, process, technique, or the like that:

- Gives a business a competitive advantage.
- Is not generally known by the company's current or potential competitors and cannot be discovered through legitimate means.
- Is the subject of the company's reasonable secrecy efforts.

A trade secret can be protected forever as long as each of the above criteria is met. This is one reason some companies elect trade secret protection over patents to protect some IP: the content of patents is made public and expires after 20 years. Imagine if Coca-Cola had patented its formula instead of using trade secrets: it would have lost its primary asset to the public domain years ago.

Competitive Advantage

A trade secret can protect any information that gives the company a business advantage, assuming the information also meets the other two criteria of secrecy efforts and general unavailability of the information. Pretty much anything you don't want other companies to know—object code, program structure and concepts, results of your QA, business development plans, research and development in progress, project management processes, and so on—can qualify for trade secret protection.

Not Publicly Known

Trade secret protection is *not* available for information that is publicly or generally available to competitors or customers. This can include:

- Any materials the company releases without an NDA and the appropriate notices, such as a design or technical document.
- Information released accidentally, such as a document left on an airplane or overheard from an employee at a restaurant.
- Data that can be figured out from a released product (in other words, if a product can be reverse engineered, the product can lose its trade secret protection).

Figure 5.1

Trade secrets, such as the Coca-Cola formula, may be protected indefinitely.

Efforts to Maintain Secrecy

Trade secret protection is also not available for information that the company has not taken reasonable efforts to protect. What is a reasonable effort? Courts have looked to:

- How valuable the information is
- The company's resources available to protect its trade secrets and whether they were used
- How difficult and expensive it would be for a competitor to develop the information
- How widely the information is known within and without the company

How Do I Qualify for and Obtain Trade Secret Protection?

Unlike the other intellectual property categories, trade secrets do not have to be registered with a government entity to be enforceable. However, for information to meet the trade secret test (gives a competitive advantage, is not generally known or available, is reasonably protected by the company), a company will need to put some thought into information and disclosure processes. The company's trade secret protection program should be developed with your attorney and should be reduced to a written policy and NDA, signed by all employees, contractors, and third parties receiving materials containing trade secrets (like licensees and publications).

The core of a trade secret protection program is (i) to create the legal duty not to disclose confidential information in all relevant recipients; and (ii) to provide for physical protection (including software-based measures) of the trade secrets.

> **CAUTION**
>
> Releasing the information to a party who is not under confidentiality obligations can permanently destroy trade secret protection because that party can make the information public, thereby disqualifying it from the trade secret category.

Your program should be specific to your company, but will probably include:

- Creating the legal duty of confidentiality in recipients of confidential information
- Physically protecting the confidential information

Creating the Legal Duty of Confidentiality

You need to be concerned with any parties who will have access to materials containing trade secrets. This includes:

- Employees
- Third parties, including independent contractors, licensees, investors, and others

EMPLOYEES

Employees are the bricks in your information perimeter wall, so your defense should start there. While all employees have an implied duty at law to protect your confidential information, this implied duty should always be made explicit and explained to the employee with an NDA.

> **CAUTION**
>
> It is equally important to protect your company against an employee's illegally importing trade secrets from previous employers. When recruiting a new employee from a competitor, take a look at the situation: does it seem possible that your competitor could construe the hire as an effort to access its trade secrets? Did you conduct an actual search, or was this the only candidate looked at for the position?

> **TIP**
>
> Your recruit should sign an agreement that he will not be revealing any of his employer's proprietary information throughout the hiring process and the employment agreement should contain a representation and warranty by the employee that he will not be using or bringing any intellectual property or proprietary information to the new position.

Agreements

Every employee and contractor (including cleaning services) should sign a confidentiality/non-disclosure agreement (NDA) promising not to disclose or make unauthorized use of trade secrets and to take actions to prevent disclosure or unauthorized use (See Chapter 4 for a sample NDA).

> **CAUTION**
>
> The NDA may be incorporated into the employment agreement or separate, but if the employee is signing a confidentiality or non-compete agreement (see next paragraph) as a stand-alone contract *after* he has been hired, the employer needs to offer something in exchange for the promises of confidentiality, such as $1.00.

Post-Employment Protection

What about after an employee leaves? This is a somewhat murky area, because even though your NDA may prevent an ex-employee from making direct use of your trade secrets for a certain number of years, there is no way to prevent an ex-employee from having the benefit of working with those trade secrets. In other words, even though an ex-employee may be prohibited from creating a duplicate of a tool, he will probably be able to create a substitution with many of the same benefits as the tool.

Some states (California excepted, unless in connection with the sale of a business) allow employers to create an additional buffer by having employees sign a post-employment non-compete agreement. This agreement prevents the employee from leaving to work for a competitor or start a competing venture for a reasonable duration (one to two years, usually) and in a reasonable geographic area (worldwide is reasonable for game development).

Even if your state does not allow for post-employment non-compete agreements, your company should conduct exit interviews and obtain exit agreements. Exit interviews are meetings with departing employees in which you explain their obligation under the NDA not to use or disclose any trade secrets. Explain that they are not allowed to take or keep (for instance, in an e-mail account or on their home hard drive) any materials containing trade secrets. The degree of invasiveness the employer wishes to use depends on the relationship with the departing employee: some employers terminate e-mail and computer access the instant they hear (or tell) of an employee's departure, others physically examine anything the employee is taking out of the building, others rely on the employee's honor. Given the size and collegial nature of most development houses, it may not be a great idea to get invasive with your departing employees, since it could have the effect of alienating remaining employees, angering the departing one, and ensuring that in the future, everyone grabs what they want before informing the company of their departure.

The exit agreement provides a better alternative (see sample exit agreement at the end of this chapter). With an exit agreement, the departing employee promises that he is not taking any materials containing trade secrets. If the employee refuses (which would be hard to do without looking shady), then the employer is justified in taking more extreme measures.

> **NOTE**
>
> All of this should be tempered by the reality that execution is far more important than information, and that fluidity of information is the rule rather than the exception. In other words, evaluate the true potential damage of a situation before going ballistic.

Figure 5.2

The colonel's trade secret blend of herbs and spices is a mystery that haunts many.

Articulate and Reinforce

Most employees are not IP experts and will need some education in what a trade secret is, why it is important that efforts are made to maintain secrecy, and how to identify new trade secrets as they are created. Regarding the latter, think of your employees as (creative, well-paid, well-treated, highly trained) miners who must be shown an example or two of the gems for which they are digging—a diamond in the rough is barely recognizable as a hillbilly cousin of the polished diamond.

Identify main categories of information that are likely to be trade secrets: source and object code, concepts, structures, diagrams, tools, design and technical documents, contract terms, new technology being developed, recruiting plans, and any other information that is not generally known or available and which would be valuable in the hands of a competitor. Ask employees to mark such items "CONFIDENTIAL AND PROPRIETARY" and send them to a designated supervisor and/or your attorney to see if the item qualifies as a trade secret. For information that you know qualifies for trade secret protection (like source code or design documents), it is important to plaster them with notices. A good idea is to embed the following notice on all media containing confidential information, labels, and in the header of each code module during development:

[COMPANY NAME] CONFIDENTIAL AND PROPRIETARY

THIS WORK CONTAINS VALUABLE CONFIDENTIAL AND PROPRIETARY INFORMATION. DISCLOSURE, USE OR REPRODUCTION WITHOUT THE WRITTEN AUTHORIZATION OF [COMPANY] IS PROHIBITED. THIS UNPUBLISHED WORK BY [COMPANY] IS PROTECTED BY THE LAWS OF THE UNITED STATES AND OTHER COUNTRIES. IF PUBLICATION OF THE WORK SHOULD OCCUR THE FOLLOWING NOTICE SHALL APPLY: "COPYRIGHT (©) 20XX CLAIMANT ALL RIGHTS RESERVED."

If you are pressed for space, the following is acceptable:

THIS IS AN UNPUBLISHED WORK CONTAINING [COMPANY] CONFIDENTIAL AND PROPRIETARY INFORMATION. IF PUBLICATION OCCURS, THE FOLLOWING NOTICE APPLIES: **"COPYRIGHT (©) 20XX [COMPANY] ALL RIGHTS RESERVED."**

The distinction between "published" and "unpublished" software is discussed further in the "Protecting Your Assets: Enforcement: Notices" section.

CAUTION

Over-protection is almost as dangerous as under-protection. A court may refuse to uphold confidential status for *any* company information if you designate all of it as confidential.

THIRD PARTIES

Releasing the information to a party who is not under confidentiality obligations can permanently destroy trade secret protection because that party can make the information public, thereby disqualifying it from the trade secret category.

Simply put: every third party receiving material containing trade secrets must sign an NDA obligating the recipient and all of its employees and contractors to protect the confidential material (see Chapter 4 for a sample NDA). When you sign an NDA with a company, trade secrets are the bulk of what is being protected. Even if you are not releasing hard assets like code, you may be disclosing protected information. Example: Developer A (a famous sim creator) wants to demo an RPG to Publisher B. Developer A cannot protect the *idea* of an RPG game because it is *generally known*, but it may request an NDA to protect the *fact* that the company is developing an RPG. Competitive strategy—in this case, a bet on the RPG market—can qualify as a trade secret.

Physical Protection of Trade Secrets

- Mark all trade secret materials and documents containing such materials "CONFIDENTIAL AND PROPRIETARY." Additional notices are highly recommended and are discussed below in the "Protecting Your Assets: Enforcement: Notices" section.
- Confidential information should be shared on a "need to know" basis—it is expected that sometimes this will be everyone in the company.
- Use passwords and available security measures to protect computer files; keep hard materials (pitch bibles, printed copies of code or files) in a locked file cabinet or in a locked office.
- Use encryption or other data-protection measures when e-mailing sensitive files and when FTP'ing files.
- Maintain a clean-desk policy: no confidential materials should be left out while the employee is away from his desk.
- Enforce a building-security policy that prevents unknown people from entering and circulating through the company. This can be as simple as stationing a receptionist in front of the door and insisting that all visitors be accompanied by an employee at all times.

- Use common sense and a healthy dose of paranoia in public: don't discuss confidential matters in Starbucks, on a plane, elevator, restaurant, or any public place. This goes double for public places around trade shows and triple for trade show parties. Remind employees that an open bar is a loaded weapon aimed at them.
- Review speeches employees are scheduled to deliver at public events—you might be surprised what can leak out this way.
- Maintain a work/home separation where possible. Keep confidential material at the office as much as possible, and ask employees to guard the information when working away from the office.

If you believe it is warranted, additional measures may include:

- Shredding discarded confidential documents
- Reviewing the file logs for abnormal activity

Enforcing Trade Secret Rights

Violation of trade secrets is punishable by injunctions (preventing a party from doing or not doing something) and money damages. The amount of money damages is based on either the infringer's profits or the infringed party's losses. In really ugly cases, punitive damages (extra fines for behaving badly) may be awarded.

Strengths and Weaknesses of Trade Secrets

Strengths of trade secrets are

- Trade secret material can be made public in other forms and maintain its trade secret status. Example: even if a game's object code were somehow publicly released (and not simply distributed in a protected format), the *source* code would still be entitled to trade secret protection as long as it is not disclosed.
- Unlike copyrights, they can protect ideas, concepts, and methods, not just a particular expression of those ideas, concepts, and methods. Example: A copyright can only protect the literal source code of a program; a trade secret can protect the ideas and methods underlying the program.
- Unlike copyrights, trade secrets can also protect special features or components of released software (remember that trade secrets only offer protection for information kept secret and not publicly available), as long as the features are not readily reverse-engineerable.
- Unlike copyrights and patents, trade secrets have no expiration date. As long as the information meets the qualifications, it is entitled to protection.

Weaknesses of the trade secret are

- The trade secret only protects against disclosure by parties with a legal duty not to disclose (employees and third parties under NDA), making it vulnerable to loss of protected status through accidental disclosure.
- Nothing that is reverse-engineerable can be protected as a trade secret.
- Trade secrets do not defend against a third party's independently developing the same concept or product.
- Maintaining a system of trade secrets can be a bit like herding squirrels and can become expensive and time consuming.

What Assets Can a Trade Secret Protect?

Trade secrets can be used to protect almost anything a developer might create, including source code, object code, machine code, firmware, any concepts, ideas, methods, processes, or documents related to the creation of software or game concepts, including characters, storylines, drawings, business plans and methods, marketing plans or customer lists, databases, and so forth.

Basic Principles of Keeping Trade Secrets

1. Mark all trade secret materials CONFIDENTIAL AND PROPRIETARY.
2. Only show trade secret materials to those who have signed a non-disclosure agreement.
3. Keep trade secret material under lock and key, whether physical or electronic.
4. Obtain exit agreements from departing employees reminding them of their NDA duties.

Copyright

Copyrights are very important to developers, as they protect both software code and art (as well as many other important assets). Not only do you have a "natural copyright" in material you create (insufficient for most business purposes, discussed below in this section)—meaning that your legal rights to the created material arise at the time of creation—but registering your copyright to ensure full legal benefits is reasonably inexpensive ($30 per copyright).

> **CAUTION**
>
> **Copyright registrations look pretty simple, but simple mistakes can make the registration ineffective, so have an IP attorney review your applications.**

What Is a Copyright?

As the name implies, a copyright gives the owner of a work of authorship, such as a play, musical composition, computer program, drawing, or business plan, the right to dictate how, whether, and for what benefit that work is to be copied. A copyright owner has the exclusive power to use, copy, make derivative works (like later versions of software), sell, or distribute that work. A copyright will protect a work owned by a corporation for 95 years from the date of publication or 120 years from the date of creation, whichever is shorter; for individuals, the copyright will last for the life of the creator plus 70 years.

Control Over Use of Work

The copyright protects the owner's ability to control the use of the work, giving the owner the exclusive right to reproduce, develop derivative works, distribute, sell, license, or publicly use, perform, or display the work. Because most software is distributed as a licensed product, and not actually sold to the customer, the copyright ownership and a good deal of control stays with the developer and/or publisher and any other parties whose copyrights were licensed for the making of the product, like an engine licensor. This gives those parties the ability to impose restrictions on the use of the game that would not be possible if they made an outright sale of a copy of the game to the customer.

DUPLICATION

A purchaser of a copy of a software product would need the copyright owner's permission to make duplicates of the work (except for backups). Duplication rights also prevent a purchaser from being able to make a verbatim copy of any source or object code; make duplicates of screens or audiovisual elements; or translate the code into another programming language. In limited situations, the purchaser may be prevented from using the code structure, sequence, and organization to create a substantially similar program.

SALE, LICENSE, AND DISTRIBUTION

Parties need the copyright owner's permission to distribute, license, or sell copies of the software to the public. The right to "license" the copyright is important because most software is licensed to end users, not actually "sold," because the owner can retain more control over the customer's use of the product. Technically, this means that copyright owner permission is required if you wanted to go to Best Buy, pick up 20 copies of a game and then resell them to your friends. Loan, rental, or lease for commercial purposes is also generally prohibited. The right to sell, license, or distribute is separate from the right to make copies of a work, meaning that the distributor may not be able to manufacture copies of the game; that right may be licensed to another party.

DERIVATIVE WORKS

The copyright also gives the owner exclusive rights to create *derivative works*, which are works that grow from and are closely related to the original work. This means that no other parties may modify, adapt, or change the copyrighted work for distribution to others except with permission of the owner. Examples of derivative works include: later software versions, translations/localizations to other languages, ports to other platforms, sequels, projects in other media based on the original copyright, and user-generated "mods" (discussed below in the "Protecting Your Assets: Enforcement: Mods" section). Each of these derivative works needs its own protection, but the right to make them is controlled by the holder of the original copyright.

Copyrights are also available for *compilations* of other work where there is some level of authorship in the selection and placement of the work. For example, a collection of public domain games from the late 70s may be copyrighted. The compilation copyright would not grant the compiler a copyright to the *games*, only to that specific *selection and order* of the games, thus preventing another person from issuing the exact same collection.

Infringement

Unauthorized use of a copyrighted work is known as *infringement* and the owner may sue the infringer for *damages* (money) and/or an *injunction* (prohibiting the infringer from continuing the infringing activity).

Copyrights should be registered with the Copyright Office (www.copyright.gov) to have the greatest power against infringers. Without registration, every creator of a copyrightable work (who is not under a work-for-hire or invention assignment agreement) has what is known as a natural copyright in that work and may affix the © notation to the work, but natural copyrights are difficult to prove and enforce against an infringer, and the Copyright Act awards greater damages for registered copyrights.

Idea Versus Expression

Copyrights can be flimsy protection because, unlike trade secrets or patents, they can protect only the *expression* of an idea, not the idea itself. Methods, applied mathematical formulae, applied algorithms—none of these can be protected with a copyright, only the actual code embodying those concepts.

The government's goal with this policy is to avoid monopolies in ideas except in extremely inventive works (patents). Copyrights do not grant their owners any control over the idea underlying the copyrighted work, only that particular manifestation of the idea. Taking the example of a compilation of late 70s games, the compilation copyright holder would be dismayed to find that he had no recourse against a copycat compilation containing 7 of the same 10 games. By slightly but meaningfully altering the copyrighted work, another party may obtain a separate copyright. Another example: a competitor who sees a design document for your next game may create a game copying most, if not all, of the ideas and concepts in the document (though none of the actual text or artwork).

A related difficulty with copyrighting software is what is known as *merger*. Merger is what is said to happen when the idea is inseparable from its expression, making the expression uncopyrightable. An idea is inseparable from its expression when there is really only one way to express it, meaning that giving someone a copyright on the expression would give them a copyright on the idea. Example: the forward-back-left-right buttons on a handheld controller cannot be copyrighted because they are inseparable from the function and purpose (to allow the user to manipulate a screen-based entity in various directions) of a controller.

There are limited ways to use copyrights as a form of idea protection in pitch meetings, for instance, which will be discussed in the following "Enforcing Copyrights" section.

How Do I Qualify For and Obtain Copyright Protection?

First, be sure that the company has taken the appropriate measures to gain clear title (ownership) to the work.

Next, analyze whether the material qualifies for a natural copyright:

1. The work must be fixed in a tangible medium from which the work can be retrieved (for example, a composition can be written or recorded, a computer program can be printed out or saved to disk).
2. The work must be original (created by the author). Note that original does not mean innovative, groundbreaking, unique, or worthy of note. Simply, something new.
3. The work must contain some level of creativity. Again, the bar is quite low: software documentation is considered creative enough to fit this criteria.

Works qualifying for copyright protection include almost every tangible, fixed expression of an idea with even a modicum of innovation. Aside from the more familiar realms like artistic works and computer programs, copyrights can protect seemingly un-creative works like sound effects and business documents like design and technical specifications, software documentation, budgets, and so forth.

Finally, consider federal registration of the copyright, which will provide you with maximum protection of your assets.

Figure 5.3

The Resident Evil *property has spawned many derivative copyrights, shown in Figures 5.4 through 5.6.*

Ensuring Company Ownership of Copyrights

Before a company thinks about protecting its copyrights, it needs to make sure that it owns them. The Copyright Act grants certain rights to the creator of a work, and an employer must be careful to structure its relationships with the creators (employees and contractors) for smooth transfer of all ownership rights to the employer.

> **NOTE**
>
> *Droit Morale.* Some countries and a few jurisdictions in the U.S. give authors "moral rights" to prevent any modification, distortion, or mutilation of their work that would be prejudicial to the author's honor or reputation (can you tell this idea originated in France?), even after it has been assigned. Be sure that these rights are waived in all assignment and license agreements.

Employees

Under the Copyright Act, an employer automatically owns most works created by employees acting within the scope of employment as a *work made for hire.* Employees should nonetheless sign an assignment of invention agreement (see Chapter 4, "Staffing Up") to avoid disputes over whether a worker is an employee and whether or not the work was created in the scope of employment. Furthermore, some forms of work may not qualify as a work for hire, and an assignment agreement will transfer ownership of these works to the employer.

CONTRACTORS

Unless a contractor signs an agreement to the contrary, work created under contract will probably be owned by the contractor, with the client having a *license* to use it, if anything. Needless to say, this is generally not a desirable outcome. To avoid it, have a contractor sign an agreement stating that (i) the work is a work made for hire and (ii) to the extent any work produced during the contractor's employment does not qualify as a work made for hire, the contractor assigns all other rights in and to the work to your company. The latter language is required because the "work made for hire" category is limited and sometimes your contractor will be creating work that does not quite fit the definition but for which you still require all rights. Software, for example, is generally outside of the work made for hire definition.

Figure 5.4

Books.

LICENSEES

What if you license technology to another company for incorporation into a game? Typically, the licensor retains all ownership to the licensed technology, and the licensee retains all ownership to the developed game except for the licensed technology. Some licensors insist on owning any modifications created by a licensee; some co-own it with an irrevocable, royalty-free, non-exclusive license to both parties; some licensors allow licensees to retain ownership of their modifications only to the extent separable from the licensed technology.

Federal Registration

Intelligent copyright management requires that a company register its copyrights. It's cheap ($30 per copyright), it's pretty easy, and it makes enforcing your rights against infringers much easier. The main benefits of federal registration are

- While the natural copyright creates legal rights for owners who can prove that they created their work before an infringer, this is not always easy to prove. A registered copyright is proof of ownership.
- The owner must first register the copyright in order to sue.
- If the registration follows the original work's initial publication date by more than three months, the owner can only recover actual, provable damages (money) from the infringer.
- Finally, and most important, you may only recover attorney's fees (which can pack a wallop in an infringement case) and *statutory damages* if your copyright was registered within three months of the work's initial publication. Statutory damages are automatically set money awards for infringement set out in the Copyright Act, currently $30,000 for every separate instance of ordinary infringement and $150,000 for every separate instance of willful infringement (more on this in the "Enforcing Copyrights" section).

SOFTWARE REGISTRATION

You will need to file a copy of the work (and of each subsequent version or revision) with the Register, which will make it available to the public. For computer programs, there are two sets of rules.

For programs that do not contain trade secrets: you must send in one copy of identifying portions of the program (first 25 and last 25 pages of source code), or the whole megillah if your program is shorter than 50 pages.

For programs that contain trade secrets, you must send in a letter explaining your need to protect trade secret elements of the program, along with your choice of

- First 25 and last 25 pages of source code with portions containing trade secrets blocked out
- First 10 and last 10 pages of source code alone, with no blocked out portions
- First 25 and last 25 pages of object code plus any 10 or more consecutive pages of source code, with no blocked out portions
- For programs 50 pages or less in length, entire source code with trade secret portions blocked out

There are two limitations on your ability to block out code: (1) the blocked out portions must be proportionately less than the material remaining; and (2) the visible portion must represent an appreciable amount of original computer code.

SCREEN DISPLAYS

Fortunately, you don't have to register a separate copyright for every art asset in the game. The Copyright Office allows you to submit one registration for the entire computer program, including audiovisual displays, which protects the sound and visuals. You must identify the material you want to copyright, generally with a written synopsis of the game and the material you wish to copyright along with a half-inch VHS tape of all the audiovisual elements you want to protect.

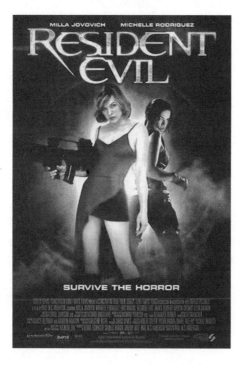

Figure 5.5

A movie.

Notice

Put a copyright notice on everything. It is not required under U.S. law, but it is so simple and creates so many advantages that there is no reason not to. A copyright notice consists of the word "copyright" or the © symbol, the owner's name, year(s) of publication, and the phrase "All rights reserved." This deters infringement on two counts: first, potential infringers will see that the owner understands copyright law and is likely to enforce its rights; and second, infringers will not be able to escape liability by arguing unknowing infringement.

CAUTION

Because some countries do not recognize the legal validity of any notice not marked with the symbol ©, it will save administrative work later on to use the symbol. Notices embedded in code should use (C), since there is no ASCII symbol for copyright. Furthermore, many Latin American countries require the use of the phrase All Rights Reserved for an effective notice, so make your life easy and only use the legend "© [Company] [years of copyright]. All Rights Reserved"

Enforcing Copyrights

Before enforcing a copyright, it must be registered with the Copyright Office.

There are four remedies available in a copyright suit: injunctions (preventing the infringer from doing or not doing something), criminal penalties, impounding and destroying the infringing material, and money damages. Money damages are measured by actual damages, statutory (preset by law) damages, and attorney's fees, the latter two being available only to owners who registered the copyright within three months of initial publication.

A party can pursue actual *or* statutory damages, but not both. Actual damages are those losses that can be documented and proved (for example, if sales of an album were consistently 100,000 per month and dropped to 50,000 per month when a pirated version became available). Actual damages can be difficult to prove, making them a less popular choice except in cases where actual damages far exceed statutory damages. Statutory damages are the fines set by the Copyright Act for each individual act of infringement, $30,000 for ordinary infringement and $150,000 for willful infringement.

If you think your copyright has been infringed, you may prove your case by simply showing that

- The alleged infringer had access to your copyrighted work; and
- The allegedly infringing work is substantially similar to your work.

While it is not necessary to provide direct evidence of copying, proving any infringement other than literal copying can be time-consuming and costly to show in court. In response to this, owners of valuable and easily alterable copyrights like software have come up with a creative way to prove copying: they insert a few lines of garbage code. If the garbage code shows up in another party's work, it is significant evidence of copying.

Sometimes, what looks like infringement is actually what is known as *fair use*. Fair use enables limited use of copyrighted materials for purposes that are in the public interest such as teaching, satirizing, criticizing, or reporting news. Naturally, the "fair use exception," as this right is called, can be abused by parties seeking to cloak commerce in a greater social purpose. When assessing whether a particular situation qualifies for the fair use exception, the court will usually look to see if the use is commercial and whether it cannibalizes or diminishes the value of the copyright to its owner; if so, the court is unlikely to grant a fair use exception.

Some examples of fair use: Example One: Showing a brief clip of GTA3 during a news clip on violence in games. Example Two: The fair use exception was denied to a Kinko's, who had been photocopying and selling copyrighted articles for college classes, in a case brought by publishers. The court found Kinko's guilty of infringement because even though the photocopied materials were being used in college classes, Kinko's use and copying was for commercial purposes.

TIP

Keep at least two hard copies of all releases and their documentation for the duration of their presence in the marketplace, in case they are needed for an infringement investigation or registrations.

Figure 5.6

Strategy guides.

Strengths and Weaknesses of Copyrights

Strengths of the copyright include:

- It offers broad protection to many types of information and work.
- It provides inexpensive protection.
- Software can be registered with trade secret portions blocked out to maintain confidentiality.

Weaknesses of the copyright include:

- Copyrights do not protect ideas, concepts, or methods, which are often key to software's value.
- In most cases, copyrights only protect literal copying, enabling competitors to clone with impunity.

What Assets Can a Copyright Protect?

Copyrights protect a broad array of developer assets, anything that can be fixed in a tangible medium (including computer media), covering everything from source, object, and machine code to automated databases (using some element of selection or arrangement of data to artwork to design docs, budgets, and business plans, and in some instances a program's structure, sequence, and organization and certain elements of the user interface.

Trademark

At one of the scariest meetings I've ever attended, a (Prada®-clad) advertising guru leaned back in his (Aeron®) chair and decreed that a brand was "a set of characteristics united by a badge of reassurance." At first, this struck me as hilarious, but it sums up the reason that companies pour millions into their brands: to make a consumer feel safe purchasing the item, a feeling sometimes referred to as "goodwill" and tabulated on a balance sheet.

When you buy a Callaway golf club, you know that you are buying a carefully constructed, perimeter-weighted hunk of metal with a nice rubber grip. When you buy a Powerbar, you know you will be

> **NOTE**
>
> Trademarks, like GE for light bulbs, protect makers of goods; service-marks like GE Capital, protect providers of services. Because the law regarding the two is so similar, this section will refer only to trademarks but applies equally to servicemarks.

getting at least 100 percent of your RDA of niacin. But what if you couldn't be sure that the branded product you were buying had been made by the brand owner? Then you wouldn't be sure about that hunk of metal or the niacin content of your candy bar. That safe feeling would dissipate. Hence, trademarks.

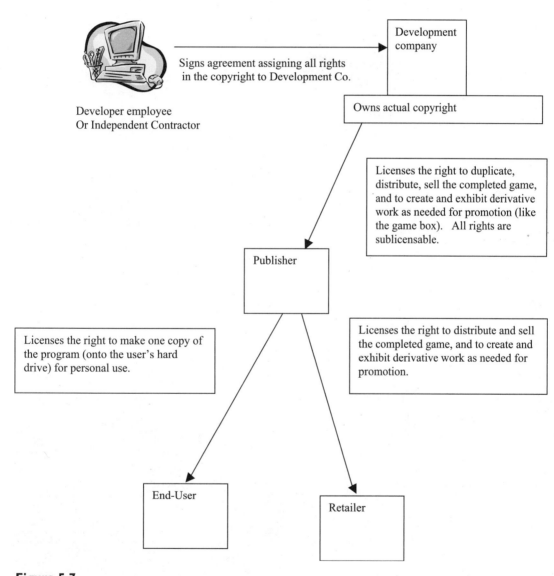

Figure 5.7

Sample of rights flow in a video game.

Figure 5.8

The trademark of status.

What Is a Trademark?

A "mark" is any word, phrase, sound, or device; a "trademark" is a mark that identifies a product as being made by one company and not another. To qualify as a trademark, it must (i) identify the product and (ii) distinguish the product from competing products. This does not mean that the trademark need bear any descriptive relation to the actual good or service—in fact, the more descriptive the mark, the less likely the U.S. Patent and Trademark Office (USPTO) will allow it full trademark protection.

Examples of trademarks and the products they represent include the name "Nike," the "swoosh" logo representing athletic apparel and footwear, and the product name "Air Jordan," or the name "Sony" and the "○□△✕" logo representing "PlayStation" and "PlayStation2" products.

If maintained correctly, trademarks do not expire.

What a Trademark Does and Does Not Protect

Trademarks protect the reputation of a brand by preventing other parties from using the trademark or one confusingly similar to it. While a mark may acquire some rights merely through use, trademarks must be registered with the USPTO to enjoy full legal rights. Unlike the Copyright Register, which functions more as a cataloguing entity keeping track of registered works, the USPTO rigorously examines every application to decide if it qualifies as a legitimate trademark and will usually fire back questions, required changes to the application, or a flat-out denial of registration.

> **NOTE**
>
> Denials are most commonly due to the proposed mark being either too similar to an existing trademark (example: a "GameBox" console would probably be too similar to both "Xbox" and "GameCube") or too descriptive (example: "Hardwood" for a flooring company) and thus not trademarkable, both of which are discussed in this section.

The strength of a trademark—in other words, how likely a court is to find that similar marks infringe on the original—depends on how distinctive the association between the mark and the described product is. The idea is that the more distinctive the trademark, the clearer it is to a court that any association between the product and the mark is the product of the company's efforts.

An *inherently distinctive* mark is one with no meaning within its product category. The three kinds of inherently distinctive marks are

- Arbitrary marks. These are *real* words that have nothing to do with the product, like Snickers candy bars.
- Fanciful marks. These are *invented* words, like Twix candy bars.
- Suggestive marks. These marks suggest a characteristic of the product but do not describe it, like Mounds or Flake candy bars.

Descriptive marks are just that: they describe characteristics of the product. One reason there is no candy bar named "Super Chocolatey Goodness" is that it probably wouldn't qualify for trademark protection. Praise (Best Chocolate), geographic origin (Swiss Chocolate), and proper names (Cadbury Chocolate) are all considered descriptive. Descriptive marks may be placed in what is known as the *secondary register* in the hopes that they will one day ascend to trademark status if they acquire *secondary meaning*, in which people come to associate the descriptive mark with a particular company's products. Example: The descriptive mark "Kool" for menthol cigarettes eventually acquired secondary meaning sufficient for a trademark.

Trade dress. Trademarks can also protect trade dress, which is a fancy name for packaging that is ornamental, not functional. The distinctive Chanel No. 5 perfume bottle is a protected mark, as is Coca-Cola's hourglass-shaped bottle.

How Do I Qualify for and Obtain Trademark Protection?

As with copyrights, there are certain rights that arise from use of the mark, but you must register the property with a government agency to receive the fullest legal protection. You can register with the state in which you are operating, but that will only protect you against subsequent users of the name within that particular state. A federal trademark is effective throughout the 50 United States.

> **NOTE**
>
> You may (and should) use the ™ or ℠ symbols if you are claiming rights to a mark, but you may only use the ® symbol, which indicates a federally registered mark, after the USPTO has actually registered your mark.

Table 5.2 Relevant Trademark and Servicemark Classes

International Class Number	Products Included in Class
Trademarks	
16 (paper)	Paper, cardboard and goods made from these materials, not included in other classes; printed matter; bookbinding material; photographs; stationery; adhesives for stationery or household purposes; artists' materials; paint brushes; typewriters and office requisites (except furniture); instructional and teaching material (except apparatus); plastic materials for packaging (not included in other classes); playing cards; printers' type; printing blocks.
21 (housewares and glass)	Household or kitchen utensils and containers (not of precious metal or coated therewith); combs and sponges; brushes (except paint brushes); brush-making materials; articles for cleaning purposes; steel wool; un-worked or semi-worked glass (except glass used in building); glassware, porcelain and earthenware not included in other classes.
24 (textiles)	Textiles and textile goods, not included in other classes; bed and table covers.
25 (clothing)	Clothing, footwear, headgear.
28 (toys and playthings)	Games and playthings; gymnastic and sporting articles not included in other classes; decorations for Christmas trees.
Servicemarks	
41 (education and entertainment)	Education; providing of training; entertainment; sporting and cultural activities.
42 (computer, scientific, and legal)	Scientific and technological services and research and design relating thereto: industrial analysis and research services; design and development of computer hardware and software; legal services.

Figure 5.9

The distinctive appearance of the Chanel No. 5 bottle is protected "trade dress."

RIGHTS GAINED FROM USE

U.S. trademark law grants ownership to the first party to use an inherently distinctive mark in commerce, unlike other nations who afford ownership to the first party to register the mark (giving rise to piracy and strategy concerns discussed below in the following "Protecting Your Assets: Enforcement: International Considerations" section). The first user of a trademark gains certain rights as long as the use is in good faith, meaning that the user is unaware of any prior owners of the mark or one confusingly similar to it. These rights are very flimsy, however, unless the mark is then registered.

To register a mark with the USPTO, you must either show commercial use of the mark or file an intent-to-use application. An intent-to-use application confers the same privileges of registration, but the registration may be deemed *abandoned* (lapse) if the owner does not prove that it started using the mark in commerce within six months from the date of registration.

> **TIP**
>
> The USPTO can extend the intent-to-use grace period up to 36 months if the owner shows good cause for the delay.

> **NOTE**
>
> A goal of the trademark laws is to ensure that trademarks are actually used in commerce, not bought and "parked" to prevent other parties from using them. To this end, trademarks are a use-it-or-lose-it proposition. Even after successful registration, a mark will be deemed abandoned if it is not used in commerce for two continuous years.

Federal trademarks are administered by the U.S. Patent and Trademark Office. A company gains the following legal benefits by registering a trademark in the Principal Register of the USPTO:

- Evidence of ownership of the trademark.
- The exclusive right to use the mark on or in connection with the goods or services set forth in the registration.
- Inability of infringers to claim innocent infringement (the law presumes that all parties are aware of all valid federal trademarks).
- The ability to use your U.S. registration as the basis for foreign registrations.
- The ability to use the ® symbol after your mark.
- The ability to prohibit the importation of any goods bearing the mark, and receipt of U.S. Customs assistance to enforce this prohibition (which is very helpful in anti-piracy efforts).
- After five years of continuous use, a federally registered trademark is declared incontestable, making it unlikely that another party will be able to successfully challenge your ownership of the mark.

Registration

To register a trademark in the Principal Register of the USPTO, an application is submitted for one or more *classes* of goods and/or services. A word trademark (Teenage Mutant Ninja Turtles), design (the appearance of the character Donatello), and slogan (Turtle Power) are all considered separate trademarks and must be registered separately in all relevant classes. Because this can add up quickly, many companies only trademark their name, which protects against other parties using the same name on the same products in either plain text or as a logo. There are 42 classes of goods and services.

The application includes a description and display of the mark if it is a drawing or particular font. The applications are not cheap ($335 in filing fees per class) and are of sufficient complexity that an attorney is used by most applicants. Trademarks must be renewed every 10 years except for the affidavit of use, which happens between years 5 and 6.

> **TIP**
>
> **Because the federal registration process can take several months, many companies elect to file a state trademark registration to provide interim protection.**

An additional expense is the trademark search, in which specialized companies comb through state, federal, and international (as required) trademark databases for identical or confusingly similar marks. They can also conduct what are known as *common law* searches to ferret out any parties using the mark who have not yet registered it. The common law search is worthwhile because those same parties can contest a registered trademark and may win if they can prove that they used the trademark first. The trademark search is worth the investment to prevent your company from building goodwill in a mark that it may have to abandon later. Furthermore, if you are sued for infringement, a trademark search record is good evidence that the infringement was unintentional.

Rejected?!

The most common reasons trademark examiners reject applications are

- **Likelihood of Confusion.** If the examiner finds prior filed or registered marks that are either identical or confusingly similar in the Federal registry, it will reject for likelihood of confusion. To persuade the examiner that there is no likelihood of confusion, you must show that the mark is dissimilar, or if the marks are similar, that the respective goods or services in question are too different to be confused.
- **Mere Descriptiveness.** If the examiner thinks that the mark is only descriptive of the product, it will deny you exclusive use of the mark. You may prevail if you can prove that your mark is recognized by the relevant public or consumer, or that your mark has acquired *secondary meaning* by being well known in its industry, through many years of operation, sales, and advertising.
- **Generic Word.** If the examiner finds that your mark is a generic description of the product (instead of the *source* of the product, which is what a trademark protects), it will deny your application. Example: "Ball Games" would probably not be allowed for a sports equipment manufacturer, since it would prevent all others in that market from using the word "ball" in their marks.
- **Indefinite Description.** This rejection has to do with the application, not the mark. *Indefinite description* means that you have not clearly and concisely identified the product or service to be protected. Fortunately, the examiners usually give you a suggested modification that would be acceptable to them.

Enforcing Trademarks

Trademark rights require some maintenance: registrations must be renewed every 10 years, and if a third party can prove your failure to use the mark for 2 continuous years, it may be deemed abandonment and given to another party. Furthermore, failure to police the use of your trademark may allow it to lapse into generic (unprotected) status. *Aspirin* was once a trademark but did not protect against generic use of its mark and lost its registration. Other trademarks that have become generic in daily use—Kleenex, Band-aid, Xerox—have maintained their trademark status thanks to active monitoring and enforcement by their owners.

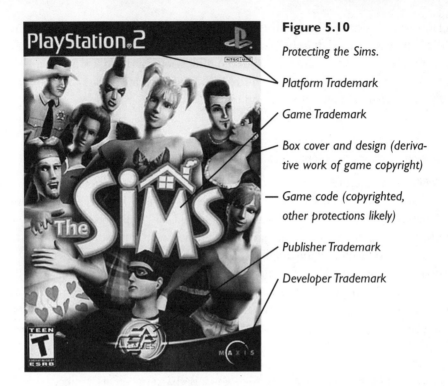

Figure 5.10

Protecting the Sims.

Platform Trademark

Game Trademark

Box cover and design (derivative work of game copyright)

Game code (copyrighted,
other protections likely)

Publisher Trademark

Developer Trademark

If you want to assert your trademark rights against an allegedly infringing party, you must be able to prove that the allegedly infringing mark is similar enough to yours that potential customers would likely be confused as to the source of the product. This is known as the *likelihood of confusion* doctrine. This is simple enough in a pure counterfeit matter, but what of a situation where a party puts out a social simulation game called "The Syms" that looks similar, but not identical to the original trademark? Unfortunately, at that point you are looking at costly litigation where a court would have to decide whether or not the allegedly infringing mark creates a likelihood of confusion in the consumer's mind.

A court will look to the following factors in determining whether the two trademarks are confusingly similar:

- The existence of actual confusion in the marketplace between the two marks
- Similarity of the marks in terms of appearance, sound, and meaning
- Similarity of the goods or services being identified by the two marks
- The strength of the prior mark
- The sophistication of the consumers who buy the particular products or services

- The similarity of the channels of distribution of the products or services (that is, whether they are both sold in the same type of stores)
- The degree of commercial competition between the two trademark users
- The distinctiveness of the trademarks (that is, whether they are somewhat descriptive or arbitrary and fanciful)

Remedies available in a trademark infringement case include injunctions, impounding and destruction of infringing material, and monetary damages.

Strengths and Weaknesses of Trademarks

Strengths of the trademark include:

- Prevents others from marketing or selling confusingly similar products or entertainment
- Can protect character names and designs

Weaknesses of the trademark include:

- Registration is costly, subject to maintenance and continued use
- May not protect against sale of similar product under different mark

What Assets Can a Trademark Protect?

Trademarks protect branding devices that establish a product as coming from your company and no other. Aside from your company name and the name of your games and technology, if you have a distinctive sound that plays at initialization of your game, a logo, a mascot—all of these can be trademarked. The names, character designs, and slogans of original IP, characters, weapons, and other valuable marks that are vulnerable to exploitation by others (in other words, whatever could generate revenue through merchandising or entertainment) should be trademarked (example: Conan the Barbarian).

Patent

A patent is the boss of the IP world. It gives its owner a monopoly over a new technology, which can be a powerful lever against other companies. Unlike copyrights, the patent protects the ideas and even applied algorithms, not just the set of code used to implement them. Unlike trade secrets, a patent protects against a third party independently developing the same technology; with a patent, you can prevent any other third parties from using your technology.

The price an inventor pays for the exclusivity, which lasts 20 years for software, is that the patent is published and its inner workings made available for the public to see. There are three main ways a patent can backfire:

- A competitor may read the patent application and be able to manipulate it to create a new technology that does not infringe, but still achieves the benefits of the patented advance.
- The U.S. generally awards patents to the first inventor, not the first to file. A company may apply for and publish a patent only to have it overturned by another company who can prove they invented it first and had been using it under trade secret protection.
- If a company is not proactive about its international patent portfolio, *registration pirates* may register the patents abroad, forcing the company to buy its patents back to do business abroad.

Because of their exclusionary nature, patents tended to have a bad name in the software development world, which emphasizes sharing and developing knowledge. The brouhaha over "business method" patents that many believe were not original enough to merit a monopoly, like Amazon's "One click" shopping or Priceline's binding bids, has contributed to this taint. For these reasons and the relatively high cost of applying for patents (at least $10,000), many software developers rely on trade secrets and copyrights to protect their source code, even for technologies like engines.

There are still many proponents for patenting software. They argue that:

- There is no substitute for exclusive protection of the concepts, methods, and ideas, because the copyrights are easily violable.
- A patent owner may always elect to give royalty-free licenses, but for business purposes should have the option of excluding competitors from using its innovation.
- Compared with the cost of developing the asset, a patent is a cheap way to protect it.
- Owning a patent still has cachet with investors, as it shows a legally responsible company that has a lock on a competitive advantage (depending, of course, on the quality of the patented technology.
- Patents are a good defense against infringement suits from competitors, enabling a company to cross-sue and settle by the two parties agreeing to a royalty-free license of the others' patent.

Keep in mind that the animating principle behind patents is to award inventors and to spur greater advances by publishing the invention's design so that other parties may see it and benefit from the learning.

What Is a Patent?

A patent is a property right granted by the USPTO that allows the inventor of a process or other invention to exclude others from making, using, or selling the invention in the United States. It also prohibits importing the invention into the United States. Once the patent is granted, the USPTO publishes the application so that other parties can see how the invention works. There are two major kinds of patents: *design* patents, which cover ornamental designs not essential to function like the iMac's CPU box, and *utility* patents, which protect useful inventions like the computer mouse (though the iMac's original *hockey puck* mouse would be eligible for a design patent). Utility patents are generally good for 20 years from the application date, design patents for 14 years.

Figure 5.11

The DualShock2 controller contains patented vibration technology.

How Do I Qualify for and Obtain Patent Protection?

For an invention to qualify for a patent, it must fit the following four criteria by being:

- **Of patentable subject matter.** There are four categories of patentable subject matter for utility patents: machines (like a Flowbie), processes (like treating a metal to make a new alloy), articles of manufacture (like a Phillips-head screwdriver), or composition of matter (like a new hair gel formula). A design patent need only be repeatable.
- **Useful and operational.** The bar is low on what is considered useful, but any machines or design must work. A non-functioning design is not patentable.

■ **Repeatable.** The patented invention must be repeatable by a third party using the application as a source document.

■ **Novel.** Qualitatively, if software provides new uses, functions, or capabilities not found in prior art, it may qualify as sufficiently novel. Technically, an invention will be considered novel if it is not patented, known, described in a publication, or used by other parties in the United States or any other country either (i) before the date of invention; or (ii) more than one year prior to the patent application. Example: An inventor has proof that he invented a widget in Year One, but doesn't get around to patenting it until Year Four. If another party used or published a description of the widget in Year Two, the invention does not qualify as novel and is not eligible for a patent.

The invention must also not be an obvious extension of or cosmetic adjustment to prior technology.

Patents do not protect ideas or suggestions as such, only machines, processes, or other instrumentalities embodying those ideas or suggestions. Patents are not available for laws of physics or nature, or mathematical principles like pure algorithms. However, applying an algorithm to create a useful, tangible result is patentable subject matter. This means that patents may be sought for software instructing a processor to convert data into figures on a screen (like a console game).

The USPTO Patent Application

Acquiring a patent is a long, expensive process that often takes more than two years and costs over $10,000, including attorney's fees. The application fees alone range from $375 to $750. The patent application is very complex and requires significant specific knowledge, making it almost a requirement that an experienced patent attorney (preferably with experience in drafting the kind of patent you're after) prepare your application. The application will describe the invention and include some illustration. The *claim* of the patent is whatever elements you seek to have protected. Claims must be written according to very particular standards, and generally require the assistance of an attorney.

> **NOTE**
> Unlike copyrights and trademarks, only the inventor may actually apply for the protection; the inventor may then assign the registration to a company who will own the patent.

> **NOTE**
> If the code must be disclosed in the application, it will lose its trade secret protection, but can be protected with a copyright.

Some software applicants are eligible for a protected application that can maintain the trade secrecy of their source code (which is normally obviated by the publication of a patent). Where the code is not required to understand the invention, the applicant may be able to demonstrate the invention using pseudo code, block diagrams, and/or flow charts.

Table 5.3 Employee-Creator's Rights in Different Categories

	Copyrights	Trademark	Patent	Trade Secret
Creator's Ownership Rights	Creator owns copyright unless the work qualifies as a work for hire (created within scope of employment; subject of written agreement; falls within one of nine work categories). Some categories of work are ineligible for work for hire status	Rights acquired through use, so generally only the company acquires rights.	Inventor owns the invention, but may be legally required to assign to employer in some situations.	Work created within scope of employment generally belongs to employer; otherwise, to employee.
Documents required for company to acquire ownership	Written, signed assignment of invention. WFH (employment agreement assumed)	None. WFH (employment agreement assumed)	Written, signed assignment of invention. WFH (employment agreement assumed)	Assignment of invention. WFH (employment agreement assumed)

Provisional Patent Applications

If you're not sure whether you want to invest all of the attorney's fees and your time into patenting a particular technology, you can buy yourself some time by filing what is known as a provisional application.

The provisional application costs between $80 and $160 but most important, it does not require you to state claims for the patent or provide a prior art disclosure, which is where most of your and the attorney's time goes. The application gives you one year to file a full application, with the benefit of the early filing date. You may use the term "Patent Pending" for property under provisional application. Even better, your 20 year patent period only starts running from the date of your full application, so you don't lose any of the protected period.

However—and this is important—the provisional application *does* start the clock on your deadline for filing international applications under the Paris Convention (see the following "Protecting Your Assets: International Considerations" section).

Searching for Prior Art

Prior art is patent terminology for previous inventions that affect your claim that the invention is novel and non-obvious. Example: If I get an idea that having adhesive on the back of notes in my notepad is a great idea and I should get a patent, a search for prior art would turn up Art Fry and Spencer Silverman's invention of the Post-it note. Insufficient prior art searches cause massive heartache and financial waste for inventors who invest in the application process only to be turned down by the patent examiner due to prior art. Prior art includes both patented and public domain technology, so it is advisable to hire a professional search firm that can search both categories rather than just searching the USPTO's online patent databases yourself.

NOTE

Another wrinkle in the search for prior art is the ability of foreign applicants to rely on activities occurring in WTO signatory countries (after January 1, 1996) to prove dates of ownership. This means that a foreign party could contest your application by showing that they invented the technology before you *in another country*. There are restrictions on this situation arising, but if you think that you have competitors in WTO signatory countries, advise your search firm.

Prosecution

After a patent application has been submitted, a patent examiner is assigned to determine if the invention is patentable. During *prosecution*, the examiner works with the applicant to modify the application so that it may be patented. Because prosecution can take more than two years, many inventors will just start selling their invention with a "patent pending" notice. The danger, of course, is that the examiner will turn up prior art that your invention infringes after you have been selling your invention.

Figure 5.12

The patented invention of Velcro revolutionized kindergarten development curricula everywhere.

Publication

A patent application may be published before it is accepted as a patent, but it will not be published for 18 months from date of application unless the applicant agrees otherwise. An applicant can also prevent the publication of the application by stating that foreign applications will not be filed (if this is indeed correct). Once the patent is issued, the application is published.

Competing Claims

Where two inventors independently create the same invention, the USPTO generally awards ownership to the "first to invent," not the "first to file." Therefore, documentation of invention processes becomes very valuable. Ongoing records of research and development progress should be kept and need to be signed and dated by the inventor as well as a witness not involved in the invention process. One exception to the "first to invent" rule is that if an inventor does not attempt to reduce his invention to practice within a reasonable amount of time after the invention, the patent may be awarded to the other party. "Reducing to practice" means either producing a working prototype or filing a patent application describing the invention in enough detail that a third party could reproduce it.

Enforcing Patents

Patent infringement is punishable by injunctions (forcing the infringer to do or not do something) and money damages in cases of innocent infringement, and attorney's fees and tripled damages if the infringement was willful.

Strengths and Weaknesses of Patents

Strengths of the patent are

- The ability to protect ideas, methods, and concepts as well as their embodiments
- The ability to prevent others from using the patented property, even if they developed it independently

Weaknesses of the patent are

- It is a long, expensive, uncertain process.
- There are pitfalls attached to the application process that require close monitoring by an experienced attorney.
- The practice is controversial within the game development community.

What Assets Can a Patent Protect?

Patents may protect many different aspects of a technology: program algorithms, display presentation, menu arrangement, editing functions, control functions, user interface features, compiling techniques, program languages, translation methods, utilities, formulae to control program execution or process data, and more.

PROTECTING YOUR ASSETS

Now that you understanding the basics of intellectual property law, here are some important applications of those principles:

Identify Eligible Assets

The first step of a strong intellectual property protection program is to identify company assets eligible for protection, such as:

- **Name and Logo.** Your name and logo, if applicable, should be federally trademarked as early as possible.

Table 5.4 Protections Available for Developer Assets by Category of Rights

Trade Secret

Source code, object code, machine code, firmware, any concepts, ideas, methods, processes, or documents related to the creation of software or game concepts, including characters, storylines, drawings, business plans and methods, marketing plans or customer lists, databases, and so forth.

Copyright

Anything that can be fixed in a tangible medium (including computer media): source, object and machine code, certain automated databases, artwork, design docs, budgets, and business plans, some UI and program structure, sequence and organization.

Trademark

Company name, logo, name of games and technology, distinctive branding sounds or colors. Names, character designs and slogans of original IP, characters, weapons, and other valuable marks.

Utility Patent

Applied algorithms, display presentation, menu arrangement, editing functions, control functions, user interface features, compiling techniques, program languages, translation methods, utilities, formulae to control program execution or process data, and more.

- **Design and Business Documents.** Design and business documents can be registered with the Copyright Office, but they will lose their trade secret protection. What may be a better solution is to mark documents with the legends and notices discussed in the following "Protecting Your Assets: Enforcement: Notices" section and to only disclose the documents to parties under NDA. The documents should be marked with both confidentiality and copyright notices.
- **Tools, Technology, Processes, and Game Code.** Tools, technology, processes, and game code may be protected with trade secrets, copyrights, patents (if the product qualifies) and several permutations thereof. Combinations may be used such as protecting every-

thing as a trade secret, and applying for registered copyrights using the trade secret registration, and patenting a small segment of the code that is particularly inventive. All creations should have confidentiality and copyright notices embedded in their code. Where any of these creations will be marketed with a certain name, like the "Unreal Engine," it should be registered for federal trademark.

■ **Content.** The audiovisual content of games should be registered at the same time as the actual game code in one registration by including a written synopsis of the game and a half-inch VHS tape of the audiovisual elements. Pitch bibles and prototypes and demonstrations may also be registered. It is also advisable to trademark the name of the property and the main character names and designs. The timing of these registrations can be important—you may not want your copyrights registered and published too early, for example—so consult an IP attorney when planning your strategy.

How Do You Protect Your Assets?

You want to be able to protect your IP from infringement by counterfeiters (for example, another company duplicating your game, or lifting portions of your code for their own uses), and gray marketers, who illegally distribute product (Example: Selling U.S. versions of a game in Australia months before the Australian release). For the most part, registration and enforcement of rights in games (not the underlying technology)—which are a considerable expense—fall to the publisher. The publisher is the party with the most at stake, and it can't afford to risk incorrect protection. However, if you are doing country-by-country publishing and distribution instead of a centralized release through one of the bigger publishers, piracy and gray marketing are *your* concerns. There are a few things you can do to buffer your property from the chaos of global intellectual property administration:

■ Obtain local IP protections. Register where necessary. Contact local counsel to vet issues and strategize.

■ Choose your local business partners wisely. If working with a regional publisher, ask for references from other game developers—preferably from a different country than the publisher—and get in touch with them. Ask them about their anti-piracy programs and how they plan to enforce your IP in their territory.

■ Price your game at a level suitable to the local market.

■ To prevent gray marketing, schedule simultaneous releases in all countries speaking a given language.

■ Have your local manufacturers create box text and art customized for that country, ideally with the country name on the outside of the box to easily identify gray marketed goods if they turn up elsewhere.

Table 5.5 Protections available by asset type

Tools, Technology, Code

Copyrights. Mark with copyright legend in code and on all media carrying the code. Register with Copyright Office using the trade secret registration.

Trade Secrets. Mark all qualifying code and media carrying code with trade secret legends.

Patents. Innovative software may qualify for patent protection.

Best Practice: combine methods. Example: Register the game with the copyright office, using the trade secret application; maintain all code as trade secret. If a segment of the game code is particularly innovative, that may be patented without sacrificing the trade secret status of the rest of the game.

All creations should have confidentiality and copyright notices embedded in their code.

Register trademark name of the technology (like "Unreal Engine").

Design and Business Documents

Copyrights. Should be marked with copyright legend.

Can be registered, but may lose their trade secret protection.

Best Practice: Trade Secret. Mark documents CONFIDENTIAL & PROPRIETARY and only disclose to parties under NDA.

Art and Audiovisual Game Elements

Copyrights. All material, registered or not, should bear copyright legend.

Audiovisual elements of the game can be registered together with game code using Form TX by including a written synopsis of the game and a 1/2" VHS tape of the audiovisual elements.

Pitch bibles, prototypes and demonstrations may be registered.

Trademark the name of the property and main character names and designs.

Names, Logos, Slogans

Trademarks protect names, logos, character designs and slogans of the company and its original IP (name of game/major characters, character slogans, special weapons and vehicles, etc.).

Registration

Patents and trademarks should be registered with the USPTO and copyrights should be registered with the Copyright Office, respectively, to gain maximum protection against infringement and piracy.

Enforcement

Prevention is the cheapest form of enforcement: the goal of your enforcement program is to avoid having to take any kind of expensive court action. Three tools of your enforcement program are notices, mod licenses, and international protection strategy.

Notices

The first step in enforcing your property is putting the world on alert that it is protected. Notices, also known as "legends," may be different for "published" versus "unpublished" software. The distinction is important because making software public has implication for its trade secret status as well as its patentability. Published software is that which is mass marketed and distributed without a signed license (like a game). Unpublished software, if distributed at all, is only available to a limited number of users under signed licenses and NDAs and marked "CONFIDENTIAL" (like a licensed technology).

Software

Unpublished software should bear the following notice:

[COMPANY] CONFIDENTIAL AND PROPRIETARY

THIS WORK CONTAINS VALUABLE CONFIDENTIAL AND PROPRIETARY INFORMATION. DISCLOSURE, USE OR REPRODUCTION WITHOUT THE WRITTEN AUTHORIZATION OF [COMPANY] IS PROHIBITED. THIS UNPUBLISHED WORK BY [COMPANY] IS PROTECTED BY THE LAWS OF THE UNITED STATES AND OTHER COUNTRIES. IF PUBLICATION OF THE WORK SHOULD OCCUR THE FOLLOWING NOTICE SHALL APPLY: "**COPYRIGHT (c) 20XX [COMPANY] ALL RIGHTS RESERVED**."

Or, where space is too limited:

THIS IS AN UNPUBLISHED WORK CONTAINING [COMPANY] CONFIDENTIAL AND PRO-PRIETARY INFORMATION. IF PUBLICATION OCCURS, THE FOLLOWING NOTICE APPLIES: **"COPYRIGHT (c) 20XX [COMPANY] ALL RIGHTS RESERVED."**

These notices should be embedded in the header of all code modules during development as well as any other media in which the software appears, including labels and screen display of demonstrations.

Once the game is published, copyright notices should be shown at the initial screen display of the game. The dates on the copyright notices should be the first year of copyright and updated to include every subsequent year of copyright, for example: "© 2000-2003 [Company]. All Rights Reserved."

Patented technology should bear a legend of either "Patent Pending" if the application is pending or "Patent No.——," as applicable.

DOCUMENTS

The same legend:

[COMPANY] CONFIDENTIAL AND PROPRIETARY

THIS WORK CONTAINS VALUABLE CONFIDENTIAL AND PROPRIETARY INFORMATION. DISCLOSURE, USE OR REPRODUCTION WITHOUT THE WRITTEN AUTHORIZATION OF [COMPANY] IS PROHIBITED. THIS UNPUBLISHED WORK BY [COMPANY] IS PROTECTED BY THE LAWS OF THE UNITED STATES AND OTHER COUNTRIES. IF PUBLICATION OF THE WORK SHOULD OCCUR THE FOLLOWING NOTICE SHALL APPLY: **"COPYRIGHT (c) 20XX [COMPANY] ALL RIGHTS RESERVED."**

should appear on the first page of all confidential trade secret business and marketing plans, design and technical documents, prototypes and demonstrations, source listings, or any other documentation of proprietary software.

CONTENT

All content should bear the legend "COPYRIGHT (©) 20XX [COMPANY] ALL RIGHTS RESERVED." as well as the above legend if the content is trade secret protected. If the content contains any trade- or servicemarks, attach the applicable notation—™, ^SM, or ®.

Mods

There is a healthy traffic in user-generated modifications and contributions to games known as "mods." Mods are generally thought of as being good for business because they extend a prod-uct's life by adding content and increasing user involvement with the property (making sequels more likely). As discussed, copyrights on software programs reserve the right to modify and distribute copies of programs. However, many game developers provide tools to create modifications and a limited license to users for non-commercial creation and distribution of mods. The key is that users may not have any com-mercial purpose in their activities.

> **CAUTION**
>
> It is very important to have a license in place for these rights; if users do not have to sign a license to modify the software, a *naked license* to the trademarks may be created that can diminish the owner's rights to the trademark.

Key terms of mod licenses:

- No modification or distribution may be for any commercial purpose.
- Users assent to the license with a "click-wrap" end user license agreement in which the "I Agree" button must be clicked to download the mod tools.
- Mods must only function with the full version of the game, not the demo version.
- Hosting of multiplayer versions of the game for non-commercial purposes is allowed.
- Users may not use the company's IP in advertising or promotion.

International Considerations

Protecting intellectual property abroad is complex and extremely expensive. Many countries do not enforce rights against infringers with anything approaching vigor. The registration and application processes must generally be repeated in every country. There are various treaties that have tried to streamline the process and create more uniform enforcement procedures, but we are still a long way off from a universal standard.

One important treaty, the Paris Convention, has over 140 signatory countries that have agreed to give the intellectual property of foreigners the same rights that it affords its citizens. The second major facet of the Paris Convention is the *Right of Priority*. The Right of Priority gives you one year to file for a patent, six months for a trademark, from the date you filed in your home country, with the effective date of the foreign registration being your home country filing date. Example:

Table 5.6 International IP Protection

US

Trade Secret
Trade secrets protected in US

Copyright
Notice recommended;
Registration required to sue and receive certain kinds of compensation;
Company can be owner of copyright;
No moral rights for author

Trademark
Limited rights from use;
First to use owns the mark;
Marks must be used or risk cancellation;
Use must be substantial commercial use;
Only federally-registered marks may use the ® symbol

Utility Patent
First to invent owns the patent;
Must file within one year of first sale, public use, or printed disclosure;
Patent application can be kept secret until issued;
Costly registration, maintenance payments

Worldwide

Trade Secret
Trade secrets not protected in many countries, and poorly protected in others;
   Tip: Disclosure should be avoided where possible, and always under an NDA;
   Companies with offices abroad should conduct extensive employee education
   about existence and protection of trade secrets;
Trade secret agreements may be unenforceable in some countries unless approved
   by government agencies;
Some countries limit the royalty period and amount of royalties payable for trade
   secret-protected intellectual property

Table 5.6 Continued

Copyright

Notice required;

US copyrights recognized in many countries;

Some countries do not allow a company to own a copyright;

Moral rights in some countries give the author rights, even after selling the copyright, to control modification of the work;

Many Latin American countries require the phrase "All Rights Reserved" in the legend. Other countries require use of the © symbol and not the word "Copyright" in the legend

Trademark

Paris Convention signatory countries give US trademark registrants six month "right of priority" to file the mark abroad;

Rights arise only through registration;

First to file owns the trademark;

Some countries make use of the ® symbol on a mark illegal if the mark is not registered in that country;

"Use" required to maintain registration, but can be as flimsy as a single advertisement

Utility Patent

Paris Convention signatory countries give US patent registrants one year "right of priority" to file utility patent abroad;

Patents must generally be registered in every country;

First to file owns the patent;

Inventions generally must be filed for registration before first sale, public use or printed disclosure anywhere in the world;

Many countries recognize US filing dates as long as foreign applications are filed within one year of US application;

Patent applications publicly available after around 18 months from US filing date;

Costly registration, translation, maintenance payments;

Some countries require that the patented invention be manufactured in that country within three years or registration may be voided

Developer A files a trademark in the U.S. on January 8, 2003. Developer Ä files the same trademark in Country Ø on May 3, 2003. Developer A then files the trademark in Country Ø on June 1, 2003. To Developer Ä's chagrin, Developer A has priority and gains the trademark.

Again, your publisher will most likely insist on administering the protection program, but here is a summary of the differences in different categories around the world:

TRADE SECRETS

The trade secret concept is relatively new to many countries, if it exists at all. It is therefore doubly important to avoid disclosure where possible, have all recipients sign NDAs that have been reviewed by foreign counsel, plaster notices of confidentiality all over materials, and educate any employees or contractors about trade secret protection.

CAUTION

Some countries require trade secret agreements to be reviewed by a particular government agency and, unless the agreement is approved, the agreement is unenforceable.

COPYRIGHTS

U.S. copyrights are valid in many overseas nations thanks to the Berne Convention treaty. Copyright notices should be placed on all materials and media. Local registration in Berne Convention nations is not necessary, but it may provide certain legal benefits like greater money awards in litigation. In the U.S., a company can own a copyright, but some countries afford ownership to individuals only. Finally, the U.S. has very limited "moral rights" in created property, but some countries give the author the right to object to any modi-

CAUTION

In ventures where royalties are paid in exchange for trade secrets, some countries limit the amount of royalties and duration of the royalty period. Check these limits before executing any such agreements.

fication of the work that would prejudice or compromise the author's honor. This has been used to hold development hostage until money could be found to assuage the author's honor; be sure your foreign counsel reviews your NDAs and invention assignment agreements to prevent such cheap chicanery.

While the copyrights may be valid overseas, vigorous enforcement is another matter. It is extremely expensive to enforce copyrights overseas, usually requiring the retention of local agencies specializing in anti-piracy measures. This is generally only cost-effective at a very high level of success. U.S. Customs agents work to intercept pirated goods here and abroad, but they can only catch so much of the traffic in pirated goods.

TRADEMARKS

Trademarks have the benefits of Paris Convention Rights of Priority, giving U.S. registrants six months from the date of filing to file abroad. There are four primary differences in the trademark schemes of the U.S. and the rest of the world:

- **Rights through registration only.** In the U.S., some rights to a trademark can be acquired merely by using the mark in commerce. In most other countries, one only gains trademark rights through registration.
- **First to file.** Most countries award trademark ownership to the first party to file, not the first party to use the mark in commerce. This has resulted in many multinational corporations preparing to sell goods abroad only to discover that a "registration pirate" has registered their mark and is willing to sell it back at a markup.
- **Commercial Use.** In the U.S., a mark can be cancelled if not used in a meaningful way in commerce. Abroad, many countries will also cancel your mark for non-use, but the flimsiest use—an advertisement, for instance—will qualify as "use."
- **Use of the ®.** In the U.S., only registered trademarks are allowed to bear the ® symbol. Abroad, use of the ® symbol if the mark is not registered in that particular country may be illegal.

> **TIP**
>
> Keep records for each country in case you need to prove "use."

> **TIP**
>
> Use the ™ symbol if you are not sure to which countries your product will be exported.

PATENTS

Patents must be filed in every country individually. There are two territorial offices—the European Patent Office and the OAPI in Africa—that will accept and review the validity of one application for registration in its member countries. If the application is accepted, the patent must still be formally registered in every individual country.

There are three main differences between the U.S. and the rest of the world, as far as patents are concerned:

- **First to file, not first to invent.** Most foreign countries award patents to the first party to file, not the party who can prove they were the first to invent.
- **First sale.** Unlike the United States, where you must file within one year of the first sale, public use, or printed description of the invention, a patent elsewhere must be filed prior to any public disclosure or use. However, Paris Convention signatory countries give you 12 months from the date of your U.S. filing to apply.

■ **Publication of Application.** In the United States, an applicant may request that its application not be published until the patent is actually issued. Most foreign countries will publish the application around 18 months after the U.S. filing date. Example: Developer A files in the U.S. on January 6, 2003. He then files in Country B on December 5, 2003. Country B will publish the application around June 6, 2004. This can compromise the trade secret status of any material in the application.

SUMMARY

Developers have four tools to help them protect their intellectual property: trade secrets, copyrights, trademarks, and patents.

Trade secret protection is valuable for developers because it enables them to protect any software product, business or technical documents, or special features or ideas in a product (including documentation) that qualify as a trade secret (gives a competitive advantage, not readily ascertainable, subject of secrecy efforts). Trade secrets require a lot of work to keep secret. They cannot protect many important ideas or features that are published or discoverable to others using the product. Trade secrets cannot prevent others from using the intellectual property if they have developed it independently. It can be used in combination with patent and copyright protection to provide more protection.

Copyrights are great because they can protect almost anything you can fix in a medium from unauthorized duplication and the preparation and distribution of derivative works. The Copyright Office will help you file special relief registrations for software that enable you to maintain the trade secret status of your intellectual property. Copyright's broad accessibility is matched by their inability to protect the underlying ideas, methods, and concepts of your software. Copyrights are also important for your artwork and business documents, though you should discuss if and when registration of these makes sense with your attorney. Copyrights may be used in conjunction with patent and trade secret protection to protect your software.

Trademarks protect brands. A developer will probably be most concerned with the trademark of its name, the names of any technology and tools that it markets, and the trademarks of any content properties it creates.

Patent protection is a powerful but controversial and expensive way to protect software. It protects ideas, methods, concepts, and many other features as long as they can be reduced to practice. Through a patent, a developer can create a monopoly on a technology or process.

All intellectual property that a developer creates, whether business documents, software, software documents, art, or anything else should bear the appropriate protective legend.

It is vital that a developer have effective NDA and assignment invention agreements signed by all employees and contractors, and NDAs with any parties to whom it will be disclosing trade secrets.

Table 5.7 Strengths and Weaknesses of Different Categories

Strength

Trade Secrets
Can be made public in certain forms and maintain its trade secret status;
Protects ideas, concepts, and methods, not just a particular embodiment thereof;
Protects special features or components of released software as long as the features are not readily reverse-engineerable;
No expiration date

Copyrights
Offers broad protection to many types of information and work;
Provides inexpensive protection for entire games with one registration;
Software can be registered with trade secret portions blocked out to maintain confidentiality

Trademarks
Prevents others from marketing works under the same or confusingly similar names

Patents
The ability to protect ideas, methods, and concepts as well as their embodiments;
The ability to prevent others from using the patented property, even if they developed it independently

Table 5.7 Continued

Weakness

Trade Secrets

Only protects against disclosure by parties with a legal duty not to disclose (employees and third parties under NDA);

Nothing that is reverse-engineerable can be protected as a trade secret;

Do not defend against a third party's independently developing the same concept or product;

Can become expensive and time consuming

Copyrights

Copyrights do not protect ideas, concepts, or methods, which are often key to software's value;

In most cases, copyrights only protect literal copying, enabling competitors to clone with impunity

Trademarks

Costly to obtain, rigorous application procedure;

Does not protect against similar materials sold under a different mark

Patents

Long, expensive, uncertain registration process;

Pitfalls attached to the application process that require close monitoring by an experienced attorney;

Practice is controversial within the game development community

Sample Exit Agreement

Mr. Preston Hamme
[Address]
[City], [State]

Dear Mr. Hamme:

While employed by [Company name] (the "Company"), you have had access to the Company's confidential and proprietary information and trade secrets. You also signed an employment agreement on [date] (the "Employment Agreement"), a copy of which is attached hereto.

This letter is a reminder that some of the obligations which arise through your employment with Company and your Employment Agreement which relate to the Company's confidential, proprietary and trade secret information will continue after you have left the employ of the Company.

The law and your Employment Agreement establish that you are obligated not to use, publish or otherwise disclose any secret, confidential or proprietary information of the Company. That obligation extends to prohibit your disclosing that information to others, including your new employer.

By signing below you indicate the following:

(1) You understand the foregoing, and you reaffirm your obligation not to use or disclose the Company's confidential, proprietary or trade secret information.
(2) You have returned to the Company all embodiments of the Company's trade secret, confidential or propriety information in your possession or control.
(3) You have returned any other materials given to you by the Company, and all materials prepared by you in connection with your employment by Company.

Sincerely,
[Name] duly authorized
[Company]

Acknowledged and Accepted:

_____
[Employee]

Date: _____

Witnessed By: _____

VALVE, L.L.C.
SDK LICENSE AND NONDISCLOSURE AGREEMENT

This SDK License and Nondisclosure Agreement (the "Agreement") is made this _____ day of _____, 2000 (the "Effective Date"), by and between _____, a _____ corporation ("Licensee") with offices located at _____ and VALVE, L.L.C., a Washington limited liability company ("Valve"), with offices located at 520 Kirkland Way, #201, Kirkland, WA 98033.

Whereas, Valve is the developer of the Half-Life™ computer game and the associated Half-Life software development kit (the "SDK");

Whereas, Licensee wishes to develop a modified game running only on the Half-Life engine (a "Mod") for distribution in object code form only to licensed end users of Half-Life, in return for license fees from such end users; and

Whereas, Licensee wishes to receive, and Valve wishes to disclose to Licensee, the SDK and other information as deemed appropriate by Valve, all on the terms set forth herein;

Now, therefore, in consideration of the mutual promises made herein, the parties agree as follows:

1. License.

   1.1 <u>License Grant</u>. Subject to the terms and conditions of this Agreement, Valve hereby grants Licensee a nonexclusive, royalty-free, terminable, worldwide nontransferable, nonsublicensable license to:

   (a) use the SDK in source code form, solely to develop a Mod;

   (b) reproduce, distribute and license the Mod in object code form via Internet download distribution only, and solely to licensed end users of Half-Life; and

   (c) to authorize its distributors (other than computer game publishers as described below) to exercise the rights set forth in Section 1.1(b), solely for the benefit of Licensee.

   1.2 <u>Restrictions</u>. Licensee shall not distribute the Mod except as provided herein. In particular, Licensee may not distribute the Mod on any tangible medium, such as CD-ROM, nor may Licensee permit any third party to do so. Licensee shall not qualify as a licensee hereunder and shall have no right to use, market, sell or distribute Mods if Licensee directly or indirectly distributes Mods as or through a computer game publisher (i.e., if any party in the on-line distribution of a Mod derives more than $10,000,000 per year in gross revenues from computer game sales in any media or platform, such party shall be deemed to be a "computer game publisher").

1.3 <u>Updates</u>. Valve may from time to time, in its sole discretion, provide updates, error corrections, and future versions of the SDK to Licensee. Upon delivery, such updates, error corrections and future versions shall be deemed part of the SDK, as applicable, under this Agreement.

1.4 <u>Indemnity</u>. Licensee shall defend, indemnify, and hold harmless Valve, its officers, directors, employees and agents, as well as Sierra On-Line, Inc. and its affiliates ("Sierra") against any and all claims, damages, losses, or liabilities whatsoever arising out of Licensee's creation, distribution, or promotion of the Mod.

1.5 <u>EULA</u>. If Licensee distributes the Mod, License shall distribute the Mod subject to a "click to accept" end user license agreement, in a form approved by Valve.

1.6 <u>Support</u>. Licensee shall be solely responsible for providing technical support (if any) to the end-users of the Mod, in accordance with its ordinary business practices.

1.7 <u>Errors and Feedback</u>. Licensee shall promptly report to Valve any program error Licensee discovers in the SDK. Valve may (but shall not be required to) correct such program error in future versions of the SDK. Valve shall also be free to use and implement any feedback or suggestions that Licensee gives to Valve regarding Half-Life, the SDK, or any other Valve software product.

1.8 <u>License back to Valve</u>. Licensee hereby licenses to Valve the worldwide, perpetual right to use and incorporate the Mod in any retail product (e.g., a level add-on pack) and to make, use, promote, market and sell such retail product alone and together with other retail products. Valve shall have the nonexclusive right and license to use Licensee's name and logo to promote such Mod as contained in any such retail product. If Valve derives any net sales revenue (i.e., gross sales revenue, less discounts, allowances, price protection, cost of goods, rebates, and any online distribution costs and expenses) from such retail product containing the Mod (and not any products sold therewith, such as the Half-Life game itself), then Valve shall pay Licensee, within 45 days after the end of each calendar quarter, a royalty on such net sales received of up to 1% of such net revenues. Valve shall determine the precise royalty percentage due to Licensee based on a total of no more than 10% royalty to all content providers for such retail product and the quality and amount of content provided by Licensee as compared to other content providers. Furthermore, Licensee grants Valve the right to sublicense the foregoing rights to third parties, subject to the terms and conditions set forth in this Section 1.8.

2. Confidentiality.

2.1 <u>Information</u>. Valve may disclose to Licensee other certain specifications, design plans, drawings, software, data, prototypes, business plans, strategies or other business and/or technical information, in oral or written form, which is proprietary and/or confidential to Valve, its business partners or its affiliated companies ("Information").

2.2 <u>Disclosure</u>. Valve shall disclose to Licensee only such Information as it, in its sole judgment and discretion, deems desirable. Licensee (a) shall hold such Information in confidence, shall restrict disclosure of such Information to its employees with a need to know (and advise such employees of the obligations assumed herein), (b) shall not disclose such Information to any third party without prior written approval of Valve, and (c) shall protect such Information by using the same degree of care (which shall be no less than reasonable care) to prevent its unauthorized disclosure as Licensee uses to protect its own confidential information of a like nature. Licensee agrees it shall only use Valve Information for the purpose of developing a Mod.

2.3 <u>Exclusions</u>. These restrictions on the use or disclosure of Information shall not apply to any Information:
   (a) Which is independently developed by Licensee as evidenced by documentation in such party's possession; or
   (b) Which is lawfully received from another source free of restriction and without breach of this Agreement, as evidenced by documentation in Licensee's possession; or
   (c) After it has become generally available to the public without breach of this Agreement by Licensee; or
   (d) Which at the time of disclosure to Licensee was known to Licensee free of restriction as evidenced by documentation in Licensee's possession; or
   (e) Which Valve agrees in writing is free of such restrictions.

2.4 <u>Announcement</u>. Licensee agrees not to announce or disclose to any third party the terms or existence of this Agreement without first securing the prior written approval of Valve.

3. Term.

3.1 <u>Term</u>. This Agreement shall become effective as of the Effective Date and shall continue for a period of one (1) year.

3.2 <u>Termination</u>. Valve may terminate this Agreement effective immediately upon written notice to Licensee.

3.3 <u>Survival</u>. Sections 1.4, 2, 3.3, and 4-6 shall survive any expiration or termination of this Agreement.

4. Disclaimer of Warranties; Limitation of Liability

4.1 <u>NO WARRANTIES</u>. VALVE AND ITS SUPPLIERS DISCLAIM ALL WARRANTIES WITH RESPECT TO THE SDK, EITHER EXPRESS OR IMPLIED, INCLUDING, BUT NOT LIMITED TO, IMPLIED WARRANTIES OF MERCHANTABILITY AND FITNESS FOR A PARTICULAR PURPOSE.

4.2 <u>LIMITATION OF LIABILITY</u>. IN NO EVENT SHALL VALVE OR ITS SUPPLIERS BE LIABLE FOR ANY SPECIAL, INCIDENTAL, INDIRECT, OR CONSEQUENTIAL DAMAGES WHATSOEVER (INCLUDING, WITHOUT LIMITATION, DAMAGES FOR LOSS OF BUSINESS PROFITS, BUSINESS INTERRUPTION, LOSS OF BUSINESS INFORMATION, OR ANY OTHER PECUNIARY LOSS) ARISING OUT OF THE USE OF OR INABILITY TO USE THE ENGINE AND/OR THE SDK, EVEN IF VALVE HAS BEEN ADVISED OF THE POSSIBILITY OF SUCH DAMAGES.

5. Compliance with Applicable Laws. In performing under this Agreement, Licensee agrees to comply with all applicable laws, regulations, ordinances and statutes, including, but not limited to, the import/export laws and regulations of the United States and its governmental and regulatory agencies (including, without limitation, the Bureau of Export Administration and the U.S. Department of Commerce) and all applicable international treaties and laws. Further, Licensee shall pay all sales tax, tariffs, duties and other taxes applicable to Licensee's performance under this Agreement.

6. General.

6.1 <u>Modification</u>. No amendment or modification of this Agreement shall be valid or binding on the parties unless made in writing and signed on behalf of both of the parties by their respective duly authorized officers or representatives.

6.2 <u>Assignment</u>. Licensee may not assign this agreement without the prior written consent of Valve. Subject to the limitations set forth in this Agreement, this Agreement will inure to the benefit of and be binding upon the parties, their successors and assigns.

6.3 <u>Severability</u>. If any provision of this Agreement shall be held by a court of competent jurisdiction to be illegal, invalid or unenforceable, the remaining provisions shall remain in full force and effect.

6.4 <u>Governing Law, Jurisdiction and Venue</u>. This Agreement shall be governed by the laws of the State of Washington. Each of the parties hereto submits to jurisdiction and venue in the state and federal courts sitting in King County, Washington.

6.5 <u>Entire Agreement</u>. This Agreement constitutes the entire understanding between the parties hereto and supersedes all previous communications, representations and understandings, oral or written, between the parties, with respect to the subject matter of this Agreement. Sierra is an intended third party beneficiary of this Agreement.

IN WITNESS WHEREOF, the parties have executed this Agreement on the date herein above indicated.

Valve, L.L.C. _____(Licensee Name)

Signature_____   Signature _____

Name _____   Name _____

Title _____   Title _____

Date_____   Date _____

Email _____

CHAPTER 6

THE PUBLISHING CONTRACT

The Publishing Contract in Action

Dana has been pounding the pavement at conferences and trade shows since March, meeting with publishing-side producers from her days at Defunct as well as anyone else she thinks might be able to help Double D. The pitches go well; everyone seems comfortable knowing that the team has worked together before and has shipped product together. The prototype crashes twice, but the publishing executives don't seem to mind. They are very appreciative of her, game sell sheet and "business plan," and more than one product development staffer told her "Wow. This makes my life a *lot* easier." Pending due diligence examination, Double D ends up with three indications of interest:

1. Publisher A likes the property and has confidence in the team's ability to execute, offering the full budgeted amount but insisting on outright ownership of the intellectual property for the content.

2. Publisher B is impressed by the prototype and the team and wants to hire Double D immediately to develop a reasonably interesting license that B has recently acquired.

3. Publisher C, unbeknownst to Dana, is strapped for cash and needs to fill a revenue hole in its fourth quarter 2005. It likes Double D's story and feels that the development team is low-risk thanks to its experience at Defunct. It can't offer Double D the full production budget Dana is asking for, but it's willing to let Double D hang onto the entertainment and merchandise rights to the property (subject to sharing 40 percent of the revenue with Publisher C) if it will develop the game for 30 percent less than its current budget.

The founders talk over the offers. Publisher A's offer is persuasive because it would allow the company to get onto a solid financial footing and to produce the game they want to build. At the same time, it is heartbreaking to think of their story becoming the property of another party, even if Double D does get a share of any revenue.

There is some talk of taking Publisher B's offer as a way of establishing a solid reputation and relationship with a publisher and pitching their game again in a year and half, but Pat asks the group: "Why not just take jobs with other developers if we're going to be doing someone else's idea?" Alex replies: "So we can live in Podunk and won't have to relocate?" Pat admits that this is sound logic, but Publisher A still seems preferable to Publisher B.

The group spends the most amount of time analyzing Publisher C's offer. Everyone likes the idea of hanging onto ownership of the property, but Dusty mentions rumors going around that Publisher C has been having trouble paying milestones. The team believes that they would be able to build a good game for 30 percent less than the original budget, but it wouldn't leave much margin for error or lag in finding their next project.

Ultimately, the group leans toward Publisher C, and calls its game attorney, Lucy Wright, to discuss concerns. Lucy warns them that there is not a whole lot that can be done if the publisher starts paying milestones late and that she, too, has heard the rumors about Publisher C's financial issues. Lucy also notes that maybe Publisher A would be amenable to a long term exclusive license to all rights instead of ownership of the property, so that Double D may negotiate for reversion of some rights if not used after a certain period of time. Lucy also warns Double D that it doesn't want to cut too lean a deal for Publisher A. If Publisher A has a choice between putting marketing dollars behind a property it owns versus a property it doesn't own, it is likely to give short shrift to a property owned by someone else. Therefore, it is very important to negotiate a deal where Publisher A has functional ownership of the property as long as it is using it. Double D decides to have Lucy call Publisher A and discuss the possibility of a long-term license.

Lucy has a good reputation with Publisher A, which helps the discussion go smoothly. Publisher A agrees that, as long as it keeps exclusive rights for the duration of its use of the property, a long-term license with reversions will be acceptable. Double D is double-delighted, and has Lucy negotiate a license. See end of chapter.

INTRODUCTION

A publishing contract is an agreement between a publisher and a developer that spells out the terms of the working relationship. What work will you perform? What will be paid and how? When will it be paid? Who owns your work? What happens if something goes wrong?

Because these contracts are complex and there are many eventualities that must be accounted for, negotiating and drafting the full agreement can take months. To avoid such a long delay in production, the publisher and developer may sign a *short form agreement* (sometimes referred to as a *letter of intent, memo of understanding, deal memo*). This short (two to seven pages), legally binding contract sets out the core terms of the contract and is then used as the basis for a *long form agreement*, which will include all of the details.

This chapter will familiarize you with the following:

- Terms and concepts found in AAA publishing agreements, whether for original or licensed IP
- Deal terms that are most favorable to the publisher and those that favor you
- Negotiation techniques in situations of minimal leverage
- Hidden pitfalls and common errors

The publishing contract will be analyzed in three parts:

- Terms of a straight work-for-hire agreement (where developer owns neither the content nor the engine)
- A publishing contract/license for developer-owned intellectual property (content and/or technology)
- Clauses added into the long forms of most contracts

The author would like to thank Kirk Owen of Octagon Entertainment (www.octagon1.com) for his help in preparing this chapter.

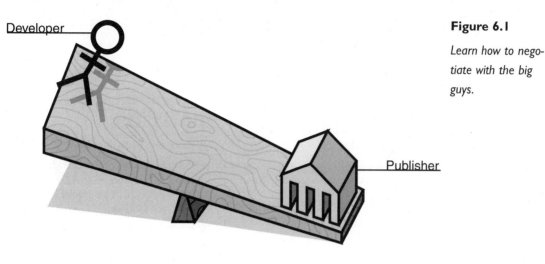

Figure 6.1

Learn how to nego-tiate with the big guys.

Developer

Publisher

Sometimes developers feel like they don't have much leverage.

LONG-FORM VERSUS SHORT-FORM

If your business is at the point where the deal has moved from the publisher's acquisitions staff to the legal department, you likely have two primary concerns:

1. Getting the deal done quickly so that you can get the cash advance; and
2. Getting the deal done correctly, so that you don't end up hamstrung down the road.

Deals fall apart sometimes, too, and it's best to find this out as soon as possible, since odds are you'll be dedicating team resources before you have a contract in place.

Rather than negotiate the entire contract in one fell swoop, which could delay the start of work (and receipt of advances), many publishers and developers negotiate a short form of their contract first.

The publisher and developer sign the short form contract, which creates a set of legal obligations on both parties (for example, what royalty rate will be paid for the game). This document is then fleshed out into a long-form agree-ment, which goes into more detail on terms that are very important but not crucial to the initial stages of work, such as audit rights. The short form is a binding contract,

> **NOTE**
> This document should be titled "Short Form Binding Agreement" or something of that ilk and *not* "Letter of Intent," because the latter may be interpreted as non-binding.

so if you and your publisher never get to the long form stage, there is still a valid contract in place setting out the basic rules of the relationship.

The short form is a great tool for developers for several reasons:

- It allows them to manage cash flow responsibly.
- Initial advances are received once the short form is signed, rather than having to wait until the long form is complete.
- It avoids the risk (and diminished negotiating position) of fronting money and devoting team resources to the project before a contract is in place.
- By vetting most of the "deal-breaker" issues early on, a short form helps avoid the unhappy situation of beginning work only to have the deal fall apart.

> **CAUTION**
> Because it is binding, it is crucial that you obtain counsel when negotiating the short form. There is little going back on terms agreed to in the short form, so don't rush to the signature line thinking that you'll go back and renegotiate later.

TIPS FOR READING AND NEGOTIATING A CONTRACT

- Hire an experienced lawyer.
- Know the basics of contract structure.
- Read the contract. *All* of it.
- Itemize every point that needs discussion before you begin negotiations.
- Size up the publisher.
- Talk about the project's needs, not your needs.
- Maintain parity.

Hire an Experienced Lawyer

The lawyer you hire to negotiate your contract should be someone with game industry experience negotiating this kind of contract on behalf of developers. These are highly specific, complex contracts, and having your general business lawyer, or your cousin-who's-a-lawyer, read and negotiate your contract can be like asking a heart surgeon to operate on your brain. Aside from knowing the ins and outs of the contracts, an experienced attorney will have relationships with the *counterparties* (see definition in the next paragraph) and an idea of what you can and can't ask for from a given publisher(royalty rates, term, net sales definitions, etc.).

Know the Basics of Contract Structure

Contracts, as a genre, have a couple of stylistic peculiarities worth knowing about.

Parties. A *party* is any entity that will be bound by the contract, usually just the entities signing the agreement. A *counterparty* is usually the entity with whom you are negotiating ("the other side") on a given agreement and can refer to either party, depending on context. Generally, the counterparty to the developer is the publisher, and the publisher's counterparty is the developer.

Defined Terms. If you see a word capitalized in the middle of a sentence, understand that it is a *defined term*, meaning that it has been given a very specific definition earlier in the document. By referring to the defined term—which is always capitalized—like Game or Net Sales, the contract can be shortened by establishing the meaning of the word as the parties understand it and referencing that specific meaning. Some contracts will have a long section in the front, like a glossary, that sets out all defined terms. Other contracts have the definitions interspersed throughout.

> **NOTE**
>
> Understanding defined terms is crucial to reading and negotiating contracts, and misunderstanding them is the cause of much legal woe. Do not assume that the meaning you normally ascribe to a term is the meaning contained in the capitalized expression. When reading a contract clause, if you come across a defined term, don't rely on your memory. Go back to the definition and read it through, then finish reading the paragraph. You may find that the defined term is not specific enough or that the definition needs to be modified.

Exhibits/Appendices. These terms are roughly synonymous and refer to any documents or agreements that are also a part of the main contract, but which are separated out and added on for convenience. Often a publisher's NDA will be attached as an appendix for you to sign. Another common use of the exhibit is to add specificity to a standard contract. If a company does a lot of the same transaction, with minimal variation, it may create a standard *boilerplate* contract and add an exhibit that states all of the specific terms (like royalty rate, intellectual property, platforms, and so forth). This is not likely to be the format of a AAA contract, but it is good to be familiar with the structure.

Read the Contract. *All* of It

Read it cover to cover. There is no substitute for knowing every last inch of your contract. It is valuable learning for your next negotiation, and I believe you cannot be a confident businessperson without a solid understanding of your main contracts. Contracts make the eyes glaze over—

this is natural—but an ounce of diligence is worth a pound of cure. If you are relatively new to the experience, don't try to read it all in one sitting the first time. Read it slowly and carefully, especially the long paragraphs with lots and lots of commas—the lists are where landmines can be buried. Eventually, you and your partners will need to read it all through at the same time to look for consistencies and inconsistencies.

> **TIP**
>
> Attorneys are not compilers: even the best, most experienced attorney occasionally misses a point, and our favorite clients are the ones who pipe up with a "Hey, what about…."

Itemize and Prioritize

Itemize every point that you want to address before beginning negotiations. Then, prioritize that list so that you can adjust your negotiating strategy if needed.

> **CAUTION**
>
> Seek legal help before you get back to the publisher. Nothing is more irritating to a counterparty than negotiating a set of issues, thinking you've come up with a balanced solution, and then hearing, "oh, wait—we also need you to change x, y, and z." Even when done out of genuine ignorance, it feels like a bad-faith effort to squeeze out a few more concessions and you will find more resistance than had you brought the topics up earlier.

> **TIP**
>
> Sometimes, the gains that you might make from addressing every last little point are cancelled out by the bad taste a drawn-out negotiation can leave in a publisher's mouth. Prioritize carefully, and use judgment in knowing when it's time to forego a couple of points for the greater good of the relationship.

Size Up the Publisher

If you're about to dedicate a chunk of your company (and, let's be serious—your life) to a project for the next couple of years, ask a few questions to see if the fit is a good one. If you are a new developer or have a team coming to the end of a project, the temptation can be great to hop into bed with the first six-figure advance that comes along. Where possible—and practical cash management means that it is not always possible—take the time to kick your publisher's tires. A few topics to consider:

- What is the financial condition of the publisher? You can research this by buying credit reports and/or contacting developers with whom it is currently working to see what the publisher's payment pattern is like.
- Does the publisher have a track record in the genre and platform?
- With whom will you be working during production? Marketing? What kind of experience do the production and marketing personnel have with this kind of release? How many other projects are they working on? How close is your release date to the release date of their other projects? One developer had this to say: "I'd sooner take an experienced producer with three other games than have a newbie's undivided attention."
- To how many platforms will the publisher commit for release? (*Commit* means rights revert on a platform by platform basis if minimums aren't met.) All at initial? Or will they be staggered? What will be the development budget for each platform? Will there be a common engine? If so, who will develop it?
- Who does the publisher see as the target audience for your game? What are their plans for reaching that consumer? What kind of marketing commitment is the publisher looking to make? This can be stated as a fixed number or as a percentage of sales, with a fixed minimum.
- What is the distribution strategy, by platform? How much time will you have in the retail channel before getting moved to budget? This window can be brutally short.
- What is the publisher's international release strategy? How many countries and localizations? Do they have distribution in those territories, or will they be sub-licensing to a local publisher or engage a third party distributor?
- What are their projected sales for your title? Price point for each platform?

Maintain Parity

To maintain parity, the discussion should be between two decision-makers or two intermediaries, not an intermediary on one side and a decision-maker on the other. The latter scenario often results in the present decision-maker giving a lot more concessions than he'd like.

A contract is a lot like a massive soundboard, with every provision represented by a sliding toggle. The toggle runs from one extreme (most favorable to the publisher) to the other (most favorable to the developer). Slide every toggle to the top, and the sound is horribly distorted; slide them all to the bottom, and no one can hear the music. The goal is a permutation of toggle positions that produces a smooth, equalized sound. In the next section, I will explain the different provisions of a typical publishing contract and give an idea of the toggle positions for each.

Work for Hire Publishing Agreement

When you are creating a game based on an intellectual property provided by the publisher and the game will not use your proprietary technology, the development is considered a work for hire development/publishing agreement. These deals are often simpler, because the parties do not need to figure out ownership and sharing of intellectual property. They are also usually less lucrative for you because the publisher must pay the *licensor* (the party who owns the rights) a *license fee* in the case of a technology and/or a *rights fee* (compensation for making a product based on an intellectual property like a character or story), the latter of which will almost assuredly include some *back-end participation* (a share of the profits, usually a percentage, much like royalties).

Time

Always be aware of time. What is the effective date of the agreement? Are the milestone dates subject to change if the agreement takes longer than anticipated? Watch the start date for all time periods. Be sure that every decision has a time limit on it—sequels, approvals, and so forth. Otherwise you could end up in limbo, with one party having a right with no end date on it and no clear intention of using that right. The goal of a contract should be for clarity and definition, and every decision should have a time limit.

Parties

Do you know the correct, complete names of the legal entities entering into the agreement? This is important because some companies have a confusing structure of similarly named subsidiaries, and only the signatory is legally bound by the contract. Careless naming of parties can result in a toothless contract, because the party that you want to obligate is not a signatory.

Property

If the contract is a work for hire, this section is where the publisher describes the content intellectual property with which you will be working (such as "Spiderman"). It is important to carefully understand the *"four corners"* (the boundaries) of the property, because one property can have many different incarnations, only some of which the publisher is licensing. Example: the recent Spiderman

TIP

If you are working on a *day and date release* (where the game release is scheduled to coincide with the release of a product like a film or DVD), find out what kind of access to production assets (story lines, art, backgrounds) the publisher is negotiating with the producer. Smooth transfer of assets will often speed game development and create synchronicity between the two releases.

game would use assets and story lines from the recent Spiderman film, not from the live-action Spiderman TV show of the early eighties.

Additions to the property

Frequently, the licensor will include language stating that any additions a licensee makes (say, a new weapon) are granted back to the owner and become part of the property; other times, the licensor will co-own additions with the creator.

Term

The term defines the duration of the parties' different rights. Terms are usually broken out into *Initial Terms* and *Renewal Terms*. The initial term covers development and commercial release of the game, and the renewal term kicks in if the relationship meets certain conditions, for example, if the game is successful and the parties develop a sequel together. Term considerations are discussed more fully in the section below on Developer-owned IP Publishing Contracts.

Territory

Territory determines the area for which a publisher is purchasing rights. In a work for hire, the publisher will most likely take a worldwide exclusive license, in other words, the right to manufacture and distribute the game worldwide. However, if you are extremely enterprising and want to pursue distribution in areas the publisher does not, you will want to negotiate either to keep rights to territories for which the publisher has no release plans, or for a territory-by-territory *reversion* (rights that are granted return to the grantor) if the publisher is not distributing product in the given territory.

Development Fees

A standard compensation arrangement will be broken out into two or more tiers, depending on whether it is your IP being licensed or you are doing a work-for-hire. The first tier is the development fee/advance against royalties, paid out over the duration of development; the second tier is royalties after *earn-out* (defined in Royalties, this section); and the third is *ancillary products revenue*, money earned from the sale of merchandise related to the game like strategy guides.

Tier One: Development Fee/Advance Against Royalties

The first tier is the development fee/advance against royalties. This is what you will receive over the period of development to cover costs. You will want to be sure that the development advance is non-refundable. The typical structure is 20 percent at signature, 10 percent at gold master, and the remaining 70 percent spread out over ten or so milestones. No milestone = no milestone payment, so schedule yourself realistically or you'll end up late and lacking the money necessary to complete the milestone. Don't assume that the publisher will jump in with more money to protect its investment: Sometimes a publisher will see this as throwing good money after bad and will terminate the project; other times, it may require additional compensation in exchange for additional funding.

> **TIP**
>
> **To protect yourself, assume that the publisher will not pay milestones in a timely manner and build a cash cushion sufficient to weather significant delays.**

> **CAUTION**
>
> **Be extremely careful when budgeting and pricing your development contract. Many developers add a margin to their budgets and end up spending all the padding *and* never receiving royalties. Remember: odds are very high that you will not receive any royalties on a game, so plan accordingly and be willing to cut features to stay on time and within budget.**

Tier Two: Royalties

Royalties are a percentage of the publisher's sales payable to you. The balls to keep your eye on when discussing royalties are

- Recouping/Earn-out process. How much money the publisher must earn before it begins sharing royalties with you.
- Cross-collateralization. Whether the publisher can apply revenues from one SKU to the costs of another. Example: can the publisher use your share of ancillary products revenue to recover costs of developing the game?
- Royalty rates for each category. The percentage you will receive for different platforms, products, and methods of distribution.
- Definitions of "Gross" and "Net." How big (or small) is the pie you'll be getting a slice of.

> **TIP**
>
> **It is wise to have the publisher include a sample royalty statement as an appendix to the contract, and be sure it includes the number of units manufactured, the number sold, and the wholesale price. A sample royalty statement is included at the end of this chapter.**

Recouping

The publishing company will want to "recoup" some or all of the development fee from royalties payable on the game (or other products—see the discussion of cross-collateralization in this section) before it begins making royalty payments to you. *Earn-out* the point at which the publisher begins paying royalties.

The three main schemes for recouping the development fee are

1. Recouping the fee from net sales at developer's royalty rate (most favorable to the publisher)
2. Recouping the fee from total net sales (most favorable to you)
3. Recouping the fee from net sales at developer's royalty rate minus X percent and paying developer X percent from unit one (a valid compromise, but a very uncommon arrangement)

Here's an amusingly lowball example: Assume the royalty rate is 10 percent of net sales, the publisher makes $10 in net sales per unit, and the development fee was $100,000. $1 (10 percent of $10) of every unit sold goes toward repaying the development fee; you will begin receiving royalties after sales of 100,000 units (barring other income from ancillary products). You won't like this setup since the publisher would break even and be long into the black before sharing any money with you.

You will want the publisher to begin paying royalties after break-even, once net sales (see discussion below) exceed the development fee (in other words 10,000 units).

TIP

When negotiating, you should expect a trade-off between the advance and the royalty rate. If your advance is higher, your royalty rate will be lower, and vice versa. There is a risk balance between you and the publisher: up-front money is high risk for the publisher, low risk for the developer; back-end compensation is the reverse. Some developers with a cash cushion and confidence in their product prefer the higher royalty rate, assuming they can negotiate a favorable definition of net sales; many other developers prefer the lower risk, guaranteed return, and ready money of the higher advance. Take a look at the expected release window: is the game going out during the competitive, but lucrative Christmas season? Or will it be part of the dreaded August release? A low royalty rate not only means that you will ultimately earn less revenue, you will also have to sell more units to recoup.

Another approach may be available in situations of lower risk to the publisher (such as where you have self-funded or partially-funded) that will not increase your ultimate revenue but does reduce your risk and provide more even cash flow. You can negotiate for a proportion of the royalty from unit one to go toward repaying the development fee and the rest to be paid to you currently. Using the above example, if the developer negotiates to receive 25 percent of its royalty rate starting with unit one sales, then $.75 of every unit sold would go toward recoupment, and $.25 would go to the developer until unit 133,334, at which point the developer would receive $1 from every unit. So the earn-out is pushed back, but the developer will still earn some royalties even if the game sells only 100,000 units.

Cross-Collateralization

Cross-collateralization means that the publisher can recoup development advances from more than one *SKU* (retail term meaning "stock-keeping unit;" each platform is considered a separate SKU) or category. Some publishers will want to cross-collateralize every revenue stream from you against every contract it has with you. So, for instance, royalties from a game done with a publisher now can be withheld to repay any unrecouped advances from a contract ten years earlier. You will want to keep the fictional third party in mind when arguing for limiting cross collateralization to:

- **Platform by platform**, so that a profitable Xbox SKU will not be used to subsidize an unprofitable Gamecube SKU, and the U.S. release will not be cross-collateralized with the Chinese localization.
- **Simultaneous releases**, for example sequels, will not be cross-collateralized against the original.
- **Games only**. In other words, the publisher cannot cross-collateralize across categories like ancillary products or revenue from the licensing developer's IP, whether technology or *entertainment* (other media, such as a film or soundtrack, based on the same property).

> **TIP**
>
> A developer can resist platform by platform cross-collateralization by arguing that if a third party developed the port or localization, the publisher would not be able to wait to pay royalties until it had recouped development fees for the original game.

> **TIP**
>
> A developer can argue that if a third party developed the sequel, the publisher would not be able to wait to pay royalties to that third party until the publisher recouped development fees for the original game.

> **NOTE**
>
> This is crucial when you own the content intellectual property. You can resist cross-collateralization from entertainment based on your IP by arguing that if the publisher had purchased, for example, film rights from a third party, it would not be able to withhold royalties from that licensor until the publisher had recouped development fees.
>
> If, for instance, a publisher purchases the rights to make games and other entertainment based on a popular card RPG and then *sublicenses* the right to make a film to a third party, the publisher will most likely have to share revenue with the card RPG licensor from the first dollar that the publisher receives from the film producer. The publisher would probably *not* be able to recoup its game development costs before paying the card RPG licensor for film-related revenue. Therefore, when the developer is also the licensor, the publisher will be no worse off than if it had licensed the property from a third party (like a card RPG licensor) if it does not recoup development costs before paying license revenues to the developer. For more on this topic, see Chapter 7: "Licensing."

Royalty Rates

The royalty rate paid to a developer varies significantly based on reputation, platform, whether it is developing its own content, and the size and leverage of the publisher. Some publishers like to grant a flat amount per unit sold, which can put your heart at ease over accounting chicanery (see net sales discussion, below), but the percentage of net sales is more common. Wherever the

> **NOTE**
>
> Given the hit-driven nature of the game business, be prepared for your publisher to actually try to *reduce* the royalty rate as sales go up, with the reasoning that 1) the developer is incurring no additional cost and is making a fair return even at a lower royalty rate, and 2) hits are what keep publishers in business so they need to capture as much revenue as possible from the hits in order to finance the games that fail. Your response to this should be 1) that a developer's business model relies on extra revenue from hits to cover the games that never earn-out, and 2) the publisher's share of net sales is already significant enough to cover its risk.

royalty rate begins, you will want to share in any success of the title, and most publishers are happy to grant royalty escalations based on units sold. The points of negotiation will be the thresholds for escalated royalties and the amount of the escalation. Rates will also vary by medium and category.

Example:

Consoles

8-20% 1-300/500k

10-22% 3/500-750/1mm

12-24% 750/1mm - 1mm/1.5mm

14-26% 1.5mm and up

PC

Some developers argue that they should receive a higher royalty for PC games because the publisher does not have to pay any license fees to the console manufacturer.

Handheld

5-8%

PDA and Wireless

This area is still developing, but the developer should receive a share of any revenue generated by PDA or wireless game distribution.

Online Multiplayer, Digital Distribution, and Subscriptions

This area is still developing, but developers should receive a share of revenue generated by subscription services using their content. Developers are arguing that they should receive higher royalties for digital distribution of games given the reduced cost of distribution.

Ancillary Products

25-50% of Net Sales or Net Receipts (see sections in this chapter)

Entertainment

25-60% of Net Receipts (see section in this chapter)

The publisher will want to reduce royalty rates in the following situations:

- The wholesale price drops below a price point specified in the contract [expect no royalties for units given away or sold at less than the publisher's actual cost of goods sold ("COGS")].
- For follow-on games developed by a third party.

Figure 6.2

Revenue from online game play is playing an increasing role in the industry.

NOTE

You will, in effect, receive a lower royalty rate for games sublicensed for publication by third parties (generally in territories where the publisher does not have a strong network) because the publisher will itself be receiving a royalty from the third-party publisher, leaving the developer with the same slice of a smaller pie. (See Sidebar: It's Not Really a Small World, After All). You may want to handle this by having two royalty structures, one for markets in which the publisher distributes the product and another for markets where the publisher sublicenses the product.

It's Not Really a Small World, After All

Selling games around the world is a complex process. Even the giant publishers lack an extensive global presence, and will often sublicense game rights to local publishers by *territory* (usually a country) or *region* (a geographically and commercially cohesive group of countries, like "Europe" or "Southeast Asia").

Your international concerns will be fourfold:

■ Guaranteeing a minimum royalty rate in case of sublicensing

■ Registering intellectual property worldwide

■ Anti-piracy and enforcement

■ Proper localization of the game by the publisher

If the publisher sublicenses the game in a given territory, it must compensate the regional publisher with a chunk of royalties. Your royalty on these products will be reduced to reflect this cost. Some developers therefore negotiate one royalty rate for territories where the publisher has direct distribution and a higher rate or minimum per-unit royalty in territories where the game will be sublicensed.

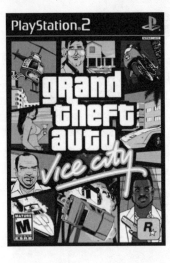

Figure 6.3

The gaming juggernaut.

TIP

Keep the cost of sublicensing in mind when selecting a publisher and negotiating the territory of a contract. It may not make sense to grant worldwide rights to a publisher with distribution in North America only.

Definitions of Gross and Net Sales

The publisher will want to deduct certain expenses from revenue received in connection with the game (or licensing products and entertainment). Just as the publisher recoups its cash outlays for development of the game, it will want to recoup certain cash outlays for selling the game. Which of these outlays are fair to recoup and which are not is the subject of negotiation between parties. Getting from "gross" to "net" refers to the set of expenses deducted to arrive at the *royalty base,* the number from which you will receive your royalty percentage.

Figure 6.4

With the spiraling costs of development, publishers look to safe, established brands for licenses.

CAUTION

This is one of the most important sections of the contract. If you get a great royalty rate, but neglect to pay attention to the deductions allowed, you will make significantly less money than had you received a lower rate on a higher base.

Gross Sales

For games you will want the gross to include all games sold and not returned. For entertainment/merchandise you will want the gross to include all licensing fees and revenues received by the publisher, its subsidiaries, partners, affiliates, and sublicensees, including barter. The interrelation of entertainment conglomerates makes the cast of *Deliverance* look like models of genetic hygiene. Including the value of barter will prevent situations where, for example, the publisher receives millions of dollars in advertising time on the network that happens to own the production company that licensed the live action TV show rights to your game.

Net Sales

The publisher will want to deduct as much as possible from gross sales to get to net, because this minimizes payable royalties. Of course, you want to limit the deductions to non-overhead cash expenditures actually paid to unaffiliated third parties. The core deductions are: reserves, credits, returns, mark downs, lost and damaged goods, write-offs, allowances, promotional units, and rebates.

> **NOTE**
> Where the publisher will be sublicensing game production to another publisher (in another territory, for instance), most of the deductions listed here will already be taken out of the royalty received by the publisher and should not be deducted again from the publisher's receipts. (See Sidebar: It's Not Such a Small World, After All.)

- Credits. Refunds issued by the publisher to the distributor.
- Return reserve allowance of 10 to 20 percent (liquidated after two periods or 180 days, whichever is shorter). When a publisher sells product to a distributor, some of the product usually comes back if it doesn't sell through in retail. However, a publisher does not know what portion will come back until some time later, usually a few months. To protect against paying a royalty to you for items that are later returned, the publisher will maintain a *return reserve allowance*. Essentially, the publisher will set aside 20 percent of the revenue from a given period and not pay royalties on it until enough time has elapsed that the publisher is comfortable that any returns from that period have come back. Example: A publisher who maintains a 20 percent return reserve allowance for 120 days sells 100 games to the distributor in January. It will pay you royalties on 80 games. Four months later, the publisher will look to see how many of the games sold in January have been returned. If only five games were returned, the publisher will *liquidate* the January reserve and pay you royalties on the allowance less actual returns (20-5=15).
- Returns. If, on the other hand, the number of returns exceeds the allowance, the publisher will want to deduct those units from any royalties it may owe.
- A commercially reasonable number of promotional units/rebates. Publishers will send out a certain number of free copies of the game—to the press, to retailers and distribu-

tors, anyone it wants to sell the game—to help market the game. Sometimes a rebate will be offered on sales of the game. A developer will want some kind of a cap on the number of promotional units a publisher can give away.

■ Lost and damaged goods and write-offs.

A publisher may want to add on other deductions for

■ Cooperative advertising and MDF funds. Cooperative advertising is funded by several groups in an industry to advertise together. MDF is short for market development funds, which is money paid to retailers to secure shelf space, *end caps* (the high-visibility displays at the ends of aisles), and advertising (in circulars, for example).

■ Cost of goods sold. All costs that the publisher puts into the finished product, from manufacturing to packaging and license fees.

■ Manufacturer's platform royalties. The publisher must pay a royalty to the owner of proprietary platforms (like Sony for the PS2 or Nintendo for the GameBoy) for every game sold. This is how console manufacturers earn their profits—they generally lose money on the R&D and manufacture of the consoles, but make money through the royalties publishers pay to create games for the platform.

■ Price of name talent in association with a licensed property. If your company is doing a licensed game for a movie, for example, and the publisher insists that you use the voices of the film's actors, the publisher will want that to be considered a development cost.

■ Sales taxes and VAT. VAT is *value-added tax*, a tax imposed by many countries on all finished goods. Some people think it's how Canada prevents more Americans from moving there.

■ Shipping charges. If these are included, a developer will at least want to limit the deduction to charges actually paid to unaffiliated third parties (alternatively, limit shipping and handling not to exceed $X).

■ Imputed fees for publisher assets and services. If a publisher wants to use its own assets to further the game, whether in-house attorneys and licensing staff to an engine, it may want to charge you an *imputed* fee for these items. Imputed means that there is no itemizable cost to point to, but there is value being exchanged that should be recognized and compensated.

> ## TIP
>
> A developer's strongest argument against most of these expenses is that they are the publisher's overhead and that all overhead is covered by the (100 percent-developer's royalty) percentage the publisher receives. Shared deductions are intended to protect the publisher against its actual risks and costs associated with your game. You may want to try and limit the amount of these expenditures by requiring the publisher to provide you with timely documentation of the money spent.

Sequels

Sequels are closely related to any discussion of the term because they act as extensions. Sequel rights can prolong a relationship, so it is wise to build in assurances that the extension will benefit both parties. In a work for hire, the sequel rights at issue are usually for the

> **TIP**
>
> Create a cap, whether in hours or otherwise, on the amount and kind of support provided.

right to be the development house on any sequels. This is usually included as a *right of first negotiation* or a *right of last refusal*. If the original developer does not want to work on the sequel, the publisher may want some kind of follow-up support for any third-party developers.

Right of First Negotiation and Right of Last Refusal

These rights are essentially what they sound like: the right to be the first party negotiated with and the right to be presented with and have the opportunity to match the final offer from all other parties.

It doesn't make much sense to negotiate the terms of a sequel development deal before the initial game is even complete, especially since gaming hardware changes so much and long-term contracts can saddle you with obligations that become impractical, if not impossible. Beyond the usual language of "will negotiate in good faith," developers are usually granted a right of first negotiation. This means that the publisher must negotiate with you for a certain period (usually 30 days) to develop the project. If you and your publisher cannot come to an agreement for the sequel, the publisher may pursue another developer, but may not cut a deal with that developer that is any sweeter than the one offered to you.

The right of last refusal states that any agreement the publisher comes to with a third party must be offered back to you for *X* number of days before the publisher proceeds with that third party.

While these rights seem innocuous enough, they can bite in two ways: delay and chilling negotiations with outsiders. A right of first negotiation must expire before the parties can look elsewhere, causing a delay of at least thirty days should no agreement be made. A right of last refusal hanging over a property will make third parties wary of negotiating, since they know that their terms will be shopped back to the last refusal rights holder.

> **TIP**
>
> The right of last refusal is a bit more airtight that the right of first negotiation, because definitions of "sweeter" vary; example: if the second developer's contract gives it a higher development fee but a lower royalty and no sequel rights, is that a sweeter deal?

NOTE

Notice is very important for follow-on developments. Timing cash flow and resource commitment is everything to a developer, so you will want to do everything you can to avoid a situation where you need work to begin as soon as possible on a sequel when you have just committed a team to another project. The best way to work this out is to agree on a notice "deadline," perhaps 90 days following the initial commercial release of the game, during which the publisher can interpret the sales data and decide if it wants to do a sequel. Another option is for the publisher to give you a heads-up period (90 days, for example) that would enable you to organize resources for the project. Do beware: many publishers are nervous about the reliability and functionality of rapidly staffed teams and may shy away from the latter scenario.

Development Procedures

The contract should specify not just what you will be delivering (milestones), but how you will be delivering it, how it will be accepted, what changes to the milestones are acceptable, and what happens when milestones are late. Will the publisher be delivering any development kits? At whose expense (usually the publisher's) and when? (Tardy development kits can lead to missed milestones.) The first milestone should be signing the short form contract, and the last is usually delivery of the gold master. As for pricing the contract, you will want to factor in as wide a margin of error as possible and to isolate as many unpredictable costs (cost of third-party licenses, name actors or vocal talent required by the publisher or over which the publisher has approval, and any other costs over which you have no control) by stating that the milestone advance amounts will be $X—plus the cost of those items to be jointly approved, or that the publisher will cover those costs for all publisher-mandated content. Remember when drafting the milestone schedule: publishers who need to deliver products in very particular retail or quarterly income windows prize a developer with a reputation for being on time.

Milestone Definitions

While the nature of game development means that milestone definitions must be somewhat elastic, many developers and publishers cite lack of clarity in milestone definitions (and the resulting mismatched expectations) as a common cause of friction.

TIP

To improve the quality of milestone definitions and project planning, many contracts make the first milestone the setting of the milestones for the entire project.

Example: "Level two characters in" means to you that the art assets will be complete and rendered, but not fully functioning, while the publisher is expecting to see the characters fully integrated and finished.

It is also useful to include definitions of core terms like Bug, Alpha, Beta, and Gold.

- A **bug** is one of the following:
  1. A repeatable phenomenon of unintended events or any action occurring during the running of the game rendering it partially or completely nonfunctional
  2. A failure of the game to conform to the design and technical specifications
  3. A detriment to the audiovisual elements or function of the game
  4. The destruction, disruption, or corruption of a data system, storage device, or mechanism
- **Alpha** is a version for which the content and code are complete according to the design and technical specifications submitted, including all features, front-end, intro/endgame sequences, screens, sound/music, with some bugs.
- **Beta** includes all of the alpha definition plus translations from the localization kit, containing some bugs but no known active level "A" bugs (those that will cause the game to crash or freeze).
- **Gold** is the final version of the product delivered on a CD-ROM (specify the number of copies to be delivered) with the complete asset pack including all source code (organized in labeled files), art/cinematic/music files, and all necessary written documentation required so that a programmer of reasonable skill can modify the game if necessary at a later date.

Publisher Acceptance

Once you meet a milestone, the publisher needs a certain amount of time to review it (ten days is sufficient) and either accept or reject it. Set out sufficient grounds for rejection, such as significant deviation from the milestone definition. It is important to establish what creative approval and input the publisher will have: if creative issues are a ground for rejection, set out a baseline so that you don't get a new producer mid-game who "just doesn't like" the previously established creative direction. Any rejection must be accompanied by a detailed set of fixes required for acceptance and a reasonable amount of time for you to make such fixes (30 days). It is reasonable for you to be entitled to two efforts to cure before the publisher can entertain termination.

TIP

For administrative facility, you will want the publisher to specify in the contract one employee (subject to change with written notice from the publisher) with the authority to approve all milestones, and have the publisher send that name to you in writing.

By laying out timelines and grounds for rejection, you can prevent two unpleasant situations:

1. Submitting a milestone on time and not getting paid for three months because the publisher has no acceptance deadline.

2. Having a publisher use arbitrary milestone rejection as a way to terminate a project for convenience while receiving the benefits of termination for cause (see the "Termination and Rights After Termination" section later in this chapter).

> **CAUTION**
>
> It is not uncommon to submit a milestone, have it accepted, and still have to wait for the milestone check. This is a vagary of the industry, and a developer's best defense is solid contract language and careful financial planning.

Modifications

The publisher will want the right to request modifications to the game mid-project. Although a certain amount of give-and-take (also known as "reasonable requests for modification") is to be expected, you will want to avert *feature creep* (where small features get added slowly and end up sinking the project) by stating that any significant modification requests not due to developer error will be accompanied by proportional deadline extensions and advance increases.

> **CAUTION**
>
> It's not always the publisher who is responsible for feature creep; teams can get very excited about a great feature and insist they'll do the overtime to implement it. The development executives can fall into the logic that it's okay to spend more of their own money on the game because they'll make it up in royalties. Be aware that this can lead to two unpleasant realities: first, your developers will likely be putting in overtime just to make the original design spec, and may be burned out by any expansions; and two, any cash cushion that you have put away will get eaten up by an expanding game, which may not generate enough royalties to cover the money you spent on those extra features.

Delay

What if you are late? It has been known to happen, although—as mentioned earlier in this chapter—a developer stands a much better chance of success if it earns a reputation for accurate scheduling. There are a few contractual approaches to the problem, generally a combination of leeway, fines, and termination: one good compromise is to give you a "bank" of late days (10 to 25) to be distributed as you need over the course of the development, with further lateness resulting in fines and/or the publisher's ability to terminate the contract for breach (see the following "Termination" section).

> **TIP**
>
> No matter whose fault the delay is, all parties may suffer from lost opportunities due to missed retail windows. Wherever possible, work with the publisher to compensate for unexpected delays.

> **NOTE**
>
> It is important to distinguish between lateness caused by you and lateness caused by third-party situations, such as the publisher's request for a modification, delay in providing development kits, or problems with third-party vendors chosen by the publisher, such as engine licensors. Only those delays due to developer error should by counted toward the bank of late days.

Third-Party Licenses, Engine/Underlying Technology

More and more developers are using third-party engines, which means a bit of planning is necessary in the way of warranties, indemnifications, and compensation schemes. The engine licensors have prepared their contracts to accommodate publishing a game, and are fairly straightforward.

If you will be licensing any IP from a third party, such as an engine or music or vocal talent, you will need to obtain the right to sublicense that IP and provide proof of any sublicenses to the publisher. You will want to include a provision that any publisher-mandated licenses (for celebrity actors, for instance) will be paid for by the publisher. Although the fees may be recouped in full or in part from your royalties, that is far better than having it come out of your development fees.

Localization

Specify all languages that are to be delivered as part of the guarantee/payments, and dates. The publisher will provide a localization kit (almost always at its own expense) and the date for delivery of this kit must be set—otherwise you could be in breach of milestones through no fault of your own. Provide terms for add-on localizations, for instance, prices for European and non-byte/double-byte languages.

Creative Approvals

A rule of thumb is that the more expensive the license, the tighter the rein a publisher will want on the creative direction. A work-for-hire will be strictly regulated, because the publisher is probably under certain restrictions from its licensor. Even for developer-originated IP, it is to be expected that the publisher will insist on some form of final creative approval for all but the most established developer.

You will want some comfort that your creative team will be able to work in a fashion you find acceptable, so one way to stave off problems without compromising the publisher's needs is to have extensive, documented communication before contracting. You should discuss creative specs with the producer and acquisitions executives to be sure everyone is on the same creative page. Draft a design and technical spec—preferably as a supplement to a playable demo or prototype, which is the best communication of your intent—and include language in the contract that the creative/technical documents have been agreed to by the publisher and that you can expect approval for all elements not significantly deviating from those documents. This helps protect you from mid-project producer changes and other corporate turmoil.

Key Man Clause

Because the publisher is buying access to your talent, it will often ask for a list of key personnel and some assurances that those people will remain at the company for the duration of the development. Should those people leave or move to different projects, the publisher will want certain rights, ranging from the right to be notified to the right to terminate the agreement.

Annotated Source Code

Publishers may ask for annotated source code in an attempt to protect themselves in case another developer is needed to finish the project. Developers fight this clause tooth and nail—and usually win—because annotation is an extremely time-consuming, often futile pursuit (even annotated source code is very difficult for a follow-on developer to pick up).

Options

Talented developers capable of delivering on-time games are very desirable, and the publisher will want the option to continue working with a given developer without the competition that a successful release might create. Therefore, the publisher may request an option or a right of first negotiation/last refusal (see the "Sequels" section in this chapter) for your next title.

Publishing Contract with Developer-Owned IP

Where you will be contributing your own intellectual property, either content or technology, the contract must account for all of the terms discussed in the previous heading as well as many more that require long term, low-probability thinking. The main differences are

1. What happens to the property should the relationship not work out?
2. How much control will each party have over the creation and exploitation of the property?
3. How does the revenue get shared if the property is a huge hit and spawns several other licenses?

For an overview of intellectual property, see Chapter 5, "Intellectual Property." For an overview of licensing, see Chapter 7, "Licensing."

Definition of Property

For a developer-owned intellectual property, here is where the "four corners" of the property being licensed or sold are defined. The precise definition of the rights is crucial for the same reason that giving the address and plot plan of the home you are selling is important. You don't write a contract selling "my house." What if you have more than one home? Furthermore, does that mean you are selling only the house, or the land surrounding the house? And what about the oil that you don't know is underneath the land surrounding the house?

For development using your original content IP, carefully define the copyrights and trademarks available for the game and sequels.

For development using your proprietary technology, a publisher will need certain rights to be able to distribute the game, but beware attempts to gain a royalty-free license to use your technology in unrelated games.

FOR CONTENT

An intellectual property is usually not a discrete entity but rather a set of trademarks and copyrights—for example, the Superman property isn't just the Superman trademark; it's Clark Kent, Lex Luthor, Kryptonite, Smallville, Lois Lane and the other peripheral characters and villains, weapons, story lines, town names and descriptions, etc. that make Superman "Superman." But is the Justice League part of the property? Superman appeared in it, but the holders of the Wonder Woman property would probably be quite irritated if a Superman licensee incorporated her in their work. Of course, this wouldn't happen because any Superman license would be very specific about the characters, and even the manifestations of characters (Dean Cain versus Christopher Reeves versus Hanna-Barbera), weapons, and so forth that a licensee can use. An important negotiating point is who owns the derivative copyrights and other additions to the property made by a licensee (say, a new weapon).

For a new property, the publisher will want to acquire as many rights to as much of the property as possible. Expect language like:

"...The *Newgame* universe created by Devco and owned by Devco, whether now existing or hereafter developed, including without limitation all characters, settings, story lines, designs, weapons, vehicles, costumes, and all trademarks, trade names, copyrights, and any and all other intellectual property rights..."

In other words, the publisher will have rights to every new character, weapon, or story that you develop around *Newgame*.

Subsequent Additions and Developments

A property evolves over time—characters are added, weapons are added, and so forth. Spin-offs can be a huge profit center for franchise properties. Contemplate with the publisher what will happen if three, five, ten years down the line you create new characters, weapons, or scenarios. What if you retain the entertainment rights, and the film licensee creates a new character? Will the publisher have rights to those additions? In which categories? Games only, or entertainment, too? What if the publisher holds the entertainment rights and its TV licensee develops a new character that you want to use in a sequel game? How will the publisher define the property in its sublicenses?

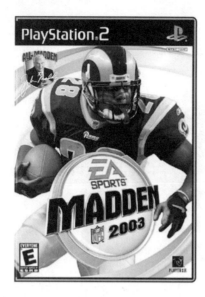

Figure 6.5

EA has created one of the smartest franchises around with its Madden games.

Rights Being Licensed

A "property," as a chunk of content, generally consists of a set of trademarks and copyrights. If the content is yours, expect the structure of the agreement to be a *license*, but be prepared for the publisher to demand to own the property outright.

A license means that you retain "ownership" of the property, and that most copyrights and trademarks (TMs) are registered in the development company's name, but the publisher is granted a license to use certain rights (like making and selling games) for a certain period of time. An *exclusive license* for some rights means that you may not grant those rights to any other parties during the exclusive period of your agreement. As an example, an exclusive license to make games based on your *Newgame* property means that, absent some other provision in the contract, you may not license *Newgame* game rights to any other publisher during the term of the agreement, even if the publisher decides to release the game on only one platform.

Nowadays, it's tough to find a publisher that will risk the money developing and promoting a new property without a lock on other revenue streams, such as film, TV, toys, and T-shirts, that may flow from that property. Break out the different categories of licenses granted, because each should have its own rules in the contract for revenue split, term, what happens after termination, reversion, and more. The four main categories of rights are:

- Games
- Merchandise/Ancillary Products
- Non-software entertainment
- Engine/Underlying Technology

Games

There are two core questions regarding game rights: how many (platforms, languages, and sequels) and how long (duration).

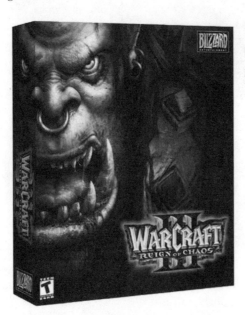

Figure 6.6

Blizzard's crowd pleaser.

HOW MANY?

What platforms are being licensed? You will prefer to give a publisher a license for only those platforms the publisher intends to release, or institute an *option* or *reversion* (see discussion in Options and Reversions Sidebar). Can you publish a port with another publisher? What about a localization in a territory in which the publisher does not intend to release the game? What about wireless, PDA, and other platforms? What about digital distribution and online revenue?

HOW LONG?

Generally, a license is for one game, with the publisher having options for sequels for a certain period or if certain thresholds are met (see the "Sequels, Ports, and Conversions" section later in this chapter).

Merchandise/Ancillary Products

Merchandise and ancillary products include hint books, T-shirts, and other merchandise or derivative products based on *Newgame* as well as *OEM* ("original equipment manufacturer" product, where the game is bundled with hardware or other software as an add-on or an arcade game) but *not* the *Newgame* movie or *Newgame* movie merchandise or what is currently being called non-software entertainment.

Non-Software Entertainment

This includes all filmed, animated, and recorded entertainment based on the property and all merchandise/ancillary products based on those products rather than on the property itself.

What is the difference to the developer between merchandise based on the game and merchandise based on filmed entertainment? Size and timing. Merchandise from other entertainment comes in the form of a smaller slice (for the publisher and, therefore, for you) of a much larger pie. When filmed entertainment is made from a property that you own, the producers and distributors of that entertainment take a chunk out of the merchandise profits before passing it on to the publisher. Profits from merchandise based on entertainment take longer to get to your pocket because there are more middlemen. Where the contract is between the publisher and a merchandising sublicensee, the sublicensee has an accounting period within which to pay the publisher, who then has an accounting period within which to pay you. Tack on a filmed entertainment producer and that adds at least one more accounting period. Ultimately, however, the profit split for the two kinds of merchandise (that based on the game and that based on entertainment) will be roughly the same between you and the publisher.

If you will be granting the publisher the right to sublicense entertainment rights to the property, the core issues to cover include:

- For which media?
- What are acceptable sublicensing arrangements? See discussion in this section as well as Chapter 7, "Licensing."
- What happens if the publisher does not produce any entertainment?
- Is there any difference in the revenue split if you find and initiate the deal?

Engine/Underlying Technology

If you will be making a game with your own pre-existing underlying technology, or developing underlying technology for the game, or using the publisher's technology, issues arise concerning:

- **Ownership (if you will be creating it for the game).** Publishers have been known to assert ownership rights in technology created on their development dime. Developers have also been known to pitch a game with the claim that they can use their pre-existing Technology X, which doesn't quite exist and won't until they get the development advance to fund its creation.

- **Use in other games based on the property.** If you will not be developing a sequel, for example, the publisher may want a royalty-free license to use the technology. While the "royalty-free" part is a concern, the bigger concern is the support that will be required for a new team to try to understand your technology.
- **Use in games not based on the property.** A publisher may want the right to use your technology royalty-free in other games created by other studios. Many developers find this a patently absurd idea, as a publisher wouldn't ask to use the game's content in another product without paying a royalty.
- **Annotation/support requirements.** As a hedge against having to complete the game with another developer, some publishers request that you annotate the code and agree to provide support for any third parties using your technology. This is highly unadvisable and extremely expensive for you in terms of the man-hours that it will cost.
- **Your ability to license it to third parties.** If you create it, you should be able to monetize it. If you are creating the technology with the development fees, your publisher may feel that, as it shares revenue from content licensed to third parties, it should share revenue from technology licensed to third parties.

Term

Where you own the intellectual property, the term is more important because it defines the duration of the publisher's rights to your IP. Without a carefully-written term provision, a developer may technically own the property but be prevented from exploiting it due to rights lingering in the publisher's control.

Options and Reversions

When developing a property, both parties want to ensure that rights stay with the party that values them most. The goal is to allow the publisher to retain rights long enough to reap the rewards of its investment, while giving the developer the ability to take its rights back if the publisher is not exploiting them. Two mechanisms for retaining or obtaining rights are the option and the reversion.

Imagine that you are hungry and have just picked an orange off a tree, but you aren't sure it's edible. Someone comes along and wants to buy some or all of the orange, incorporating uncertainty about the orange's condition into the purchase. If he buys an *option* on the orange, the orange would stay in your hands, and he would pay a certain fee for the right to have the option, after you have peeled the orange and he has tasted it, to buy the fruit. If he buys it subject to reversion, he takes the orange from your hands, paying you outright for the right to the fruit on the inside, but he must give you any part of the orange he can't finish.

Whether the rights are put into an option or a reversion framework is somewhat value-neutral—it is the specific terms of the option or the reversion that make it more or less to the benefit of a given party. Under the option, the rights still belong to the developer, and the publisher has the option to purchase them for a given price and/or subject to certain conditions. Under the reversion, the publisher receives a grant of the rights but can lose those rights if it doesn't meet certain conditions. Giving the publisher a license that reverts back to you if he doesn't use it for one year is a better deal than if you hold on to the rights but the publisher gets an automatic option if sales are greater than $10,000 (a threshold it is almost sure to reach). Low option fees or a lot of successive options can also be counter to a developer's interest: five successive two-year options means that the publisher can pay an option fee every two years to lock up rights for a full ten years.

All things being equal, however, while possession isn't quite 9/10s of the law with intellectual property, there are all sorts of formalities to getting a property back, and the process sometimes gives rise to conflict. Developers will want the publisher to specify some release window in their contract, after which the developer can regain the rights.

Rights commonly subject to reversion/option:

- Platforms
- Languages
- Territories
- Sequels
- Entertainment rights

As a general rule, the more successful a release is, the more rights the publisher receives gratis; frequently, all reversions can be overridden if total royalties from all projects are greater than a pre-specified amount.

Games

The term will likely be either a long grant with reversion, for example, 10 years from the date of signature, reverting to you if property is not exploited or royalties fall below $X for three years in a row, or a short grant with an automatic renewal, for example, five years from the date of signature, automatically renewing for successive three-year terms if earned royalties exceed $Y.

Ancillary Products

This usually runs and ends with the game term, since it is based on products relating to the games.

Entertainment

It is helpful to think of these rights in two chunks: the right to make *new* entertainment and the right to continue receiving money from entertainment already made. While the term will often be stated as "for the life of copyrights and trademarks in the entertainment," there is usually a reversion clause that will send the rights to make new entertainment back to the developer, on a medium-by-medium basis, should the publisher not exploit those rights within a given time period. So a situation may arise under which, 20 years in the future, the publisher and developer still have a relationship surrounding a film made during the term, but the developer is doing a comic book with a separate entity and the publisher has nothing to do with that comic book deal.

Territory

The publisher will want a worldwide exclusive license. You may want territory-by-territory reversion if the publisher is not distributing or adequately localizing your product in the given territory.

Sequels

Sequels are closely related to any discussion of the term because they act as extensions. Sequel rights can prolong a relationship, so it is wise to build in assurances that the extension will benefit both parties. Decide what will trigger the publisher's right to make the sequel. Meeting a certain sales level for the original game? Paying the developer a certain amount of royalties? How many sequels will publisher have rights to? Who will develop the sequel? Odds are, you will want the development contract. What will the royalty structure be?

Reversion

Take care to ensure that your sequel rights come back to you if the publisher decides it isn't interested in publishing a follow-up title. This can be done by giving the publisher an option to pick up sequel rights or granting the publisher so-called *exploding* sequel rights that revert to you after a certain period of time (two to four years after release of the game for which a sequel is being considered). The option may be free (that is., there is no specific option fee) if it is a short window after initial commercial release or is contingent on hitting an earned royalties threshold within a certain number of months following release, or the publisher may buy an option for a set amount of time, say two years after initial release.

Notice

If you want to do the sequel, it is important that the publisher have a quick deadline for deciding whether it wants to exercise its sequel rights; otherwise, by the time the publisher decides it wants to do the sequel, you may be committed to another project.

THIRD-PARTY-DEVELOPED SEQUELS

What if you can't or don't want to develop the sequel to your property? If the publisher hires a third party, a few issues may arise:

ROYALTIES

If the original game is based on your intellectual property, you will receive a license royalty for all sequels and all ancillary products/entertainment based on the sequels. This royalty should be negotiated up front and included in the contract. Be sure that the royalty is based on the same "net" definition as your original royalty.

CONTROL/APPROVALS

A developer probably won't get much in the way of control over sequels done by third parties unless he has a very strong negotiating position. Meaningful consultation is a reasonable request, however, and may be agreed to by the publisher.

DEVELOPER OBLIGATIONS

The publisher may want you to provide follow-up support for any third-party developers. You will want to create a cap on the amount and kind of support you will provide.

Additional Compensation

A developer contributing its own IP to the game usually receives additional compensation in the form of a higher royalty rate and a larger share of derivative products like merchandise and entertainment. Because there are additional parties involved in the production and distribution of these derivative products, getting from "gross" to "net" looks a bit different (see discussion in the "Work for Hire" section).

Usually, the publisher and developer will share what are called "net receipts." Net receipts are all revenue from the licensed products, including barter, less certain expenses. You will want net receipts to be for expenses actually paid to avoid paying for internal expenses such as the in-house attorneys' time spent negotiating a TV deal.

Standard deductions "off the top" of gross receipts are:

- **Agent's commissions.** An entertainment agent usually takes about 10 percent. A merchandise agent will take anywhere from 25 percent to 50 percent.
- **Third-party distribution fees and costs** (which can be as high as 45 percent in territories like Japan); (see discussion of these costs in Chapter 7, "Licensing").
- **Intellectual property registration and enforcement.** The cost of intellectual property enforcement and registration is a surprise for most. The major cost centers are local and international copyright and trademark registration; anti-piracy measures; and suits against infringers. The enforcement/registration costs for the game are often borne by the publisher and recouped off the top of revenue.

Intellectual Property Ownership and Control

There are a lot of property rights to keep track of in a game development deal, particularly if you created the original IP. Most people are accustomed to understanding property rights as a binary: either you own something or you don't. Law students learn to think of ownership as a "bundle of sticks," with each stick representing a certain right in and to the property. Particularly with IP, the sticks can get split down to splinters.

Take the example of television rights. Even that stick gets broken down further into series, mini-series, and movie of the week, and those are subdivided further into live action and animated rights. Aside from the granular definition of a category of use of the property, the terms of its use and duration of that use create even more complexity. If the publisher is granted the use of your engine, will it still have that stick if the contract terminates?

Another way to understand duration rights is to think back to the reversion/option structure. A reversion takes the stick out of the bundle and gives it to the publisher, but it creates another stick for the developer's bundle—the right to reclaim the property should certain events occur or not occur. An option leaves the stick in your bundle but creates one for the publisher's pile—the right to make certain uses of the property should certain events occur or not occur.

How these sticks get divided—for instance, who owns the property and who has a license or exclusive license or reversion—is the subject of intense negotiation. The main goal is to ensure that, no matter what happens between the parties and whether the contract terminates or not, everyone involved will end up with all of the rights they need to receive the benefit of work performed under the contract and to maximize the exploitations of the property.

The four main properties to analyze are

1. Underlying technology
2. Content/the property trademarks and copyrights
3. Game/Product (source and object code and audiovisual assets)
4. Property licensed from third parties (such as engines or vocal talent)

Related Issues

SUBLICENSING RIGHTS

If the IP belongs to you, the publisher will need to be able to *sublicense* property rights to other parties, such as the right to license the game (since software is generally licensed to the end-user, not sold—see discussion in Chapter 5), manufacture and sell merchandise based on the game, or the right to produce and distribute a direct-to-video film based on the game. The publisher can only sublicense those rights you have granted. For more on this topic, see Chapter 7.

This is really an issue of third-party contracting. Let's say a film based on the game is produced. Most likely, it will be the publisher and not you who negotiates and contracts with the producer, distributor, and merchandise agents. If you want to influence decisions made by those parties, you will have to lever the publishing contract. When a publisher has certain restrictions on its use of the property—in other words obligations to you, the developer, under the publishing contract—it will carve space for those obligations in its contracts with third parties. An example of this would be getting creative approval over the plots for a book series based on the game. When the publisher contracts with the book publisher, it will insert a clause giving itself creative approval over the books' plots so that it can solicit your approval and thereby fulfill its contract with you, the developer.

Understandably, the publisher will want to limit or eliminate all such provisions in the publishing contract to ensure it maximum flexibility when contracting with third parties and to save the administrative hassles of coordinating with you for decisions. See the "Approvals" section for a discussion of the forms that approvals take. Areas impacted by sublicenses include the following:

CREDITS

You will want to receive credit of the same size and prominence as the publisher on all games, merchandise, and entertainment and a credit "Based on the game "Newgame" created by Devco" in all entertainment in addition to any other credits appropriate to your involvement in the production. This latter is particularly important in filmed entertainment because producers are obligated to pay certain amounts for certain credits. The publisher will want to insert language to the effect of "wherever possible."

CREATIVE RIGHTS

Publishers are extremely reluctant to grant the developer any kind of creative approval over entertainment or merchandise, but two areas of compromise exist. The first: For you to have some approval right for all creative areas for which the publisher has a creative approval. For instance, if the publisher has a right of mutual approval over the film script, you would have some approval over the film script as well, whether mutual or consultation (discussed below in Section: Business Approvals). The second: To include language requiring the publisher to use its "best efforts" to have the key originator of the idea attached as a creative consultant, paid by the producer at industry-standard rates, to any entertainment project.

BUSINESS APPROVALS

You will want some form of input into business arrangements, though publishers will be reluctant to grant it. Non-specific language like "meaningful consultation" rights on all business and creative decisions may be thin, but it communicates intentions between the parties that you wish to be involved in business dealings, and it is far better than having no rights language at all.

If you are licensing your own IP to a publisher, the business issues on which you will want input are

- Marketing and distribution strategy (how much will be spent and how—TV, print, retail)
- The licensing program, which includes merchandising and lateral media production, like a TV show or comic book series

Licensing covers a broad range of products and decisions that are discussed in Chapter 7. The scale of approval rights for a developer goes from lowest to highest:

- Consultation rights, which means the publisher will keep you informed of and solicit your opinion on certain topics.
- Mutual approval, which means both you and the publisher must agree before any action can be taken.
- Unilateral approval, which means you must approve the decision.

Because the publisher has so much money at stake and your business is to make games—not to manufacture, distribute, and manage a licensing program—the publisher is understandably reluctant to allow you any approval rights. Take some time to think about your priorities: how emotionally attached are you to

> **TIP**
>
> With very few exceptions, I tend to counsel creative people that, while they will always have more brilliant ideas, they need to publish titles and hopefully entertainment to gain the control that comes with stature. Pick your management at the publisher, ask questions, and get as much written documentation as possible of the publisher's plans for the property.

the property? Is it more important to you that the property is done your way or that it is done at all, because that is often the decision until you reach the highest echelons.

COSTS

The publisher will want you to pay for some or all of the cost of doing the licensing deals, often *pro rata* based on the way net receipts are shared (example: if you share the revenue 50/50, you will pay for half of the deal costs). You will want to avoid this for a few reasons. First, the attorney will be hired by the publisher and quite likely more inclined to represent its interests, even if you are paying a portion of the fees. Second, you will argue that you should not be responsible for paying the publisher's overhead, and attorneys—especially in-house counsel—are considered overhead. Particularly with large conglomerates, all costs deducted should be costs actually paid, not just accounted for.

CREDITS AND NOTICES

If the IP originated with and belongs to you, you will want correct copyright and trademark notices prominently displayed on all manifestations of the property, including your company's trademark and logo.

Termination

The termination provision should be thought of as a prenuptial agreement, but with a bonus for blame. Termination scenarios fall into a few categories, generally: for developer's material breach, for publisher's material breach, "at will" or "for convenience," and bankruptcy. The fairest rule of thumb is that, in case of termination, parties are still fairly compensated for whatever they accomplished during the term of the contract. Damages caused by the breach should be the subject of a separate legal proceeding, but not built into the termination facts.

It is, however, standard that the party retaining the rights will pay the other party a diminishing royalty over time, whether that is marked strictly chronologically or by the renewal terms of said contracts:

- **Example One (time-based):** the parties terminate the agreement after a successful television show has been made based on the property. The party who holds the television licensing rights after termination must still pay the other party its share of revenue from the show, but four years after termination, the rightsholder only needs to pay the other party 50 percent of its original participation. The logic is that the rightsholder has done the bulk of the work to create the value in the last four years and should receive more of the revenue.
- **Example Two (contract-based):** Same TV show scenario: instead of reducing the participation to 50 percent after four years, the reduction happens whenever the TV contract or associated merchandise agreements are renewed.

For Material Breach

The terms should be the same for you and the publisher for breach. Essentially, the offended party will give notice (in accord with the notice rules of the contract, see the "Notice" section in this chapter) to the breaching party, who will then have a period of time to "cure," or correct the breach. If the party doesn't cure, then the contract terminates, but with the following consequences:

PUBLISHER'S MATERIAL BREACH

If it is for the publisher's material breach, the publisher will still owe you for any milestones submitted and approved. You will want to receive a termination fee, generally the current milestone plus one or two more with a set minimum dollar value, to reflect the fact that you have committed resources to the project and will need to find another project.

The *cure period*, the amount of time after receiving a breach letter that the publisher has to correct the breach, is very important to getting paid on time and should be as short as possible—15 days if you can negotiate it. If your publisher has 30 days to cure, it is quite possible that it will take 30 days to pay after receiving a breach letter from you.

The publisher will want to continue receiving royalties for any games it published or entertainment/merchandise contracts that it originated. This is fair, but you will want all monies redirected to you f/b/o the publisher ("for the benefit of," which means that the money legally belongs to the publisher, even though it is delivered to you). If there is a lawsuit over damages caused by the publisher's breach, you will also want the right to hold onto any royalties you may owe the publisher to offset any damages the court may find that the publisher owes you.

Publishers fear *remedies in equity* which are non-monetary remedies like temporary or permanent injunctions that prohibit the publisher from doing something (like releasing a game), or specific performance, in which a court compels a company to do something, and will want to limit your remedies to money damages.

DEVELOPER'S MATERIAL BREACH

You may want to define material breach, for clarity, as failure to get approval for a milestone, failure to deliver the gold master, your going out of business, or excessive delay in delivering the game.

If you are in material breach before the game is completed, the publisher will have a period of time to decide whether to complete and publish the game or to abandon development (30 to 60 days).

If the publisher elects to complete and publish and if the publisher owns the IP, it will want to terminate the contract with no further payment to you. You will want to receive a proportional royalty. The calculation for this is found by multiplying the original royalty rate by a fraction, the numerator of which is the number of milestones you completed and the denominator of which is the total number of milestones.

If you own the IP and the publisher elects to complete the game, the publisher will want to retain the license and sublicensing rights. The publisher will continue essentially as planned, but it should pay you a rights fee for the license to use your IP as well as a royalty (reduced as per the above formula) on the game reduced to reflect the fact that another party will need to be hired to complete the game.

The publisher will also want to reduce the entertainment royalty, but the validity of this will be determined by a few factors, such as how far into development the game is at the time of termination and the relative positions of the parties. You will need to furnish some form of assistance to the third-party developer, but will want a firm ceiling on that obligation, such as "commercially reasonable" or "not to exceed *xx* hours total."

If the publisher elects not to complete and publish the game, you will want all rights back. The publisher will want to receive the equivalent of a turnaround fee, that is, repayment of money it has paid you for milestones submitted. While the publisher may want to be repaid from *first monies* (the first money you receive to finish the game), this may not be practical if the money is needed to actually develop the game. A good compromise would be to repay the publisher from first monies to the extent they exceed your documented development costs.

If the game is complete, some may argue that the breaching party should forfeit royalties as a penalty for breach, but as noted above, penalties are a matter for a separate proceeding. Whatever contracts are in place, both parties should continue to receive the benefits for work contributed.

At Will

This privilege will likely only be afforded the publisher. If the publisher terminates the agreement, the consequences are similar to those occurring if it breaches the contract.

Bankruptcy

If either party enters bankruptcy, the counterparty will want to be able to continue with the project without intervention from the creditors and bankruptcy court. Both parties will want to be able to terminate for the bankruptcy of the other, with the provision that the agreement and the rights created thereby shall not be deemed assets and that the bankrupt party will not have the right to sell or assign any of the rights created under the contract. These provisions may or may not be effective in bankruptcy court.

Rights After Termination

Parties often still have involvement with each other even after a contract is terminated, particularly if any of the fruit of the agreement is still making money.

SELL-OFF PERIOD

This is a window, usually six months, for the publisher to sell off all games and merchandise in its pipeline, after which it will no longer have the rights to do so.

RIGHTS REVERSION

The publisher may request a residual percentage of royalties on new entertainment even after reversion, based on the argument that the game launched the property. The parties may negotiate this point.

Clauses Added to Most Long Form Contracts

Most of these provisions, while important, won't find their way into the short form. Instead, a "future agreement/residual clause" in the short form will note that the parties intend to fill out the short form into a long form agreement, but if they don't, the short form agreement is binding. The "residual clause" states that the long form agreement will include provisions relating to *force majeure*, assignment, severability, and lots of other dense little paragraphs like the ones explained in this section.

Representations, Warranties, and Indemnifications

Representations and warranties is the section where the parties promise that certain facts upon which the counterparty is relying are true. Indemnifications (see the "Indemnifications" section that follows) is where the parties promise that, if the representations are not true, the offending party will protect the innocent party from the consequences of the misrepresentation. Most representations concern ownership and use of intellectual property. Ideally, representations, warranties, and indemnifications should mirror each other from publisher to developer and back again.

Common Representations and Warranties

Both parties will agree that they are legally authorized to enter into the agreement and perform all of their obligations.

Developer Warranties

You will warrant and represent that:

- All IP you attach to the game is wholly owned by you, is reasonably free of bugs, and *to the best of your knowledge* (important because otherwise you are liable for infringements of which you were not aware) does not infringe upon the copyrights, trademarks, or other rights of any person, firm, or corporation.
- If the IP is yours, you can license the property and its trademarks and copyrights to the publisher without violating any third party's rights or interfering with a contract. An example of where a license could interfere with another contract would be if you were under option to another publisher to offer it your next original IP for a period of 60 days. If you did not offer the IP to the option holder, you could not safely make this representation.
- You are a licensed developer for the applicable platform(s).
- You have obtained any and all permissions and clearances to any third-party IP for its authorized use in the game (or entertainment, if necessary). In other words, if you are using a third-party engine, you have gotten the legally correct licenses. If you use voices, you have clearances from the actors.
- You have no knowledge of any claim that would be contrary to your warranties, representations, and agreements contained in the contract. For instance, if you knew that an angry ex-founder was going to sue the company for ownership of the engine, you could not safely make this representation.
- You will reasonably correct programming defects in the work product or released Game. (Be very careful with this clause, as it could indenture you to bug-fixing for the term of the contract. Be sure that you and the publisher understand each other vis-a-vis what is an acceptable bug and what is not).

Publisher Warranties

The publisher will warrant and represent that:

- The publisher has acquired all necessary third-party platform rights and licenses. This means that the publisher has permission from the console manufacturer to make the game, or will acquire it. Furthermore, the publisher has all of the necessary licenses to the content of the game if you are working on a licensed IP. An example would be the right to make a game based on a particular Dungeons and Dragons edition.
- The publisher will make no changes or alterations to any submission by the developer that will infringe any third party's rights. In other words, the publisher will not take your game and insert copyrighted text on the box without obtaining the necessary rights.

- All games, content, entertainment, and merchandise produced by the publisher, the publisher's sublicensees, subsidiaries, affiliates, agents, partners, or joint venturers will be free from any material that would violate any laws or infringe any third-party rights. This means that you will not be responsible for intellectual property or other infringements made by third parties chosen by the publisher (example: if the publisher sublicenses the film rights to a producer who uses a plagiarized script).
- You will want the publisher to warrant that any merchandise created and sold by the publisher or its sublicensees will conform to all safety standards, and a corresponding indemnification should be put in place. For example, if the publisher's merchandising licensee manufactures a toy that violates safety laws, you will not be liable for any damages this causes.

Indemnifications

Both parties indemnify each other against any losses arising from breach of representation, warranty, or obligation under the contract. You will want to analyze the language to be sure you won't have to pay for defense against false claims and that the publisher cannot withhold all funds during the defense of third-party claims.

Both parties agree to give the other prompt notice of any claim arising due to breach of warranty or representation, and you agree to give the publisher the right to participate in the defense at the publisher's expense.

FROM DEVELOPER

You will maintain a general liability policy of at least $X, and the policy will name the publisher as an additional insured.

You will defend, indemnify, and hold the publisher and its affiliates harmless from any claim by any of your employees, subcontractors, or independent contractors for work-related injury or disability.

FROM PUBLISHER

The publisher will indemnify you from any action or inaction by the publisher or its sublicensees, agents, subsidiaries, joint venturers, partners, and so forth deemed to infringe or harm a third party's rights or cause any damage to any third party.

Accounting

Game royalties are usually accounted for quarterly. The publisher will deliver a statement and any royalties due within 45 days of the end of the calendar period.

For entertainment/third-party receipts, the publisher should remit payment to you within 45 days of its receipt of such monies.

> **TIP**
>
> Try to institute a penalty for late delivery of royalty statements or late payment of royalties.

Audits

Audit rights give you the ability to hire someone to examine the financial records of the publisher to be sure you are receiving accurate royalties. Giving your audit provisions teeth is a good way to encourage careful bookkeeping. Standard provisions are

- You have the right to audit the publisher's books during normal business hours at the publisher's place of business with reasonable notice once every two years. Statements are deemed closed (can no longer be audited) after two years.
- You pay the cost of the auditor (though not for any time spent by the publisher's personnel) unless a discrepancy of 5 percent or greater is discovered, in which case the publisher should pay for the audit. Any monies found owing will be paid with interest at prime plus 2 percent from the date originally due.

Marketing/Advertising Expenditure

It is helpful to negotiate a minimum, whether a fixed dollar amount, a percentage of net sales not to fall below a certain number, or the marketing for comparable releases that year. If you do negotiate a minimum expenditure, the only way to verify it is to require the publisher to provide you with receipts for marketing and advertising related to your game. Some discussion of the kinds of marketing (television, online, *end-caps*) and the anticipated demographic should happen between the publisher and developer, whether or not it is reduced to writing in the contract.

Relationship among the Parties

There will be a clause noting that there is no partnership or joint venture among the parties. This avoids some of the legal ambiguities of partnership law.

Force Majeure

Force majeure stops time in a contract for a period (usually around 90 days) where acts of god, terrorism, and so forth, prevent any party from fulfilling its obligations.

Governing Law and Dispute Resolution

This is one of the most important clauses in any contract. This is where the parties decide which state or country's law will govern the contract, and whether disputes will be resolved in litigation or arbitration.

Laws vary significantly from sovereignty to sovereignty. California's refusal to honor most non-compete clauses in employment agreements and France's granting of *droit moral* or "moral rights" in intellectual property are two examples. California and New York law are best for entertainment and intellectual property contracts because both have an established body of law, thereby removing much uncertainty as to how a court will interpret certain situations. Expect the governing law to be that of the publisher.

Arbitration is like a mini-trial before a qualified arbitrator (often an ex-judge or attorney), usually a member of one of the major arbitration associations. Many prefer it over litigation for dispute resolution because it can be drastically less expensive and leaves less room for the deep-pocketed party to intimidate with the specter of excessive attorney's fees. However, there may be no appeal from an arbitration and no rules of evidence protecting you. The arbitrator should be neutral and a member of the American Arbitration Association or another reputable association. The arbitration clause usually states where the arbitration will occur. In case the parties are far-flung, insert a clause stating that parties and witnesses may appear electronically, whether by telephone or video conference. The findings of the arbitrator must be final and binding, and the judgment may be entered in any court having proper jurisdiction.

Assignment

Assignment is the ability to transfer the contract and your obligations to another party. For instance, if your company got bought in the middle of development, you would "assign" the contract to the purchaser in the sale. Understandably, a publisher will be leery of your assigning the rights to a third party, though it will usually consent if it is simply a matter of being purchased. Since most publishers have no problem allowing a developer to assign its rights to receive royalty streams, this can be a solution if your publisher does not want to allow any kind of obligation assignment.

Confidentiality

Expect your publisher to attach a form confidentiality agreement and ask you to have every member of your team sign it.

Severability

This is a legal detail that allows a judge to throw out one clause of the contract if it is found to be unenforceable without having to throw out the entire contract.

Proprietary Platform Owner/Manufacturer's Consent

This reserves the proprietary platform owner's (e.g. Sony) right to approve or disapprove of the software.

Notices

Both parties give their official contact information and state acceptable methods (certified mail, fax, and so forth) of communicating important information. This information is important for delivering communications that may need to be proved in court, like a notice of termination. If sent to the address in the notice provision, in a permitted manner, the recipient will have a hard time arguing that it did not receive the communication.

Modification

This states the only manners in which the agreement may be changed (usually in writing signed by both parties).

Survival

This sets out certain sections of the agreement that remain in force even if the term of the agreement expires or is otherwise terminated. It is customary for the confidentiality, warranty, and indemnification clauses to survive termination.

No Waiver

This clause usually says that even if a party does not immediately exercise its rights against a counterparty, it reserves the right to do so in the future. Example: if a developer is late enough to allow the publisher to claim breach under the contract, the publisher can keep working with you to try to finish the game without waiving its right to sue for breach down the road if the game ends up incomplete.

Entire Agreement

This clause prevents either party from insisting that there were verbal promises made that are not reflected in the written document. Essentially, it says that every piece of the intent of the parties is captured in the agreement.

SUMMARY

Negotiating your publishing contract is an exciting process that should be tempered with caution and a good lawyer. The high degree of financial and execution risk involved in a development project leads to a high level of complexity in the contract.

To start production quickly, it is advisable to execute the contract in two stages: a short form agreement setting out the most important terms, and a long form agreement that contains all of the details. This prevents the developer from starting work "bareback" (without a contract or an advance).

A developer may contribute an original intellectual property and/or a proprietary technology to the game development. In either situation, care and foresight must be exercised in making sure that the developer retains rights where necessary and is adequately compensated for any use or profit stemming from use of its property. A work-for-hire development, in which the publisher licenses the core technology and game rights to a property from third parties, can be a simpler contract because there is no need to account for ownership and control of the intellectual property.

You and your publisher will be wrestling over rights in the four main sources of revenue created by a game: the game itself, the underlying technology, and the merchandise and entertainment licensing rights if you are developing an original IP. Most developers will not have a tremendous amount of leverage when negotiating with a publisher. One mitigating strategy is to attach conditions to grants of rights such as options and reversions.

Three points, among many, to remember:

- Give yourself a reasonable budget and schedule so that you can start or maintain a reputation for delivering on time, on budget, and on spec.
- Build in as many structures as possible to assure timely milestone approvals and payments.
- Don't just fixate on the royalty rate: fixate on the deductions allowed in getting from gross to net sales.

BINDING SHORT FORM AGREEMENT

Date: September 1, 2003

Parties: Game Publisher, Inc. located at 500 Long Road, Sunnywhere, California 99934 ("Publisher")

And

Double D Development, Inc., located at 9174 Winding Road, Podunk, Pacifica, 10000 ("Developer") (Publisher and Developer each a "Party" or jointly, the "Parties")

1. <u>Property</u>. NewGame, and all sequel and derivative rights ("Property").

2. <u>Rights Granted</u>. Developer hereby licenses to Publisher the exclusive rights to create, produce, license, sublicense, use, advertise, market, manufacture, distribute, exploit, sell and otherwise vend:
   A. "Games". Interactive entertainment software based on the Property for the Sony PlayStation 2, Nintendo GameCube and GameBoy Advance, Microsoft Xbox, PC, Internet, Wireless and PDA platforms and future and successor platforms, including multi-player internet gaming capabilities.
   B. "Ancillary Products". Merchandise based on the Games but not on any derivative products thereof (e.g. filmed entertainment), derivative products (i.e. hint books and strategy guides), and OEM.
   C. Non-Game Entertainment and Merchandising ("Entertainment"). Including all other filmed, animated and recorded entertainment based on the Property and all related merchandise and toylines.

3. <u>Territory</u>. Worldwide; all languages.

4. <u>Term</u>.
   A. Games. ___ years after the initial commercial release of the first Game on the first SKU ("Initial Release"). Rights will revert on a platform by platform basis if Publisher does not publish or make significant progress toward development of a new Game on that platform within ___ years of the last SKU commercially released. The term will automatically renew if Developer receives royalties in excess of $_____.
   B. Ancillary Products. Co-terminous with Game term.
   C. Entertainment. In perpetuity, subject to rights reversion on a media by media basis if Publisher does not execute licenses within ___ years of Initial Release.

5. <u>Sequels</u>. Developer will have the right of last refusal to develop any sequels, ports, conversions, or derivative products of any Games Publisher elects to produce (each a "Sequel Product"). If the Parties cannot come to mutually agreeable terms for a given Sequel Product, Publisher may hire third parties to develop that Sequel Product. Publisher shall pay Developer a license fee for Sequel Products at _____ percent (____%) of Net Sales for handheld titles and _____ percent (____%) of Net Sales for all PC and console titles.

6. <u>Development</u>.
   A. *Platforms*. Developer will develop and Publisher will publish one Game on two platforms, the Sony PlayStation 2 and Microsoft Xbox platforms (the "Initial Games").
   B. *Third Party Expenses*.
      i. Developer shall obtain all licenses, releases, and music necessary for development of the Initial Games.
      ii. Publisher shall obtain all hardware licenses at its own cost.
   C. *Approvals*.
      i. Publisher shall have approval over all material stages of development, including game content and characters of the Initial Games.
      ii. Publisher will submit in writing the name of one employee who shall have approval over all material stages of development of the Initial Games, such approval to be exercised within ___ days of milestone submission and not to be withheld so long as milestone meets commercially reasonable standards. Publisher will notify Developer in writing of any change of such designated employee.
      iii. Approval rights and procedures for subsequent Games will be negotiated in good faith.

7. <u>Localization</u>. Developer shall perform all localizations of the Initial Games with a localization kit to be provided by Publisher as part of the Milestone schedule. Developer will perform _____, _____, _____ and _____ localizations without separate guarantees or any other payments from Publisher. Guarantees for all other European languages will be negotiated in good faith. $_____ fully recoupable guarantee will be paid to Developer per language for the localizations of all other non-European languages.

8. <u>Developer Royalties</u>
   A. *Definitions*.
      i. "Net Sales" shall be defined as all monies paid to and received by Publisher or its sublicensee from exploitation of the Game, net or less

deductions for reserves, credits, returns, mark downs, lost and damaged goods, write offs, allowances, promotional units and rebates.

ii. "Net Receipts" shall be defined as revenue, including the value of any barter not used solely for promotion of the Property, received less agents' commissions actually paid, third party distribution fees and costs actually paid, audit and debt collection expenses, and intellectual property enforcement costs actually paid.

B. *Rates.*

   i. Console Systems:

     __% of Net Sales on units 1 - _00,000

     __% of Net Sales on units _00,000 - __00,000

     __% of Net Sales on units __000,00 - __00,000

     __% of Net Sales on units __00,001

   ii. PC:

     __% of Net Sales on units 1 - _00,000

     __% of Net Sales on units _00,000 - __00,000

     __% of Net Sales on units __000,00 - __00,000

     __% of Net Sales on units __00,001

   iii. Handheld Systems, excluding wireless:

     __% of Net Sales

   iv. Wireless Gaming when

     __% of Net Sales

   v. Subscription and Multiplayer revenue

     __% of Net Sales

   vi. Ancillary Products:

     __% of Net Receipts.

   vii. Entertainment:

     __% of Net Receipts.

C. *Cross-collateralization.*

Royalties from sales of Initial Games, including localizations, are cross-collateralized against the Advance as defined in Section 9. All other royalties shall only be cross-collateralized against the advances or guarantees for Games released within six (6) months of each other. Ancillary Product and Entertainment revenue shall not be cross-collateralized against each other or development advances or guarantees.

9. <u>Advance</u>. Developer shall receive $_____ as a non-refundable and fully recoupable advance (the "Advance") to develop the Initial Games. Payment will be made within thirty days of submission of each approved milestone according to the schedule attached as Exhibit A.

10. <u>Marketing</u>. Publisher commits to support the Initial Games with a marketing program that may include television, print and online advertising; in-store merchandising and/or circulars; co-op; tradeshows; promotion via product-specific websites; national public relations programs; demo-discs and/or other marketing efforts. Such commitment shall be not less than $_____ worldwide, to be allocated at Publisher's discretion.

11. <u>Entertainment</u>. Developer will defer to Publisher's business judgment in connection with the sublicensing of Entertainment rights. Publisher agrees to: Ensure that Developer receives proper credits on all Entertainment and licensed products; Inform Developer of the progress and business terms of the sublicensing efforts; Meaningfully consult Developer on all major business and creative decisions relating to the Property; and, Exercise mutual approval with Developer for creative issues over which Publisher has approval rights.

12. <u>Intellectual Property</u>.
    A. <u>Ownership</u>. Developer owns the Games in all their forms including the Game engine and source code, subject to the license granted to Publisher hereunder. Publisher has a license to unsupported source engine and source code in any Games.
    B. <u>Registration and Enforcement</u>. Publisher shall, at its own cost, register trademarks and copyrights in the name of Developer in all appropriate classes and geographic areas. Publisher will also be responsible for clearance, enforcement, and renewal of title to intellectual property related to all Entertainment and Ancillary Products provided under this Agreement, such costs to be deducted from the gross in calculating Net Sales and Net Receipts.

13. <u>Manufacturer Clearance</u>. Developer shall deliver the Initial Games (and all materials and elements, including all music contained therein) fully cleared and ready for Publisher to submit to Sony and Microsoft by [date]. Manufacturer approval of all products is a condition precedent to Publisher's obligations hereunder.

14. <u>Accounting</u>. Accounting statements and the corresponding payments due will be provided to Developer within forty-five (45) days of the close of each business quarter. Developer may audit Publisher once every two (2) years at Developer's cost, unless such audit shows a discrepancy of greater than Five Percent (5%), in which case Publisher shall pay the cost as well as all monies owed with interest at prime plus two percent (2%) from date such monies were due. Statements will be closed after two 2 years.

15. <u>Governing Law and Dispute Resolution</u>. This Agreement shall be governed by the laws of the state of _____. Any conflicts shall be resolved by binding arbitration in [City, State] under the rules and institutional supervision of the American Arbitration Association ("AAA"). Parties or witnesses may appear by telephone. Judgment upon the award(s) rendered by the arbitrator may be entered in any court of any country having jurisdiction thereof. The arbitral tribunal shall consist of one neutral arbitrator appointed by the AAA. The arbitrator shall award attorney's fees to the prevailing Party.

16. <u>Future Agreement</u>. This Agreement shall be binding on both Developer and Publisher. Subsequent to acceptance of these terms by both Parties, the Long Form will be concluded, pending or failing which this Agreement shall govern the relationship between the Parties.

17. <u>Residual</u>. Standard terms will be added to the final agreement including the following: retention of records, reasonable audit rights, royalty and distribution reports, representations and warranties regarding intellectual property, dispute resolution, indemnification, confidentiality, limitation of liability, termination for cause, waiver, modification, severability, notice, *force majeure*, assignment, relationship of Parties, interpretation and construction, and merger clause.

ACCEPTED AND AGREED TO THIS ____ DAY OF _____, 200____

Double D Development, Inc.

By:_____
    Name, duly authorized

Date:_____

Game Publisher, Inc.

By:_____
    Name, duly authorized

Date:_____

EXHIBIT A

Milestone Schedule

Milestone	Date	Amount	%	Cumulative
Signature of short from agreement	TBD	$_____	___%	$_____
Milestone 1 : [Description] _____	_/_/_	$_____	___%	$_____
Milestone 2 : [Description] _____	_/_/_	$_____	___%	$_____
Milestone 3 : [Description] _____	_/_/_	$_____	___%	$_____
Milestone 4 : [Description] _____	_/_/_	$_____	___%	$_____
Milestone 5 : [Description] _____	_/_/_	$_____	___%	$_____
Milestone 6 : [Description] _____	_/_/_	$_____	___%	$_____
Milestone 7 : [Description] _____	_/_/_	$_____	___%	$_____
Milestone 8 : [Description] _____	_/_/_	$_____	___%	$_____
Milestone 9 : [Description] _____	_/_/_	$_____	___%	$_____
Alpha _____	_/_/_	$_____	___%	$_____
Beta_____	_/_/_	$_____	___%	$_____
Gold Master _____	_/_/_	$_____	___%	$_____
Localization [Specified languages] _____	_/_/_	$_____	___%	$_____

SAMPLE ROYALTY REPORT

Developer Name _____

Address _____

Address _____

Tel # _____ Fax # _____

LICENSEE: _____

PROPERTY: _____

CONTRACT #: _____

YOUR ROYALTY STATEMENT IS NOW DUE FOR THE MONTH/QUARTER OF: _____

PLEASE FILL OUT AND REMIT BY: _____

ITEM NUMBER	DESCRIPTION	NUMBER OF UNITS SOLD	WHOLESALE PRICE	TOTAL FIGURE

TOTAL SALES:_____

LESS RETURNS:_____

NET TOTAL SALES:_____

ROYALTIES DUE AT (%):_____

BALANCE OF UNEARNED ROYALTIES IF ANY:_____

NEW UNEARNED BALANCE IF ANY:_____

YOUR CHECK FOR FULL AMOUNT PAYABLE AND ROYALTY REPORTS SHOULD BE DISTRIBUTED AS CALLED FOR IN THE LICENSE AGREEMENT(S) BETWEEN OUR COMPANIES.

_____

NAME AND TITLE OF PERSON PREPARING REPORT

CHAPTER 7

LICENSING

Licensing in Action

Three years later, Double D is still alive and kicking. Its original IP game came out to critical acclaim and sales good enough to get a sequel development with Publisher A, who is in the middle of negotiating a film option on the property. The founders have been debating adding a second team, but aren't sure they really want to handle the exponential management hassles.

At the same time, the group would like to leverage its current engine and AI for at least one more game before major changes are required. The founders decide to find out what the rest of the company is interested in working on. Dana sends out an e-mail asking people to submit game proposals compatible with Double D's current technology within the next two weeks. She disseminates the proposals a few days before an all hands meeting called to review the company's options.

Dana opens the meeting by announcing that the meeting is to talk about potential projects as well as to hear what people think about expanding to 1.5 or 2 teams, which would probably be a prerequisite for developing any of the submissions.

The proposal that gets the most traction is based on an obscure comic book called *ComicBook* released by an independent publisher. Jean brought it into the office one day and a cult rapidly developed. The group seems enthusiastic enough about the project that Dana asks the proposal's author, a line producer named Lorne, if he wants to work up a top-line budget and spec so that Dana and the founders can evaluate what additional resources would be required to make the game.

Dusty comes into Dana's office after the meeting and expresses concern that Lorne's budget would be pretty inaccurate. "Yeah, I know," she tells Dusty, "but I think it's a good exercise for him, and—more important—he'll need a lot of help from everyone to get it put together. I figure it'll be a pretty good indicator of just how motivated everyone is to make the game."

Pat comes in to the office and mentions that there is definitely a card-based game to be made out of the *ComicBook* property. The three of them discuss the possibility of buying the property and trying to develop it into several different media. Dana sends an e-mail to the founder group summarizing the ideas and seeing what people think about her talking to their IP attorney, Jamie, about acquiring the *ComicBook* property.

Dana sends Jamie an e-mail explaining Double D's idea, along with the fact that Double D doesn't want to spend much money on the license or the drafting and negotiating fees because it is fronting the money to acquire the property without a development contract in hand. Jamie drafts a short form option agreement to use in approaching *ComicBook's* owner. (See end of chapter.)

INTRODUCTION

Licensing is the practice of selling less than all of an intellectual property right to a third party. This chapter will discuss two kinds of licensing: *content licensing*, where a trademark and/or copyrights are exploited in other media (example: Batman comics becoming Batman the movie and toys); and *technology licensing*, where a third party acquires the rights to use a technology or incorporate that technology into its product (example: the 3-D engine used in the Quake games is licensed for use by other game developers in making their own games).

The structure of this chapter is a bit different from its predecessors. The contract terms and logic of the licensing world will be introduced and then illustrated through examples of four different contracts, an engine license, a film option, a children's television series license, and a license for a developer to purchase a little-known property from a third party.

> **NOTE**
> Some definitions: The party who owns the rights is known as the *licensor*, while the recipient of those rights is the *licensee*. A *property*, for purposes of this chapter (and as generally used in the industry), is a set of trademarks and copyrights that identify products and entertainment as coming from a single source (though not necessarily a single author).

Licensing Versus Owning

The idea of licensing property can seem counter-intuitive: either you *own* something, or you don't. Law professors like to explain the subtleties of property use and ownership with the "bundle of sticks" metaphor. A property that you own is comprised of many different sticks, each representing a separate right that can be taken out of the bundle and sold. With a house, for instance, you can sell the stick corresponding to the right to live in the house (renting), but keep the stick representing the right to sublet the house; you can sell the stick representing the right to walk across your lawn to get to the beach (called an *easement*), but keep the stick that represents the right to walk across your lawn to get to the bar on the other side.

The author would like to thank Fred Fierst of Fierst, Pucci & Kinder LLP for his help in preparing this chapter and for his generosity in being an outstanding boss and mentor.

A property has an almost infinite number of sticks in its bundle: instead of giving a license to the book rights to your game, you can license just the Latin American trade paperback rights for stories about just one character in your game. The goal of a licensing program is to give a licensee only those rights that it will actually use. Wouldn't it be terrible if you sold the worldwide exclusive book publishing license to a publisher who ended up releasing just a single book in Spanish in Venezuala? This pain would double if Random House then approached you two months later to do a series of books in 12 languages around the world.

The art of licensing a property is like building a fire with your bundle of sticks. You only have enough gas to build a fire with some of your sticks, leaving you the option of having a small fire all to yourself, or building a bigger fire to share by selling the other rights to licensees with enough gas to light their own sticks and throw them onto your fire.

Technology licensing is usually quite a bit simpler than character licensing. Technology is generally created for a narrow purpose and has only so many possible uses. In other words, the bundle doesn't have that many sticks in it. Therefore, the bulk of this chapter will address the subtleties of content licensing, though it will review the highlights of a contract licensing a third-party engine.

Risks and Benefits of Licensing

Benefits to the licensor:

- New sources of revenue with minimal investment.
- Licensed products provide free advertising and marketing ("brand extension").
- Expansion of the property and its creative assets.
- Trademark becomes stronger through use in more *classes* (see Chapter 5, "Trademarks").
- Having several licenses in production can minimize cash flow volatility (rather than being dependent on revenue from only one product).

Risks to the licensor:

- Overexposure of property.
- Inferior licensed goods can erode the value of the property.
- International enforcement against piracy and gray marketing is difficult and costly.
- Inadequate control over use of trademarks can lead to loss of trademark status.

Benefits to the licensee:

- Brand recognition.
- Pre-built audience.
- Synergy with advertising/marketing budget of all other uses of the property.

Risks to the licensee:

- Usually must pay a minimum guaranteed royalty (the "guarantee") no matter how much money licensee earns.
- Licensee assumes production and distribution/marketing risk for the product.
- Licensee suffers from piracy and gray marketing issues as much as licensor.

CONTENT LICENSING

Content licenses grant rights to the trademarked and copyrighted assets associated with a particular property such as main and supporting characters, story lines, weapons, backgrounds, and any other relevant trademarked and copyrighted assets. It is a multi-billion (with a "b") dollar industry worldwide.

Why License?

If I showed you 4 cards with different names on them and asked you to remember those names for 20 minutes, you probably could. If I showed you 40 cards, you'd have a harder time, and if I showed you 400, only an eidetic or a politician could remember them.

This is the situation of the retail goods and entertainment producer: they are just another name among 400 others competing for your attention and memory. But what if these sellers could arrange for their names to appear on 2 cards in the group of 400? That would double their chance of being remembered. What if they could get it on 4 cards? That would probably start improving their chances exponentially, not just geometrically; in other words, appearing on 4 cards would increase the chance of being remembered six, seven, or eight times, not just four.

This is the core logic of brand licensing: it is so difficult to be seen in the overcrowded market that it takes either massive advertising and marketing budgets *or* some way to associate your product with one the buyer already recognizes.

The benefit goes both ways—not only does the licensee gain from association with the licensor's known product, the licensor benefits by having its product become even better-known without having to spend money on advertising and marketing. A licensed product is like a free ad for the licensor.

Basis of Rights

Copyrights confer to their owner the exclusive right to
- Reproduce the work in copies or records.
- Create derivative works based upon the work.

- Distribute copies of the work to the public by sale or other transfer of ownership, or by rental, lease, or lending.
- Perform the work publicly, in the case of literary, musical, dramatic, and choreographic works, pantomimes, and motion pictures and other audiovisual works.
- Display the copyrighted work publicly, in the case of literary, musical, dramatic, and choreographic works, pantomimes, and pictorial, graphic, or sculptural works, including the individual images of a motion picture or other audiovisual work.

Licensing allows the owner of the copyright to divide and subdivide these rights and lease them to third parties. To create a T-shirt based on a game requires the owner to license: (i) the right to create a derivative work (the T-shirt) based on the original copyright; (ii) the right to make copies of that derivative work (to manufacture the T-shirt); (iii) the right to distribute that work (by selling it); and (iv) the right to display the work publicly.

The right to create derivative works is generally the source of the most revenue. Derivative works, like a film based on a game, are divided (example: the right to make toys) and subdivided again (the right to make plush toys and the right to make injection molded plastic toys may be sold separately). The distribution rights are equally important, allowing licensors to limit the right to make derivative works (the right to make plush toys for sale only in Latin America for a period of two years).

How It Works

Content is usually licensed for two different kinds of products: entertainment and merchandise. Entertainment licenses allow third parties to create entertainment based on your property across different media. Example: the right to make a film out of the *Resident Evil* game was an entertainment license granted to the film producers by the property's owners. Merchandise licenses allow third parties to manufacture different consumer products based on your property. Example: the right to make hint books or a board game from a video game is a merchandise license.

> **NOTE**
> Complexity is added when a party wants to make merchandise or entertainment based on a derivative product (derivatives are new works based on the original copyrighted work). Example 1: T-shirts featuring Milla Jovovich in her costume, which are based on *the Resident Evil* film, not the game. Example 2: a *Buffy the Vampire Slayer* game based on the television show, which is a derivative product of the original film.

NOTE

The licensor will generally maintain ownership or co-ownership of all derivative copyrights and trademarks created by licensees (in other words, the licensor of the Buffy property—which started as a may have acquired ownership of the copyrights and trademarks in Angel, Spike, and all of the other characters and concepts created by the television licensee). A talented licensee, as with the *Buffy* television series, can make derivative products the core of a property's value.

If this doesn't seem fair—why should the licensor own the results of a licensee's creativity?—it gets fair with the revenue split and associated production (like television shows based on the film) rights. Even though a licensee may not "own" the rights to additions it makes to a property, it can reap the rewards of those creations in two major ways: (i) participation in merchandise based on the derivative work; and (ii) rights to create more products based on the derivative work. Example: even if the *Buffy* television producer didn't own the rights to the other characters it created, it would still receive a healthy chunk of any merchandising (or other) revenue based on the series (as opposed to the film) *and* it could have spinoff rights to create new shows based on characters it introduced, like the *Angel* spinoff.

Figure 7.1

Buffy DVD: The television show, a derivative work of the 1992 film, has created massive value for the property and a slew of merchandising including...

Figure 7.2

...a game, natch...

Figure 7.3

...creative merchandise...

Figure 7.4

...spinoff TV shows...

Figure 7.5

...dolls and other items for the obsessive fan.

The Licensing Meritocracy

This seems convoluted because it is. A lot of times it is the licensee, not the original creator, who creates a blockbuster property. These licensees are generally compensated with additional rights to leverage that success into more products, as well as appropriate shares of all relevant revenue streams. The competing principles at work are the desire of a licensee who creates a property-enhancing product to share in the ripple value effect created by that product, and the licensor's need to maintain a "clean," easily administered property—that is, one that doesn't have residual rights lying about in all different corners.

Example: the creators of the *Buffy* television series probably deserve *participation* (a cut) in licenses that result from the success of that show, like merchandise, DVD sales, spinoff TV shows or movies. Sometimes, licensees who add major value to a property are also compensated with a share of any increased sales in pre-existing products (known as a "bump"). Example: the creators of the *Buffy* television series could ask for a share of any increased sales and rental income from the original *Buffy* movie, because they can logically argue that the bump is caused by their efforts with the property.

KEY CONCEPTS AND CONTRACT TERMS

The most important thing in licensing contracts is to articulate the rights granted with extreme specificity; otherwise, you could end up giving away a whole stick and getting paid for a splinter. Terms and concepts that appear in most licenses include:

Definition of the Licensed Property

The definition of the property identifies what assets a licensee may use. The licensor is generally looking to define the property narrowly; the licensee, broadly. In a technology license, this could be something as simple as "the *Shake* engine and all modifications, upgrades, and fixes not sold as stand-alone products." In a content license, the definition will center around copyrights, trademarks, and the ideas they represent. Example: "the property "Binky the Vampire Slayer" and all related copyrights, trademarks and symbols, including without limitation characters, plots, story lines, concepts, designs, backgrounds, locations, sets, weapons, and artwork."

Sloppy language can result in what amounts to a free license. For example, the definition of the licensed technology property in this paragraph might be insufficient for a single platform license—without limitations like "the *Shake* engine *for the GameCube platform* and all modifications, upgrades, and fixes not sold as stand-alone products," the licensor could inadvertently grant rights to all versions of the engine.

In defining a content property, time is an important consideration. For example, if the above definition had been used to grant a merchandise license to the original film, that licensor might not have rights to any aspects of the property later created by the television show. Had there been language like "the property 'Buffy the Vampire Slayer' and all related copyrights, trademarks and symbols *which are created now or in the future for the Property,* including without limitation characters, plots, story lines, concepts, designs, backgrounds, locations, sets, weapons, and artwork," that merchandise licensor might have been able to argue that it owned the merchandise rights to the television series as well.

Figure 7.7

With its roster of licensed sports properties requiring annual updates, EA makes brilliant use of licensing.

Rights Granted

This is where the parties specify those products that a licensee is allowed to create, as well as the associated rights like duplication, promotion, distribution, and the right to sublicense any of those rights to third parties. Again, specificity is key: If the parties have agreed to a price for an animated network television series, don't just grant rights to "motion pictures for television"—that could include a live action series, movie of the week, or mini-series, and could be broadcast on cable or network television. This is not to say that you shouldn't include these associated rights in the grant, but they should each have a separate price.

A producer may demand an exclusive option or right of last refusal to create associated merchandise and productions to allow it to take advantage of a successful production.

Definitions of Gross and Net

This is particularly important in content licenses, where parties are frequently sharing pieces of a pie that has already been split several times. Certain product-specific, non-overhead expenses should be shared *pro rata* (according to the profit allocation) and should come off the top of gross revenues before licensor shares, such as:

- **Agent's Fees.** Agents may be used to handle the merchandise licensing, and their fees can range from 30 percent on the low end to 45 percent or more in some territories, such as Japan. Entertainment agents, such as those used to sell a game property to a film licensee, typically receive around 10 percent.
- **Distributors.** These are the parties who get the product, whether it is merchandise or entertainment, to retailers, be they Wal-Mart, Blockbuster, or the local television station. The fee for their services is usually in the range of 20 to 35 percent.
- **IP Enforcement and Registration.** As you may recall from Chapter 5, "Protecting Intellectual Property," protecting and registering intellectual property can be very expensive, particularly for global properties. Registering and protecting a successful property worldwide can cruise by the $100,000 mark with just enough time for a nod and a wink.
- **Licensor's Administrative Fee.** Licensors may receive a reasonable administration fee—10 percent off the top—for overseeing the property.

Figure 7.8

Bond films have become product placement orgies, but the 007 license has been attached to some good games.

Territory and Languages

Specify both the territory and any permitted languages. A global marketplace means that every territory and language has value and the licensor should be adequately compensated. A licensor should only receive rights to those areas/languages where it commits to exploiting the product—in other words, it might not make sense to grant the worldwide book publishing rights to a publisher with U.S.-only, English-language distribution.

Term

Setting the term of rights correctly is important for two reasons: to be sure that parties only share in the benefits that they create; and that any rights not being adequately exploited revert back to the licensor for use elsewhere. A term should generally be set for every licensed product category (example: movie of the week or animated network series).

The term for entertainment licenses may be further subdivided into pre-production, production, and distribution terms. This enables the licensor to gauge the licensee's commitment to completing a production, and allows it to get its rights back earlier. Example: A licensor can grant film rights as a three month option, a four-year production period, and a permanent distribution period. If the licensee can't raise financing for a production, it doesn't pick up its option and the licensee gets the rights back in time to get a film made by another party within the same time frame. If it picks up the option but doesn't produce a film within a certain amount of time, the rights revert after four years. If it picks up the option and produces a film, it may distribute that film in perpetuity.

Extensions and early terminations should be considered when negotiating the term, such as:

- **Renewal.** A licensor will want a licensee to earn the right to any term extensions and may set performance thresholds (money received by licensor, number of productions, aggregate production budget, and so on).
- **Reversion.** A licensor will also want to provide for the reversion of rights after a set time if the licensee does not use the rights or meet a certain threshold of payments to the licensor.

Sequels, Prequels, Re-makes, Ports, and Conversions

If the license includes rights to make follow-on content like sequels and the like, this should be elaborated (how many sequels, when does the option to make sequels lapse, what are the fees for sequels). For merchandise, if licensee gets a right of first refusal for sequel-related merchandise, include that right in the contract. For technology licenses, if the licensee gets a reduced price for ports, conversions, or sequels of the title, make a note.

Figure 7.9

The Baldur's Gate games are a great example of selecting licenses sympathetic to the game medium.

Other Terms

- **Approvals.** A licensor must exercise some approval over a licensee's use of its trademark or risk losing its trademark rights. If the licensor is granting rights that will be sublicensed, it may request some influence over sublicensing activity—even if it is just timely, meaningful consultation rights—over key creative elements and business contracts.
- **Quality Assurance.** Manufacturers of merchandise and toys, or the agent hired by the licensor to deal with those parties, must give assurances that any products created will meet certain safety and quality standards.
- **Marketing Guarantees.** A licensor may want to see a marketing and advertising guarantee to ensure the licensee's commitment to the product.
- **Ownership of Derivative Works.** A licensor must have the right to own and incorporate all new intellectual property created by licensees. It is common for the licensor and licensee to co-own the copyrights to licensed entertainment such as films.
- **Reservation of Rights.** To protect against misinterpretation or inadvertently over-broad license language, a licensor may want to include a clause noting that it reserves all rights not specifically granted in the license.
- **Representations and Warranties.** The most important representations and warranties from licensor to licensee are that the licensor owns the property and has the legal authority to grant the license, and that nothing in the property violates the rights of any

third parties. The most important representations and warranties from licensee to licensor are that the licensee will make no additions or modifications to the property that would infringe on the rights of any third parties and that it will manufacture only safe and appropriate products.

- **Execution of Further Agreements.** The licensor will want the licensee to agree in writing to execute any other documents necessary to secure the licensor's ownership of any intellectual property. This can avert annoying games later in the development process.

- **Assignment and Sublicense.** Licensees often need the right to sublicense or assign rights, for example, a production company licensing the right to make, exhibit, and distribute a film needs to be able to sublicense the exhibition and distribution rights to the film's distributors. Sublicensing these rights should be no worry to the licensor, as long as the rights to produce the entertainment stay with the production entity. If the production rights can be freely assigned or sublicensed, the quality control that a licensor exercises in selecting a producer is negated.

- **Audit Rights, Governing Law, Dispute Resolution.** These provisions are extremely important and can vary significantly. See Chapter 6, "The Publishing Contract," for a discussion of what to ask for in a contract.

FOUR EXAMPLES

Licensing an Engine

It should be noted that while a lot of energy has gone into promoting proprietary technology for third-party licenses, only a few developers are actually making any money through licensing. It is still advisable for a company to work to develop its own technology, both because it can dramatically reduce development time if several projects can use the same core technology, and because proprietary technology can provide a persuasive competitive advantage if it is the best within a category. For example: if you build an outstanding RPG AI, publishers will think of your company first when they need to develop an RPG project.

Cast of Characters

- **Licensor.** Engine owner.
- **Licensee.** The developer creating a game using the engine.
- **Publisher.** The publisher may be a party to the engine license to preserve its rights to use the engine in the game if another developer ends up working on the game.

Mis en Scène

Developer has been approached by Publisher to develop Game A, a licensed property that it needs to release six quarters from now. Developer does not have an in-house engine appropriate to the game. Furthermore, it has worked with Publisher before and knows that the deal alone will take at least two months, meaning Developer won't receive any funds for at least that long. Developer decides to license to the Shake engine, which has a good reputation, and factors this into the proposed budget and schedule.

Contract Highlights

Definition of "Licensed Technology"

Most software can adequately be described by a name, for example, the Shake engine, and the term "Licensed Technology" should be defined to include all modifications, patches, improvements and updates not marketed as separate products, to be given to the licensee at the same time as all other licensees. Clarify which version and platform of the engine is intended, for example, the Shake II engine for PlayStation2.

Permitted Use

Licensor will want to limit licensee's use of the engine to certain applications. The licensor will need to confer many of the copyright rights discussed above, namely the rights to: create a derivative work, including the right to modify the original work; the right to duplicate and distribute the derivative work; and the right to sublicense the duplication and distribution to the required third parties (such as a publisher or OEM manufacturer). Typical terms of use include:

- **Game.** The licensee may generally use the engine only to develop Game A and any localizations. Are sequels, ports, and expansion packs (stand-alone and/or dependent?) included in the license? If not, what are the terms and fees for these additional products?
- **Distribution in Object Code Only.** In addition to confidentiality provisions, an engine licensor will want to protect its product by only allowing the licensee to distribute the engine in object code as embedded in Game A.
- **Restrictions.** Licensees must usually agree to other protective restrictions on their use of the technology, such as prohibitions against reverse-engineering or decompiling the technology, disclosing the source code to any third parties, and so on, as well as agreeing to make proper use of the licensor's trademarks ("proper" being defined in the license agreement).

Fees

Engine fees are usually broken down by title and platform. If there is a possibility that the game will be ported, and the licensor supports those platforms, negotiate the port fees in the original license.

License fees for third-party engines are almost always non-recoupable and non-refundable—even if the game is terminated mid-development. It is always a good idea for the publisher to pay the licensor directly and recoup the cost as part of development expenses.

Territory

A licensor will want the license to be valid in all territories in which it plans to distribute its product; worldwide is most appropriate.

Term

When the license is limited to use on a single title, the licensor can allow a perpetual term because the game has a limited shelf life, even with *catalog* sales (sales of the game after it has been in the market for at least one year) factored in.

IP Ownership

Ownership issues surrounding products that become enmeshed with other products can become messy. Engine licenses generally deal with this issue by allowing the licensee ownership of all elements of the game *except* the engine. It is important for the licensor to make it clear that the licensee acquires no rights to the engine even if it makes modifications or enhancements to the engine. However, the licensor may allow the licensee to retain ownership of any modifications or enhancements to the engine that are separate and independent from the engine.

Support

Support is a critical component of licensing a technology. A licensee needs to be sure its employees will have sufficient support to make effective and efficient use of the engine. Many licensors provide a training session at the developer's office soon after executing the agreement as part of the license fee. Licensees will want to be able to ask questions and receive timely answers by phone, fax, and e-mail. Licensors will want some kind of limit on the amount of support available to prevent extreme resource drain, for example, by extremely inexperienced developers.

Expected Features

Have your team work out its feature requirements and be sure the licensor can guarantee that those features will be in the product (and in the license agreement). For example, what does your particular game need in terms of polygons per frame, sound, streaming, VU0/VU1 acceleration, and other technical enhancement? Ask the art department if they have any theme-specific needs, such as realistic image distortion for an underwater level.

Mature Game into Film

Cast of Characters

- **Licensor.** In this instance, Developer and Publisher jointly.
- **Producer/production company.** The company that makes (or sublicenses the making of) the film.
- **Financier(s).** Any third parties contributing to the production budget.
- **Distributor.** The party who gets the film from the can to the screen (or VHS, if it's a direct to video). Usually, this is one of the big studios.

Mis en Scène

Developer is working on a game, to be released by Publisher, based on its Developer's original IP. Developer held onto the ability to pursue entertainment licensing opportunities, on the condition that Publisher approve any deals and share half of all revenue for three years following the release of the last game put out by Publisher.

Developer thinks that the property, which is very character-driven, would translate well to film and puts together a modified bible to pitch the project. They think about hiring an agent, who would have better film industry contacts. Furthermore, they worry that the time and effort required to shop the project around would take focus away from getting the game done. To try to save the 10 percent agent's commission (which could apply to all revenue stemming from the film, including sequels and film-related merchandise), Developer decides to spend one month trying to sell the project without an agent.

Two parties express interest in optioning the property: Producer A is a small independent production company willing to pay $5K for a one-year feature film option with the direct to video and television film (not series) rights, with a $50K purchase price plus 3 percent of the production budget if they exercise the option. Producer B is a production company tied in to a large entertainment conglomerate. This company is willing to pay $5K for a one-year option, with a $50K purchase price and one percent of the production budget on exercise; however, it wants not only all film rights but the merchandise rights associated with the film and an exclusive option to make other entertainment.

Developer consults with Publisher on the two offers. They agree that Producer A is more likely to make the property a priority, and the deal would allow them to hold onto what could become valuable entertainment and merchandise rights. However, even though Producer B wants to tie up more rights for less money, Developer and Publisher agree that their best chance of getting those rights turned into entertainment lies with the power of a conglomerate to finance and co-ordinate a licensing program across its divisions.

Developer consults with its attorney, who counsels that Producer B sounds like a fine choice pro-vided that any rights not exploited within a certain time frame revert. Producer B and Developer (with Publisher's approval) negotiate a contract with the following highlights.

Contract Highlights

Highlights of licensing a property for film production may include:

Property Definition

Where the original public version of the property will be a game, the definition of the licensed property would make reference to the game by name and would incorporate all copyrights and trademarks including all characters, artwork, plots, music, story lines, costumes, vehicles, props, weapons, concepts, sets, and ideas.

Rights Granted

For this kind of broad agreement, the licensee is acquiring the right to most forms of entertainment and merchandise. If the licensor already has certain licenses in place, such as a graphic novel or series of figurines based on the game, these should be noted in the contract as *excluded categories* of rights.

> **TIP**
>
> While the developer may not have the leverage to resist a conglomerate's desire to license all entertainment and merchan-dise rights, the developer can try to negoti-ate to have some rights revert if the film's production budget is less than a certain amount or to only grant those rights if the budget exceeds a certain amount (see Chapter 6 for a discussion of the relation-ship between options and reversions).

Compensation

A licensor will often receive three forms of compensation: rights fees, profit participations, and service fees.

- **Rights Fees.** Rights fees are "front-end" compensation for the right to use the licensed property in the product. These may be complemented by "back-end" compensation, a share of profits from the film, and/or merchandise.
- **Option Price.** The option price does not actually buy the license to make the film; it buys the producer a license to do pre-production work—like writing a screenplay—and a period of time to make a decision about whether to purchase the license to make the film. However, the option agreement usually lays out most, if not all, terms of the full license—a licensor does not want to lock up rights without knowing what kind of compensation it will receive should the deal go through. There is usually an initial option fee for a certain amount of time, renewable for another fee for another period.
- **Exercise Price.** If the producer decides to proceed with making the film, it *exercises* the option by paying the *exercise price* or *guarantee.* The exercise price/guarantee is the minimum rights fee that the licensor will receive. The full rights fee is usually a percentage of the production budget, less any option fees paid, with the exercise price acting as a set minimum (if for example, the production budget is very low). This protects the licensor by setting expectations for the production budget (read: quality); in other words, the guarantee named in the option agreement should be around one percent of the producer's envisioned budget.

> **NOTE**
> If the license is for a product that has not yet been released, the licensor may negotiate for bonus fees if the product is very successful (which increases brand exposure and enhances the value of the license).

- **Other Rights Fees.** The option will usually set rights fees for sequels to the film at half of the rights fees for the original and at one-third for remakes. Other fees to consider: television spin-offs based on the film.
- **Profit Participation.** Profits may come from the actual production or from other sources like merchandising.
- **Production Profits.** The licensor should receive some share of the producer's profits. As always, beware the path from gross to net: it is a good idea to include a "most favored nations" clause in the definition, which states that the definition of net profits for licensor will be no worse than that for any other parties sharing in the producer's net profits. As with packaged goods, the manufacturer (in this case, the producer), sells its product through a distributor (the studio) that takes a percentage of the revenue as a

CALCULATING RIGHTS FEES FOR MOTION PICTURES

Rights fees for motion pictures are usually calculated by a formula and paid in two or three stages: the option fee, the guarantee (paid on exercise of the option), and any additional rights fees due on the start of principal photography. Typically, payments from one stage are deducted from payments at another stage, as you will see in this example. Keep in mind that an option generally won't be exercised until the producer starts production—no sense paying the guarantee if the project falls through.

Assume:

Initial Option Fee: $5K

Renewal Option Fee: $5K

Guarantee: $50K

Rights fee: 1% of production budget on first day of principal photography

Additional rights fees: Another $50K for game sales in excess of 300,000; an additional $100K for game sales in excess of 600,000. Sales to be determined on the first day of principal photography.

Illustration One: Producer uses the initial and renewal options ($10K total). Licensor is paid $40K (exercise price less option fees paid) on the day the option is exercised. The game sells nicely, but is not a blockbuster (200,000 units). The production budget turns out to be $5M, for a direct to video. Licensor does not receive any additional money ($50K, less $10K option fees already paid = $40K).

Illustration Two: Producer uses only the initial option. Licensor is paid $45K when the option is exercised. The game does extremely well, selling 550,000 units by the first day of principal photography. On the strength of these sales, the producer secures a $20M budget for a feature film. Licensor is entitled to an additional $205K ($200K plus an additional rights fee of $50K, less the $45 already received).

Adjusted Gross vs. Net Profits

Example:

Assume:

Production Cost: $5M

Distributor's sales: $20M

Distributor fees: 25%

Investor share: 50% of adjusted gross

Director's share: 3% of adjusted gross

Licensor's share: 5% of net profits

The distributor would remit $15M to the producer ($20M less a 25% fee), who would be left with a $10M adjusted gross after recouping the $5M production expense. The investor would receive $5M and the director $300K, leaving net profits of $4.7M. The licensor's share of net profits would come out to $235K.

Had the licensor's share been from adjusted gross, its share would have been $500K.

distribution fee. After recouping production costs, the producer is left with what we'll call "adjusted gross" (though other times this number may be considered "net profits"). From the adjusted gross it must pay shares of profits to any investors as well as to any powerful creative contributors (like a big-name director). Whatever is left after these fees may be called "net profits." A licensor will want to negotiate whether its royalty base is off of the adjusted gross or net profits.

■ **Merchandise Profits.** The licensor should share in revenue from all merchandise from the film or any other entertainment produced under the license (such as a television spin-off). Merchandise should include soundtracks and theme park rides in addition to apparel, books, and all of the other customary merchandise.

TIP

Consider capping the distribution fees, particularly if there is any possibility of sweetheart deals across branches of a conglomerate.

- **Service Fees.** At least one party from the developer should be engaged as a "creative consultant" on any projects and should receive industry-standard compensation and screen credits. Where possible, gaining production credits is advisable because they can carry union-mandated fees.

> **NOTE**
>
> The developer will want to reserve rights to make games based on the filmed entertainment; the parties can negotiate a participation for the producer.

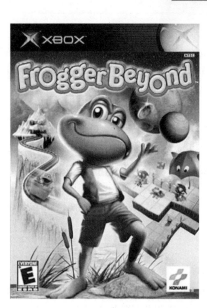

Figure 7.11

Licensing an old stand-by like Tetris and Frogger can provide a reasonably inexpensive license to a publisher.

Term

This kind of contract has three relevant terms: the option term, the production term, and the distribution term. The option term is the period during which the producer has the exclusive right to purchase the production license (called *exercise* of the option) and may prepare certain pre-production materials like a script. This term may have renewal periods, and those renewals may be contingent on the producer showing some form of progress, like a *treatment* (a story synopsis). If this term expires

> **NOTE**
>
> The distribution term for entertainment actually produced is usually perpetual. This means that a producer will always have the right to sell entertainment that it created, even if it has lost the right to make sequels or merchandise.

without a purchase of the production rights, the relationship goes no further and all rights usually revert to the licensor.

The production period is the time after exercising the option when the producer creates the licensed entertainment. The production period is limited to prevent parties from locking up rights and never actually producing any material. If the production period ends, the rights will usually revert to licensor. There may be some kind of *turnaround* provision (see the "Turnaround/Reversion" section that follows).

Credits

Developer should receive a prominent credit in any entertainment and advertising. The credit should read something like "Based on the video game by Developer" and should be of the same size and emphasis as the screenwriter credit.

Intellectual Property

The ownership of the film's copyright and any other new trademarks or copyrights created (new characters, for example) may be the subject of intense negotiation. Licensor will want to own all additions to the property, as will licensee. The producer will likely insist on ownership of the actual licensed product and will probably want control over the registration and enforcement of the intellectual property rights.

Turnaround/Reversion

As mentioned earlier in this chapter, rights that are not in use for an extended period of time should revert to the licensor. If the producer has spent money to create a script that the licensor would like to use, the licensor may purchase the script for a *turnaround fee*. Some producers negotiate for a licensor to pay a turnaround fee, regardless of whether the licensor uses any of the producer's materials, if the licensor takes the property elsewhere.

Creative Approvals

Developer should try to receive some form of consultation or approval right over the major creative aspects of the production, such as treatment, script, and visual elements. The licensor's need to maintain the integrity and value of the property must compete with the producer's viable argument that, since it is making a massive investment in the production, it needs to operate according to its own logic.

Game into Children's TV Show

Children's television is the brass ring of licensing because it generally creates the most merchandise and toy revenue, in addition to spawning related entertainment (like direct to video). One fact of children's television licensing that surprises many people is that the television shows don't make much money by themselves; most of the parties involved in the production and distribution of the television show (and other entertainment) are compensated with shares of the toy and merchandise revenue.

Children's television licensing can become very math-intensive, involving a lot of fractions-of-fractions. For example, the producer may receive a fraction of the licensor's toy royalties, which are a fraction of the toy licensee's revenue.

Cast of Characters

This entertainment license often incorporates many other parties.

- **Licensor.** This can be anyone from the property's actual owner to another party—like a toy company or publisher—to whom the owner has licensed the television/filmed entertainment and merchandise rights.
- **Licensee.** The licensee may be either the network or the production company.
- **Distributor.** The distributor is the company that sells the production to broadcasters (networks). There is often a domestic distributor and an international distributor. Like a packaged-goods distributor, these parties charge *distribution fees* to the producers, usually as a percentage of the *rights fees* paid by the broadcaster to the producer for the right to air the show. Distribution expenses, the cost of marketing and advertising the show to broadcasters, may be charged separately or included as part of a higher distribution fee percentage.
- **Broadcaster.** The broadcaster is the retailer of children's television: it brings the manufacturer's (producer's) product into the end-user's home. As with packaged-goods retailers, broadcasters expect to be compensated for shelf space (air time), though the money also flows in the other direction: broadcasters pay a rights fee to the producer for the right to air the show, just as retailers pay manufacturers for products they sell. The loving cup from which all television producers hope to drink is *syndication*, when a broadcaster airs the show five days a week and pays a fee for every broadcast (known as a *strip fee*). This is more likely with adult shows; the demographic windows are so short in children's television (example: 8-11 as opposed to 18-35), the shows don't usually have enough shelf life to support syndication. In other words, adult shows can retain the same viewer for seventeen years, while children's shows must constantly woo new viewers to replace the ones who've outgrown the show.

- **Master toy licensee.** A property hot enough to merit its own television show will probably have a *master toy licensee*. This is a toy company like Hasbro, Playmates, or Bandai that manufactures and distributes many different kinds of toys and desires control over all toy production, marketing, and distribution. Contrast this to a mature game that may have a market for one kind of toy, like a set of high-end figurines. In a situation of limited toy profits, there is not much incentive for a master toy licensee to invest the money in marketing the property, so it makes sense for the property owner to create a limited license for high-end figurines. A master toy licensee can be a vital part of the production and distribution negotiations because it is often one of the biggest purchasers of the broadcaster's advertising time and may be requested to make a commitment to buy a certain amount of advertising during the series' time slot.
- **Merchandise Agent.** The merchandise agent, which is almost a requirement for the level of merchandising activity created by a children's television show, handles all of the contracts with different licensees, including oversight and enforcement of the contracts. A licensor may hire a single agent to handle worldwide merchandise (understanding that the agent will hire sub-agents in different areas and that those sub-agents will take their own commission), or it may contract territory-by-territory or country-by-country.

Mis en Scène

Developer creates a game that achieves massive popularity with girls age 7 to 11. Because Developer self-funded the game, it held on to most of the intellectual property rights. After toy companies started showing interest in the property, Developer hired a full time licensing executive and created a separate corporation for the licensing business. The executive, who had been a high-ranking employee at Mattel, has lined up a master toy licensee and has been pursuing television series opportunities with different production companies.

Contract Highlights

Highlights of the children's television production license include:

Property Definition

For the level of money that must be invested in an animated children's television show (on the average of more than $250,000 per 22-minute episode, multiplied by 13 or 26 for a season), the licensee will be sure to acquire the rights to all aspects of the property, including any future additions or creations.

Rights Granted

The rights granted in a television production contract fall into two categories: the right to create licensed entertainment and the right (including the right to sublicense) to distribute, exhibit, and sell it.

Distribution and exhibition rights are rather straightforward: the licensee will need the right to sell and exhibit (and permit others to sell and exhibit) any productions.

Production rights are a bit more involved. As with a film, the licensor and licensee may be contracting before they know that the product will find interested parties to finance or distribute the production. Therefore, the rights may be broken out into categories so that, should the production hit a dead end, the licensor can get its rights back. These categories may include:

- **Pre-production.** Pre-production rights must be granted for the licensee to have the authority to create derivative products like treatments, scripts, bibles, and artwork to pitch the production.
- **Series.** This is where the licensor would specify that the licensee may produce animated but not live-action motion pictures for television broadcast.
- **Associated Productions.** The producer of an animated series almost always acquires either an exclusive option or a right of last refusal (see Chapter 6, "The Publishing Contract") to create animated feature films, television specials, spinoffs, and direct to video productions for as long as the producer is actively creating a threshold number of new series episodes per season (and possibly for a limited time afterwards).

Compensation

The licensor receives two different kinds of compensation, rights fees and service fees. Unlike the previous example of a film option, the licensor does not look to the production for the bulk of profits. Instead, most of the revenue will be from the merchandise and toy sales driven by the show, a portion of which *licensor* will pay to *licensee.*

- **Rights Fees.** The licensor will receive a minimum rights fee from the producer for every episode produced (whether or not distributed) and should receive separate minimum rights fees for other entertainment, such as an animated film, if the producer acquires and uses these rights. In addition to these minimums, the licensor should receive a share of the net profits from each production. A licensor will be most comfortable with a net profits calculus that simply subtracts the production costs from the producer's revenue from distribution (television, DVD, VHS, and everywhere else). It is more likely that the producer will have a dense boilerplate definition that your attorney will need to negotiate back down to earth.

■ **Service Fees and Screen Credits.** Licensors should be involved with the production and should receive industry-standard credits and service fees. If parties from the licensor contribute to the production—as writers or financiers, for example—they should receive commensurate credits and service fees. Fees are bound up with credits in television production because screen credits carry union-mandated payments. Therefore, a licensor will want to get as many credits as possible in its contract with the producer, though all may be subject to broadcaster approval. Reasonable credits include:

- Depending on the licensor's involvement with the negotiation, administration, and financing of the series, an Executive Producer credit for an individual may be appropriate.
- An authorship credit such as "Based on the video game by [Developer]" or "Based on characters created by [Author]."
- A service credit like "Creative Consultant" for the property's creator if she is involved with the production.
- The licensor should receive a full screen credit at the end of every episode with its logo (and up to a two-second animation).

> **NOTE**
> Where do a producer's profits come from? Most television productions run at a deficit, meaning that the fees paid by broadcasters for the initial run of the show do not cover production expenses. The profit center in television is strip fees (per-broadcast fees) if the series goes into syndication, which is more likely for an adult show, and from shares of the toy and merchandise revenue for children's television. An increasingly big bottom-line contributor is the DVD sale or rental income for a series.

> **TIP**
> Consider capping distribution fees if the production will be distributed through an entity related to the distributor.

> **NOTE**
> "Executive Producer" does not connote any particular duties—it often resembles a negotiated fee for parties involved with the series. Watch the credits on the Sopranos and you'll notice that there are around 50 executive producers and co-executive producers.

■ **Merchandise and Toy Sharing.** As mentioned in the previous paragraph, the parties financing the production—which usually includes the producer—will most likely receive a share of the licensor's income from worldwide toy and merchandising royalties. Note that it may be appropriate to give the financiers a lower share of international royalties because that income comes to the licensor drastically reduced already, due to higher commissions and cost of doing business abroad. Two important terms of sharing merchandise and toy royalties are the definition of "net" and the duration of the sharing period:

- **Getting from Gross to Net.** Just as the licensor wants to clarify deductions taken in getting from gross to net on the producer's income statement, the producer will want to establish what deductions the licensor can take from toy and merchandise royalty before paying the producer its share. It is accepted the non-overhead, product-specific costs—such as distribution fees, intellectual property registration and enforcement, agents' commissions and audit costs, and any rights fees paid for the merchandise (example: Sarah Michelle Gellar gets a rights fee if her voice is used in any merchandise like a doll or game)—may be deducted before any shares are paid, as well as a reasonable administrative fee (10 percent) for the licensor.

- **Sharing Period.** What if the producer makes 13 episodes of a series that gets cancelled after 3 episodes are broadcast? Should it receive shares of your merchandise royalty for the next five years? Probably not. Sharing periods are often limited to the production and broadcast period, with an extension period that gets longer depending on how many episodes are produced and broadcast. Example: if a producer makes 13 episodes, it shares merchandise and toy revenue for three months after broadcast of the last episode. If it makes 44 episodes, it shares for one year after broadcast of the last episode.

Term

Different rights granted in the license may have different terms attached, such as:

- **Pre-Production.** As with film options, the licensor wants to allow the licensee enough time to develop and pitch the product, but with a cutoff date to pick up stakes and move on if the pitch is not selling. The parties should decide on a broadcast season goal for pitching the show (shows get developed and pitched between January and May, and bought in September for debut the following September or January) and agree to terminate the agreement if they don't receive any offers within three to six months of the last pitch. Example: If the licensor and licensee are contracting in September 2003, they should be able to have pitch materials together for the 2004 pitch season. If they have not received any offers by October 15, 2004, the contract terminates.

- **Production.** Production rights should persist as long as the producer is releasing a threshold number of new episodes per year (between 8 and 13).

- **Distribution and Exhibition.** The producer should have the right to distribute and exhibit the productions in perpetuity.

Other Terms

- **Territory.** The territory is almost guaranteed to be worldwide.
- **Creative and Business Approvals.** The licensor will want to have an approval or consultation right over all major business decisions like choice of broadcaster or international distributor, as well as creative elements such as treatments, scripts, weapons, vehicles, artwork, sets, and backgrounds.
- **IP Registration and Enforcement.** Unless the licensor is very experienced with international intellectual property registration and enforcement, the producer may want to take responsibility for registering the property in the licensor's name (or co-owned with the licensor, as the case may be) and recouping those costs.
- **Ownership of New Material.** The licensor is likely to co-own the copyrights to any derivative works created by the producer, though the producer may own all the rights to certain aspects of the production, such as the theme song.

Book Into Game

This section addresses your licensing someone else's property for your own purposes, such as turning a book into a game or other media.

Cast of Characters

- **Licensor.** Usually the author, possibly the publisher.
- **Licensee.** Developer.

Mis en Scène

The art lead at Developer is a huge sci-fi fan and thinks that an obscure novella he read would make a great game. He draws up some illustrations of his idea and discusses it with one of the level designers, who brainstorms some gameplay ideas. They present their ideas to the CEO, who agrees to approach the author about a low-cost license to the property.

The CEO contacts the author, who is intrigued by the idea of the game, and agrees to send the CEO's attorney a copy of the author's publishing contract so that he can check for any rights conflicts with the publisher. Everything looks good, so the parties proceed with the negotiation.

Contract Highlights

Because these contracts frequently have a low dollar amount attached, be sure that the detail and cost of negotiation is in proportion to the contract. In other words, it may not always make sense to spend $10K negotiating a contract for a $500 license.

Definition of Property

The developer will want as expansive a definition of the property as possible, including all sequels, prequels, and other books in the series (if it is a series), any art if applicable, and rights to any other manifestations of the property.

Rights Granted

Because the developer may be investing millions of dollars in the development of a little-known property, it will want to obtain the exclusive option to produce, exhibit, and distribute most forms of entertainment and merchandise, including subsequent publications in the series. The production rights can be broken out into three categories:

- **Pre-production rights.** These are the rights to use the property to create and pitch pre-production materials.
- **Game production rights.** The rights to produce, copy, and distribute the game and any sequels, ports, conversions, and expansion packs.
- **Other production rights.** Film, merchandise, hint books, board games, and so forth.

Compensation

The developer should be prepared to pay a nominal option fee for an initial term (say $750), and a lesser fee for each extension ($300).

If the developer goes forward with the game's production, it will pay an exercise price of roughly 5 to 10 times the option fee, less any option fees already paid. The developer may want to pay the author a percentage of the ultimate development cost, or share a percentage of developer's net royalties with the author.

The developer should pay a share of net merchandising revenue to the author. Should the developer produce or sublicense production of any other entertainment, it should pay the author additional rights fees, which may include a percentage of the production budget or the developer's net profits from the production.

At the same time, the developer may request that the author or publisher pay the developer a share of any bump in book sales (any increase in book sales following release of the game).

Term

There are at least four operative terms:

- **Game option term.** There should be an initial option term, with successive extensions available. The author may request that the extensions only be granted if the developer shows some production progress, such as a design document.
- **Game production term.** After exercising the option, the developer should have a sufficient period to develop the game. The production rights should continue as long as the developer releases at least one game based on the property every four or five years.
- **Entertainment/merchandise option term.** The developer will want the exclusive right to make any entertainment or merchandise for a period lasting at least two years after the release of the first game and automatically renewing upon certain conditions. Examples of these conditions would be the developer entering pre-production for an entertainment product, proved by presenting a script or treatment, for example; or paying the author a minimum level of royalties in the first two years.
- **Distribution term.** Developer will have distribution rights to licensed products it creates in perpetuity.

Other Terms

- **Approvals.** The author will want consultation and/or approval rights to the creative elements of licensed productions. Some authors will want business-related input; some won't. If the developer grants any kind of approval right, it is vital that the author have a short number of days to approve or disapprove the submission by fax or e-mail, with no reply being considered assent.
- **Credits.** The author should receive some kind of on-screen credit, and may negotiate for higher profile credits (for example, on the box or in the title).
- **IP Ownership, Registration and Enforcement.** Depending on the relative leverage of the parties, a developer may try to acquire outright ownership of any products and additions to the property it produces under license. As the party with more money at stake, the developer will probably want to control the registration and enforcement processes and deduct these expenses from gross income before sharing with the author.

Figure 7.12

Eidos' Tomb Raider property is one of the very few to profitably transition to the screen. A sequel is due in 2003, to add to the heap of licensed and derivative works, including...

Figure 7.13

...the first movie...

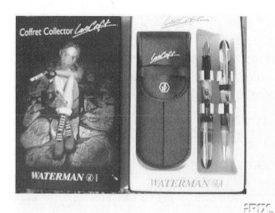

Figure 7.14

...writing instruments...

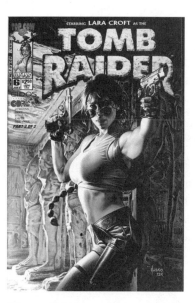

Figure 7.15

...comic books emphasizing her pneumosis...

Figure 7.16

...an amusement ride and other items for the obsessive fan.

GLOBAL LICENSING

Developers and other licensors are often buffered against many issues surrounding global licensing by their publishers, who handle international distribution, or third parties such as international merchandise agents or distributors. This section will give you some insight into what often seems like the "black box" of international contributions to revenue.

How Your IP Crosses Boundaries

Property is usually subject to different rules in different jurisdictions. For the simplest example of this, consider what would happen if you tried to take the hashish that you purchased legally in Amsterdam into France. Similarly (or not so similarly, really…), intellectual property is affected by the rules of the jurisdiction it enters. A trademark registered in the United States may receive no protection in another country (see Chapter 5, "Protecting Intellectual Property," for a look at international intellectual property law). Even if your IP is nominally protected by the *law* of another jurisdiction, whether that jurisdiction *enforces* that law is a separate matter altogether.

Your intellectual property enters other jurisdictions, usually in the form of games, merchandise, and entertainment, in one of three main ways:

- **Distributor imports.** A product produced elsewhere is imported into the country by a local distributor (under a valid distribution license).
- **Local manufacture.** A product locally manufactured and distributed under license.
- **Internet.** A product either sold or distributed (for example, downloaded) through the internet.

Parties Involved

Taking the example of a U.S. licensor, the licensor has the option of licensing rights country-by-country (usually too time-consuming and expensive), region-by-region (still time-consuming and expensive the first time, less so once the relationships are established), or globally.

- **Agents and Sub-agents.** The licensor also has the option of licensing directly to manufacturers/distributors, which usually won't make sense for the licensor, or hiring a licensing agent to handle the local manufacturers/distributors and sub-agents where appropriate. Sub-agents are used where, for example, you have granted an agent the right to sell your merchandise globally, but it wishes to sublicense those rights to territorial sub-agents, who will then license them to the parties that actually make and sell the merchandise. No matter how the sublicensing works out, you should only have to deal with the agent you hired, and that agent should be responsible for making all of its sublicensees adhere to the terms of your deal with your agent (for instance, regarding quality of goods sold).
- **Entertainment Distributors.** Packaged entertainment travels much the same as merchandise, but broadcast or screened entertainment is usually handled by a specialized international distributor who will most likely be chosen by the producer of that entertainment.
- **Regional Publishers.** Your publisher may sublicense the manufacture and distribution of your game to a regional publisher in areas where your publisher does not have an established distribution network.

Contracting with International Parties

It is crucial to have counsel experienced in the subject matter and the jurisdiction(s) of the contract. This may mean hiring counsel local to the jurisdiction. Some concerns of the international contract:

- **Is the contract enforceable?** Local law may determine that the intellectual property (copyright, trademark, trade secret, patent) forming the basis of the license is not protected in that jurisdiction. Some nations have laws governing what royalty rates can be charged and whether or not the royalties can be *repatriated*, taken out of the country.
- **How will the licensor protect your property?** Piracy and misuse of intellectual property—by other parties or by your licensee—is a major concern. The best defense is to choose a reputable local party. Given that, what anti-piracy and enforcement measures will the licensee or agent take? If you are licensing through an agent, who will audit the licensee (or sub-agents)? Who pays the costs of these measures?

- **What are the licensee's obligations?** Obligations may include: the licensee will neither produce nor sell any competing product; the licensee will not sell the product outside of the licensed territory; the licensee will provide adequate warranty and customer service for the product; the licensee will indemnify the licensor from any harm caused by licensee's product; the licensee will prominently display the licensor's mark on all licensed goods.

- **Other concerns.** A licensor needs to be concerned with several other issues, including:
  - A licensee's failure to exploit the license or create value for the licensor (generally addressed by having short initial terms with renewal thresholds such as $X in royalties or X number of products).
  - Disclosure of confidential information that may destroy trade secret protection, or losing other intellectual property rights due to licensor's use. This must be handled delicately and expertly, as non-disclosure agreements may not be sufficient to protect the property.
  - Currency fluctuation and government control on outflow of cash.
  - Responsibility for import and customs fees, as well as VAT or any other taxes.
  - How the product will be advertised and who will pay for it (usually the licensee).
  - Governing law and dispute resolution. Be aware that the validity of these terms may be subject to your licensee's local law. Example: your contract states that California law will govern the contract, but the law of your licensee's jurisdiction makes that clause illegal. Example: your contract states that any awards from arbitration may be entered in any court with jurisdiction over the parties. You enter the judgment in your jurisdiction, but the licensee doesn't have any assets in your jurisdiction. In this situation, you would probably have to enforce the judgment in the licensee's jurisdiction.

SUMMARY

Licensing intellectual property, the practice of selling some but not all of the rights to a given asset, can provide several benefits to a game developer. Licensing proprietary technology is a great way to monetize tools and technologies, though there are very few developers for whom the cost of promoting the technology is repaid in licensing fees. Licensing a game property into other media is generally a more complex affair, usually involving the publisher as a co-licensor. Frequently, the main benefit of a content license is increased visibility for the game property, which improves the odds of sequels and franchising.

The key terms of an intellectual property license

- Definition of the Licensed Property
- Rights Granted
- Definitions of Gross and Net
- Territory and Languages
- Term
- Sequels, Prequels, Re-makes/Ports, Conversions, Sequels
- Approvals
- Quality Assurance
- Marketing Guarantees
- Ownership of Derivative Works
- Reservation of Rights
- Representations and Warranties
- Execution of Further Agreements
- Assignment and Sublicense

change in the context of different licenses, as do the economics. The most important sources of revenue vary from category to category. For example, a children's television show looks to toy and merchandise sales, not advertising or syndication fees, for the biggest part of its profits.

Licensing often creates complex economics. It involves a host of parties, all of whom must be compensated. Whose pocket pays for the compensation is often the subject of pitched battle. There are entertainment agents, merchandise agents, international agents, sub-agents, packaged goods distributors, entertainment distributors, and so on. Intellectual property must be registered and enforced in all jurisdictions in which it is sold or appears, and that can be a major expense. In part as compensation for handling the complexities of administering the property, the licensor is frequently entitled to an administrative fee.

SHORT FORM OPTION AGREEMENT

This Agreement ("Agreement"), made between Double D Development, Inc., a Pacifica corporation with its principal offices at 9174 Winding Road, Podunk, Pacifica, 10000 ("Licensee") and Fantastic Comics, a [State] [Business Entity] whose principal place of business is located at [Address] ("Licensor"), (each a "Party," collectively the "Parties"). This Agreement is effective [Date] 200_ ("Effective Date").

RECITALS

WHEREAS, Licensee desires to license the Property, as defined below, for the creation of entertainment and merchandise including interactive games, filmed entertainment; and

WHEREAS, Licensor desires to grant such license to Licensee.

For the reasons set forth above, and in consideration of the mutual covenants and promises of the parties hereto, Licensor and Licensee agree as follows:

1. <u>Property</u>. The graphic serial publication *ComicBook* by Brett Novist, and all associated character names and likenesses, plot concepts, artwork, logos, visual representations, and dialogue from said work whether now known or hereafter created, including all copyrights, trademarks, and any other intellectual property rights therein (the "Property").

2. <u>Rights Granted</u>. Licensor hereby grants Licensee the exclusive right:
   a. To design, manufacture, distribute, license, sublicense, offer for sale, sell, advertise, and promote any and all:
      i. Interactive entertainment based on the Property or any derivation thereof ("Games");
      ii. Entertainment based on the Property in any medium, including but not limited to novelizations, music and soundtracks, filmed entertainment for theatrical, broadcast, or direct-to-video or DVD release ("Entertainment");
      iii. All merchandise ("Merchandise") rights associated with (i) and (ii) above.
      iv. Games, Entertainment, and Merchandise may collectively be referred to as the "Works."
   b. The right to use the name, likeness, and biography of Brett Novist in connection with the Works.
   c. Licensor reserves the rights to create and sell graphic serial publications based on the Property and printed on paper, subject to the following rights which are granted to Licensee:
      i. The right to use such excerpts, synopses, scenarios and other versions of the Property in print publication form for advertising and publicity purposes;

    ii. The right to publish, or authorize the publication of, any screenplays, teleplays, "making of" books, production history, novels, personal commentary, and/or souvenir publications.

3. <u>Option</u>. Licensee will have an exclusive eighteen (18) month period, commencing on the Effective Date, in which to purchase the Rights (the "Option").
   a. Option Fee. Five Hundred Dollars ($500.00), applicable against the Exercise Price, due to Licensor on execution of this Agreement.
   b. Option Extensions. The Option will be extendable for two further six-month periods (each an "Extension") at Licensee's request.
   c. Extension Fee. The payment for each of the Extensions will be Two Hundred Fifty Dollars ($250.00), due on or before the last day of the relevant Option period that Licensee intends to extend, all of which shall be applicable against the Exercise Price.

4. <u>Exercise Price</u>. Five Thousand Dollars ($5,000.00) less all Option and Extension payments ("Exercise Price"). The Exercise Price shall be due on initial pickup as an advance against applicable rights fees set forth in Section A below. The Option is deemed exercised only upon actual payment of Exercise Price to Licensor or Licensor's designee ("Exercise Date").

5. <u>Production Term</u>.
   a. The production term shall be five (5) years from Exercise Date.
   b. Reversion. Rights granted herein shall revert back to Licensor if: (i) No Work is commercially released within five years from the Exercise Date; (ii) No new Work is commenced by Licensee within five (5) years of the release of the last Work; or (iii) Immediately upon termination pursuant to Section 13, below. Licensee shall maintain the right to distribute the Works in perpetuity.

6. <u>Territory and Languages</u>. Worldwide, all languages.

7. <u>Compensation</u>
   a. Rights Fees.
      i. Interactive Games. Five Percent (5%) of Licensor's royalties received from any game based on the Property, less any amounts paid under Sections 3 and 4, above.
      ii. Other Entertainment. Rights fees for other entertainment shall be commensurate with industry standards and negotiated in good faith.
   b. Profit Participation. Licensee will pay Licensor Five Percent (5%) of Licensee's Net Profits, defined as all proceeds received by Licensee or its designee in connection with any Work, less: (i) Licensee's actual cost of production with interest at Prime-plus-Two Percent; (ii) additional expenses connected with the production,

distribution and promotion of the Work; and (iii) all unrelated third party participations granted by Licensee. In the event Licensee produces entertainment with a third party, the definition of net profits set forth in the agreement between Licensee and such third party producer shall govern.

8. <u>Creative Control</u>. As between the Parties, Licensee shall reasonably consult with Licensor or its designated representative on treatments and scripts, but shall retain all creative control of the Works.

9. <u>Business Decisions</u>. Licensee shall have final approval over all business decisions made in reference to the Works and shall execute all agreements therefore.

10. <u>Credits</u>. All Works, advertisements, and publicity (in whatever medium) where under the direct control of Licensee will bear an on-screen credit "Based on the graphic serial *ComicBook* by Brett Novitt."

11. <u>Notice</u>. All notices, royalty statements, and copies payments to be made hereunder shall be given or made to the respective Parties the addresses in the Agreement heading, above. A copy of all notices to Licensee shall also be sent to :

[Licensee's Attorney] _____

[Address]_____

And a copy of all notices to Licensor shall also be sent to:

[Licensee's Attorney] _____

[Address]_____

12. <u>Termination</u>.
   a. For gross misconduct such as fraud by any Party that remains uncured after written notice and 90-day cure period.
   b. Licensee may terminate this Agreement by giving thirty (30) days written notice ("Notice Period") to Licensor. Nothing herein shall effect the rights and obligations hereunder existing at the time of termination, including, without limitation, full payment of any amounts due under Sections 3, 4, and 7; provided that if Licensee terminates the Agreement due to Licensor's breach of representations and warranties under Section 16.A, then Licensor shall reimburse Licensee for all payments received by Licensor and all of Licensee's unrecouped expenses and disbursements incurred as a direct result of the performance of its obligations hereunder.

    c. Licensor may terminate this Agreement upon thirty (30) days written notice to Licensee if Licensee breaches or defaults on any of its obligations hereunder or as set forth in any related agreement between Licensee and Licensor covering the Property and Works, unless, before the end of the Notice Period, Licensee has cured or initiated cure of the breach and so notifies Licensor in writing. Licensor hereby waives all rights to equitable and injunctive relief.

    d. At the end of the Notice Period, the notifying party may exercise its termination rights. Exercise shall be made by written notice ("Notice of Termination") sent pursuant to the Notice provisions in Section 11 and shall take effect on the effective date of said Notice of Termination.

13. <u>Governing Law and Dispute Resolution</u>. This contract shall be governed by the law of the State of Pacifica in the United States of America. Any conflicts shall be resolved by binding arbitration in Podunk, Pacifica under the rules and institutional supervision of the American Arbitration Association ("AAA"). Parties or witnesses may appear by telephone. Judgment upon the award(s) rendered by the arbitrator may be entered in any court of any country having jurisdiction thereof. The neutral tribunal shall consist of one neutral arbitrator appointed by the AAA. The arbitrator shall award attorney's fees to the prevailing Party.

14. <u>Assignment and Sub-License</u>. Licensee may assign and sub-license its rights and obligations under this Agreement, in whole or in part and at its sole option and discretion. Licensee will notify Licensor of any assignments in writing at the address first written above.

15. <u>Accounting and Audits</u>
    a. Licensee shall render quarterly statements accounting for all revenue for the Works, and shall pay Licensor any amount(s) then owing on the last day of each quarter based on Licensor's fiscal year.

    b. Licensee agrees to keep accurate books of account pursuant to the Generally Accepted Accounting Principles at its principal place of business. Licensor is free to audit the books of Licensee, during regular business hours and with reasonable notice, once during each calendar year. Licensor shall bear the costs of the audit, unless a discrepancy of greater than Seven Percent (7%) is found to exist, in which case Licensee will either pay for or reimburse the Licensor for the cost of the audit. Any amount found to be outstanding shall be paid immediately to Licensor by Licensee.

16. <u>Representations and Warranties</u>.
    a. <u>By Licensor</u>. Licensor represents and warrants that (i) neither the Property nor any element thereof infringes the copyright in any other work; (ii) neither the Property

nor its exploitation will violate the rights to privacy or publicity of any person or constitute a defamation against any person, or in any other way violate the rights of any person whomsoever; (iii) Licensor has the right to enter into this Agreement and to grant the rights and privileges granted herein; (iv) the rights and privileges granted herein are irrevocable and Licensee may proceed in reliance thereon; (v) Licensor has not and will not encumber any of such Rights and privileges; and (vi) all information which Licensor provides to Licensee will be correct and truthful to the best of Licensor's knowledge.

    b. <u>By Licensee</u>. Licensee represents and warrants that (i) it is a company duly organized, validly existing, and in good standing under the laws of its jurisdiction of charter, having all requisite power and authority to enter into this Agreement; and (ii) it will make no additions or changes to the Property that infringe the copyright in any other work, violate the rights to privacy or publicity of any person, or constitute a defamation against any person.

17. <u>Indemnities</u>. Licensor and Licensee (each an "Indemnifying Party") hereby agree to indemnify and hold each other harmless from and against any and all claims, demands, actions and rights of action (including reasonable attorneys' fees and costs) which shall or may arise by virtue of anything done or omitted to be done by the Indemnifying Party (through or by his agents, employees or other representatives) outside the scope of, or in breach of the terms of, this Agreement; (ii) any breach of warranty or representation contained herein; and (iii) any misrepresentation, omission or inaccuracy in any schedule, instrument or paper delivered or to be delivered hereunder or in connection with the transaction herein contemplated.

18. <u>Further Assurances</u>. At any time, and from time to time, each party will execute any additional instruments and take any action as may be reasonably requested by the other party to confirm or perfect title to any rights transferred hereunder, or otherwise to carry out the intent and purposes of this Agreement.

19. *Force Majeure*. Inability of a Party to commence or complete his obligations resulting from delays caused by strikes, acts of God, war, emergencies, or other causes beyond reasonable control, which shall have been timely communicated to the other Party, shall extend the period for the performance of the obligations for the time equal to the period(s) of any the delay(s).

20. <u>No Waiver</u>. One or more waivers of a breach of any provision of this Agreement by either Party shall not be construed as a modification of this Agreement or as a waiver of a subsequent breach of the same or any other provision.

21. <u>Long Form/Entire Agreement</u>. At the request of either Party, the Parties will negotiate a long form agreement ("Long Form") covering the matters set forth herein. However,

until and unless such a Long Form is executed, this Agreement shall be binding and shall constitute the entire agreement between the Parties with respect to the subject matter hereof. This Short Form Option Agreement supersedes all prior negotiations, letters and understandings of the Parties.

22. <u>Amendment</u>. This Agreement may not be amended, supplemented or modified in whole or in part except by an instrument in writing signed by the Party or Parties against whom enforcement of any amendment, supplement or modification is sought.

23. <u>Severability</u>. If any provision of this Agreement should be determined by a court of competent jurisdiction, or by award of an arbitral tribunal, and enforced by the court, to be invalid, illegal or unenforceable, then that determination shall not affect or impair the validity, legality, or enforceability of the remaining provisions.

24. <u>Binding Nature</u>. This Agreement will be binding upon and will inure to the benefit of any successor or successors of the Parties.

25. <u>Headings</u>. The section and subsection headings in this Agreement are inserted for convenience only and shall not be deemed to be part of the substance of this Agreement.

26. <u>Construction</u>. The Parties and their respective legal counsels participated in the preparation of this Agreement; therefore, this Agreement shall be construed neither against nor in favor of either of the Parties, but rather in accordance with the fair meaning thereof.

27. <u>Counterparts</u>. This Agreement may be executed in two or more counterparts, each of which shall be deemed and original but all of which together shall constitute one and the same agreement.

28. <u>Currency</u>. All payments made hereunder shall be made in US Dollars (i) by wire transfer to an account designated by Licensor or Licensor's designee or (ii) by check made to the order of Fantastic Comics, and sent to Licensor or Licensor's designee.

ACCEPTED AND AGREED TO THIS _____ DAY OF_____, 200__.

Double D Development, Inc.   Fantastic Comics

By: _____   By: _____

Name: Dana Darby   Name: _____

Title: CEO   Title: _____

GLOSSARY

Accredited investor Individual meeting the SEC criteria for investors who do not need as much protection by virtue of certain qualifications.

Advance Amount paid, generally to fund production, and recouped from royalties.

Agent 1. An employee or partner having the authority to act on behalf of the company or partnership; 2. Party hired to sell the goods and services of another.

Ancillary products Often denotes merchandise but not entertainment related to a game, such as hint books, T-shirts, and figurines.

Angel investor An individual, usually affluent, who provides capital to one or more start-up companies.

Assignment of invention Document transferring rights in intellectual property.

At will Form of employment where either party may terminate at any time for any reason.

Back-end Compensation received after a product has earned a profit.

Basis Purchase price used to determine tax liabilities.

Blue Sky laws State regulations governing the sale of securities designed to protect investors from fraud.

Board Corporation's board of directors.

Boilerplate Standardized or form contract language.

Break-even Point at which a game's publisher recoups its total costs.

Bylaws Set of rules establishing.

C-corporation A business which is a separate legal entity from its owners.

Chapter 7 Chapter of the U.S. Bankruptcy code governing liquidation after bankruptcy.

Cliff vesting Vesting plan in which most of the ownership accrues in a lump toward the end of the vesting schedule.

COBRA Plan allowing departing employees to pay to continue coverage under the company's health plan, for a certain time period and under certain conditions.

COI Certificate of Incorporation.

Completion bond A bond issued by an insurance company to guarantee completion of a project by a contractor.

Consideration Legal term for compensation that a party receives in exchange for its obligations under a contract.

Content Intellectual property surrounding the story, audiovisual elements, gameplay, characters, and so forth.

Corporate veil Legal protection of corporate owners and officers from personal liability for corporation's debts.

Counterparty The "other guy" in a contract.

Cross-collateralize Application of revenues from one product to recoup investment or losses in another.

Cumulative voting A voting system allowing minority shareholders more power by consolidating all of their board of director votes for a single candidate, as opposed to having to divide their votes among different candidates and seats.

Damages Financial or other penalties paid by a wrongdoer to the wrongdone.

Derivative work New work based on another copyright.

Directors Members elected by corporation's shareholders to oversee company, including selecting officers and payment of dividends.

Distributor For product: the middleman between the manufacturer and the retailer; For entertainment: the middleman between the producer and the display.

Dividends Taxable payment to shareholders declared by a corporation's board of directors and paid out of company's current or retained earnings.

Double tax Refers to C-corporation's obligation to pay income tax at the corporate level in addition to shareholder's obligation to pay tax on distributions or appreciations in share value.

Due diligence Investigation into material facts, operations, and assets of a target company by prospective purchaser.

Earn-out Point at which publisher begins paying royalties.

Entertainment Films, television shows, books, amusement park rides, comic books, and so forth, based on an intellectual property.

Entity Form of business organization.

Equity Ownership interest in a corporation in the form of common stock or preferred stock.

Exercise price The price specified in an option contract at which the full contract may be exercised.

General partner Investor in a partnership who manages the business and is liable for its debts.

Gray market Sale of trademarked goods through unauthorized channels.

Guarantee The minimum amount of royalties to be paid to a licensor under a license. Generally non-recoupable.

Indemnification Agreement by one party to pay certain specified losses or damages incurred by another party.

Injunction A court order prohibiting a person from doing something or requiring a person to do something.

Instrument A document creating a legal right or obligation.

IP Intellectual property.

IRR The rate of return that would make the present value of future cash flows plus the final market value of an investment or business opportunity equal the current market price of the investment or opportunity.

Legend A notice that materials contain +C27-protected intellectual property.

License A permission to use an intellectual property right within a defined time, context, market line, or territory.

Licensee Party acquiring the license.

Licensor Party granting the license.

Limited liability Investor cannot lose more than the amount invested.

Limited partners Investors in a partnership who are not directly involved in management and are liable only to the extent of their investments.

LLC Limited Liability Company. Type of company where owners and managers receive the limited liability and (usually) tax benefits of an S-corporation without S-corporation restrictions.

LOI Letter of intent.

Long form The long version of a contract; generally refers to the expanded version of a contract originally drafted as a short form binding agreement.

LTCG Long term capital gains.

Mark A word, name, symbol, or device or any combination thereof used to identify and distinguish goods or services and to indicate their source.

Megillah Everything.

Member Owner of an LLC interest.

Mod Modification of game components for non-commercial use.

Moral rights Rights given in some countries to an author that survive sale or license.

NDA Non-disclosure agreement.

Non-compete Contract restricting a party's ability to compete in a certain market under certain conditions.

NPV The present value of an investment's future net cash flows minus the initial investment.

Offering A sale of newly issued securities.

Officer An executive of a company who shares legal liability with the company for her actions.

OI Ordinary income.

Options The right to acquire something at a later date under prespecified terms and conditions.

Passive investment Investment made by one who does not play an active role in the management of the business.

Pass-through A business organization that pays no entity-level tax.

Payment priority The hierarchy of which debts are repaid first.

Pitch build Demo or prototype materials built to pitch a game.

Pre-emptive rights The right of current shareholders to maintain their ownership percentage by buying a proportional number of shares of any future issue of common stock.

Preferred stock Stock that carries a specific dividend to be paid before any dividends are paid to common stock holders, and which receives payment priority over common stock in the event of a liquidation.

Private placement Direct sale of securities not requiring SEC registration, provided the securities are bought for investment purposes rather than resale.

Pro rata In direct proportion.

Property A set of copyrights and trademarks constituting a licensable chunk of content, for instance, "Batman."

R&D Research and development.

Recoup Recover costs.

Representation A guarantee that a particular fact is as stated or promised.

Reversion The right to regain assets or rights upon specified terms and conditions.

Right of first refusal The right to have an exclusive first look to decide whether to purchase a given asset or right.

Right of last refusal The right to match the final offer to buy an asset or right.

Rights fee License fee paid up front. Usually supplemented with back-end participation.

SBC stock Small business corporation stock. Qualifies for special reduced taxes.

S-corporation A form of corporation enjoying pass-through taxation allowed by the IRS for most companies having 75 or fewer shareholders.

Secured debt Loan backed by a pledge of other assets.

Security An investment instrument issued by a company as evidence of debt or equity.

SKU Stock-keeping unit.

Spread Difference between any two prices.

Statutory Mandated by law.

Sublicense License granted to a third party by a licensee.

Subscribe Agree to buy securities in an offering.

Sweat equity Paying for ownership with work instead of cash.

Turnaround Fees that may be due to the licensor if licensed rights revert to the owner.

Unaccredited investor An individual who does not meet the SEC criteria of an accredited investor.

Unsecured debt Loan not backed by a pledge of other assets.

USPTO United States Patent and Trademark Office.

Vest Become exercisable (options) or no longer subject to company's repurchase (stock).

Warrants A certificate, usually given along with a security, allowing the owner to buy a set number of other securities at a set price.

Warranty A guarantee that a fact is true as stated or promised.

Work for hire Copyrightable works of authorship created for and assigned to another party.

INDEX

Gamedev.net

The most comprehensive game development resource

- The latest news in game development
- The most active forums and chatrooms anywhere, with insights and tips from experienced game developers
- Links to thousands of additional game development resources
- Thorough book and product reviews
- Over 1000 game development articles!
  Game design
  Graphics
  DirectX
  OpenGL
  AI
  Art
  Music
  Physics
  Source Code
  Sound
  Assembly
  And More!

Gamedev.net

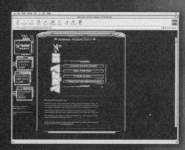

GAME DEVELOPMENT.
IT'S SERIOUS BUSINESS.

"Game programming is without a doubt the most intellectually challenging field of Computer Science in the world. However, we would be fooling ourselves if we said that we are 'serious' people! Writing (and reading) a game programming book should be an exciting adventure for both the author and the reader."

—André LaMothe,
Series Editor

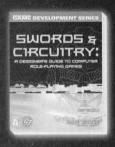